The Canons of Criticism and Glossary
by Thomas Edwards

Address:
HardPress
8345 NW 66TH ST #2561
MIAMI FL 33166-2626
USA
Email: info@hardpress.net

J. Harrison

THE
CANONS of CRITICISM,

AND

GLOSSARY;

THE

Trial of the Letter ϒ, *alias* Y,

AND

SONNETS.

By THOMAS EDWARDS, Efq;

LONDON:
Printed for C. BATHURST, oppofite St. *Dunftan's*
Church in *Fleet-ftreet.*

M.DCC.LVIII.

ADVERTISEMENT.

THE Canons of Criticiſm, and the Sonnets printed in Dodſley's Miſcellanys were ſo well received by the beſt Judges, that it is preſumed the Republication of them, together with the other pieces, which the Author left behind him, and which he had prepared for the preſs before his laſt illneſs, will be agreeable to the Public. The twenty-ſeven Sonnets, which now appear for the firſt time, are in the ſame taſte with thoſe in Dodſley's volume, correct, ſimple, not aiming at points or turns, in the phraſe and ſtructure rather ancient, for the moſt part of a grave, or even of a melancholy caſt ; formed in ſhort upon the model of the Italians of the good age, and of their Imitators among us, Spenſer and Milton. The Trial of the letter Y is a very ſenſible piece of Engliſh criticiſm ; a ſtudy, of which the Author was particularly fond, and in which few have ſhewn ſo exact a taſte.

Mr. Edwards was a Barriſter of Lincoln's-inn, Son and Grandſon of two worthy Gentlemen of the ſame profeſſion ; he had a liberal Education, and an independent Fortune.

For his Character we may with the ſtricteſt juſ-

tice

ADVERTISEMENT.

tice refer to his Epitaph, in the Church-yard of
Ellesborough in Buckinghamshire.

Under this stone are deposited the Remains of
Thomas Edwards, Esq; of Turrick in this parish,
where he spent the last seventeen years
of a studious, usefull life.

He was sincere and constant in the profession and
practise of Christianity, without Narrowness or Superstition;
steadily attached to the cause of Liberty,
nor less an enemy to Licenciousness and Faction;
in his Poetry simple, elegant, pathetic;
in his Criticism exact, acute, temperate;
affectionate to his Relations, cordial to his Friends,
in the general Commerce of life obliging and entertaining.

He bore a tedious and painfull distemper with a Patience,
which could only arise from a habit of Virtue and Piety;
and quitted this life with the decent unconcern of one, whose
hopes are firmly fixed on a better.

He dy'd on the IIId day of January MDCCLVII, aged LVIII.
and this stone is inscribed to his memory,
with the truest concern and gratitude,
by his two Nephews and Heirs, Joseph Paice and Nathanael Mason.

The Gentleman, whose assistance Mr. Edwards
acknowledges in the Preface, was Mr. Roderick,
Fellow of Magdalen-college in Cambridge, and of
the Royal and Antiquarian Societys. He dy'd
some little time before his friend, bequeathing to
him such of his Papers, as related to the Canons
of Criticism: And the Additions to that work
from those papers are inserted in their proper
places.

THE
CANONS of CRITICISM,
AND
GLOSSARY,
BEING A
SUPPLEMENT
TO
Mr. WARBURTON's Edition
OF
SHAKESPEAR.

Collected from

The NOTES in that celebrated Work,
And proper to be bound up with it.

By the OTHER GENTLEMAN of *Lincoln's-Inn*.

There is not a more melancholy object in the learned world, than a man who has written himself down.——In this case——one would wish that his friends and relations would keep him from the use of pen, ink, and paper, if he is not to be reclaimed by some other methods. Addison's *Freeholder*, No. 40.

The SIXTH EDITION, with Additions.

LONDON:
Printed for C. BATHURST, opposite St. *Dunstan's* Church in *Fleet-street*.

M.DCC.LVIII.

SONNETS

TO

Three LADIES, sent with the Book.

To the M. H. the * * *

LADY, whose fair approof I wish should
    give
  A glorious sanction to whate'er I write;
  Since what your well-pois'd judgment marks with
    white
Secure from envy will to ages live,

So may I in this arduous emprise thrive,
  As I not follow in the chase for spite;
  But led by Love of True, and Fit, and Right,
In which good cause each gentle breast should strive:

While I with hasard of my own good name
  Like *Calidore* pursue the Blatant Beast
In dear defense of Ladies' honest fame,
Which his foul mouth profanely taints with blame;
  Let me, howe'er with dread and dangers press'd,
Enjoy the smiles of ev'ry virtuous dame.

            A   SON-

S O N N E T S.

To the R. H. the   *   *   *   *

LET HIM rail on, till ev'ry mouth cry
      shame;
  Of *his* ill word I little reckoning make
  For Ladies' honor, and for *Shakespear*'s fake;
So these I may defend from blot or blame:

But ill I bear, that any worthy name
  Of those, who virtue for their miftrefs take,
  And hate the fland'rer like the poifonous fnake;
Should deem my juft reproof deferving blame.

Yet, if fair   *   *   *fpeak* in my defenfe,
  If   *   vouchfafe her fanction to my page,
If   *   *   fweetly deign to fmile applaufe;
Aided by thefe and confcious innocence,
  I'll boldly brave the CRITIC's utmoft rage;
And glory fuff'ring in fo juft a caufe.

S O N-

S O N N E T S.

To Miſs   ●   ●

SWEET Modeſty, the third of that fair
    band,
  Whom virtuous friendſhip, ill by churls deny'd
  To Ladies' gentle boſoms, hath ally'd ;
May I unblam'd your favoring voice demand,

While arm'd with Truth's good ſhield alone I ſtand
  In *Shakeſpear*'s cauſe determin'd to abide
  Th' outrageous efforts of inſulting pride,
And marks of Calumny's deteſted brand ?

Deep are the wounds ſhe gives, and hard to heal.
  Yet though enrag'd her hundred tongues ſhe join
With canker'd ſpite to blaſt my honeſt name,
I reck not much, nor bate my pious zeal ;
  But to the Fair and Good my cauſe reſign,
Who ſmile on Virtue, and whoſe ſmiles are Fame.

To the REVEREND

Mr. WARBURTON.

S I R,

IF Fame is one of the ingredients, or, as you elegantly call them, *Entremes* of happiness ; I am more obliged to You, whom I do not know; than to any person whom I do. Had not you called him forth to the public notice, the OTHER Gentleman of *Lincoln's-Inn* might have died in the obscurity, which, You say, his modesty affected ; and the few people, who had read the last Edition of Shakespear, and the Supplement to it, after having sighed over the one, and laughed at the other, would soon have forgotten both.

As I have no reason to repent the effects of that Curiosity, which you

The Dedication and the Preface were added to the later editions of the Canons, on occasion of a Note on the Dunciad B. IV. l. 567.

* MACBETH, Vol. VI. Page 392.

A 3　　　　　　　　　　have

DEDICATION.

have raiſed *on my Subject*; to borrow another expreſſion of yours; I take this opportunity of thanking You for that civil treatment, ſo becoming a Gentleman and a Clergyman, which I have received at your Hands; and offer to your protection a work, " [b] from " which, if Shakeſpear, or good Let-" ters, have received any advantage, " and the Public any benefit or en-" tertainment; the thanks are due to " Mr. Warburton."

I am, Sir,

Not your enemy; though you have given me no great reaſon to be

Your very humble Servant;

Thomas Edwards.

[b] See Mr. Warburton's Preface, Page 20.

PREFACE.

I Now appear in public, not a little againſt
my inclination ; for I thought, I had been
quit of the taſk of reading the laſt edition of
Shakeſpear any more ; at leſt till thoſe, who
diſapprove of what I have publiſhed concerning it, ſhould be as well acquainted with it as I
am ; and that perhaps might have been a re-
prieve for life : but Mr. Warburton has drag-
ged me from my obſcurity ; and by inſinuating
that I have written a libel againſt him, (by
which he muſt mean the Canons of Criticism, becauſe it is the only book I have written ; I ſay, by this unfair inſinuation) he has obliged me to ſet my name to a pamphlet ; which
if I did not in this manner own before, it was
I muſt confeſs owing to that fault Mr. Warburton accuſes me of ; a fault, which He, who
like Cato can have no remorſe for weakneſſes
in others, which his upright ſoul was never
guilty of, thinks utterly unpardonable ; and
that is *Modeſty*: Not that I was either
aſhamed of the pamphlet, or afraid of my ad-
verſary ; for I knew, that my cauſe was juſt ; and
that truth would ſupport me even againſt a
more tremendous antagoniſt, if ſuch there be ;

A 4

but

but I thought it a work, which though not un‑
becoming a man who has more ſerious ſtudies,
yet was not of that conſequence as to found any
great matter of reputation upon.

Since then I am thus obliged to appear in
public, I the more readily ſubmit; that I may
have an opportunity of anſwering, not what
Mr. Warburton has written againſt me, for that
is unanſwerable; but ſome objections which I
hear have been made againſt the Canons, by
ſome of his friends.

It is my misfortune in this controverſy to be
engaged with a perſon, who is better known
by his name than his works; or, to ſpeak more
properly, whoſe works are more known than
read; which will oblige me to uſe ſeveral ex‑
planations and references, unneceſſary indeed to
thoſe who are well read in him; but of conſe‑
quence towards clearing myſelf from the im‑
putation of dealing hardly by him; and ſaving
my readers a taſk, which I confeſs I did not find
a very pleaſing one.

Mr. Warburton had promiſed the world a
moſt complete edition of Shakeſpear; and, long
before it came out, raiſed our expectations of it
by a pompous account of what he would do, in
the General Dictionary. He was very hand‑
ſomely paid for what he promiſed. The ex‑
pected edition at length comes out; with a
title-page importing that the Genuine Text, *col‑
lated* with all the former editions, and then
corrected and *emended*, is there ſettled. His pro‑
face

face is taken-up with defcribing the great difficulties of his work, and the great qualifica-
tions requifite to a due performance of it; yet at
the fame time he very cavalierly tells us, that
thefe notes were among the amufements of his
younger years: and as for the Canons of Criticifm and the Gloffary which he promifed, he
abfolves himfelf, and leaves his readers to collect
them out of his notes.

I defire to know, by what name fuch a be-
haviour in any other commerce or intercourfe
of life would be called? and whether a man
is not dealt gently with, who is only laughed at
for it? I thought then, I had a right to laugh;
and when I found fo many hafty, crude, and
to fay no worfe, unedifying notes fupported by
fuch magifterial pride, I took the liberty he
gave me; and extracted fome Canons and an
effay towards a Gloffary from his work. If He
had done it, he had faved me the labor: it is
poffible indeed, that he might not have pitched
upon all the fame paffages as I did to collect
them from; as perhaps no two people, who did
not confult together, would; but I defie him to
fay, that thefe are not fairly collected; or that he
is unfairly quoted for the examples: if Mr.
Warburton would have been more grave upon
the occafion, yet I did not laugh fo much as I
might have done; and I ufed him with better
manners, than he ever did any perfon whom he
had a controverfy with; except *one* gentleman,
whom he is afraid of; if I may except even him.

But

But all this avails me nothing : I have read Shakefpear at Lincoln's Inn ; and have publifhed my Canons of Criticifm ; and for this I am to be degraded of my gentility. A fevere fentence this.——I find, that reading of Shakefpear is a greater crime than high-treafon : had I been guilty of the latter, I muft have been indicted by my addition, tried by my peers, and fhould not have loft my blood, till I had been attainted ; whereas here the punifhment is incurred *ipfa facto*, without jury or trial.

I might complain of Mr. Warburton to his Mafters of the Bench, for degrading a Barifter of their houfe by his fole authority ; but I will only reafon coolly with him upon the equity of this new proceeding.

A Gentleman (if I do not mean myfelf, with Mr. Warburton's leave I may ufe that word) I fay, a gentleman, defigned for the fevere ftudy of the law, muft not prefume to read, much lefs to make any obfervations on Shakefpear ; while a Minifter of Chrift, a Divine of the Church of England, and one, who, if either of the Univerfities would have given him that honour, would have been a Doctor in Divinity ; or, as in his preface he decently exprefles it, * *of the Occult Sciences* ; He, I fay, may leave the care of his living in the country, and his chapel in town, to curates ; and fpend his Heaven-devoted hours in writing obfcene and im-

* *Pref.* p. 26.

moral

moral notes on that author, and imputing to him sentiments which he would have been ashamed of.

Who is Mr. Warburton? what is *his* birth, or whence *his* privilege? that the reputations of men both living and dead, of men in birth, character, station, in every instance of true worthiness, much his superiors, must lie at the mercy of his petulant satire, to be hacked and mangled as his ill-mannered spleen shall prompt him; while it shall be unlawful for any body, under penalty of degradation, to laugh at the unscholar-like blunders, the crude and far-fetch'd conceits, the illiberal and indecent reflections; which he has endeavoured with so much self-sufficiency and arrogance to put-off upon the world as a standard of true criticism?

After being degraded from my gentility, I am accused of dulness, of being engaged against Shakespear, and of personal abuse: for the first; *if*, as * Audrey says, *the Gods have not made me poetical*, I cannot help it; every body has not the wit of the ingenious Mr. Warburton; and I confess myself not to be his match in that species of wit, which he deals-out so lavishly in his notes upon all occasions. As to the charge of being engaged against Shakespear; if he does not, by the most scandalous equivocation, mean His edition of Shakespear, it is maliciously false; for I defy him to prove, that I ever either wrote or spoke concerning Shake-

* *As you like it.*

spear,

ſpear, but with that eſteem which is due to
the greateſt of our Engliſh Poets. And as to
the imputation of perſonal abuſe; I deny it, and
call upon him to produce any inſtance of it. I
know nothing of the man, but from his works;
and from what he has ſhewn of his temper in
them, I do not deſire to know more of him;
nor am I conſcious of having made one remark,
which did not naturally ariſe from the ſubject
before me; or of having been in any inſtance
ſevere, but on occaſions where every gentleman
muſt be moved; I mean, where his notes ſeemed
to me of an immoral tendency; or full of thoſe
illiberal, common-place reflections on the fair
ſex, which are unworthy of a gentleman or a
man; much leſs do they become a divine and
a married man: and if this is called perſonal
abuſe, I will repete it; till he is aſhamed of ſuch
language, as none but libertines and the loweſt
of the vulgar can think to be wit; and this too
flowing from the fulneſs of his heart, where
honeſt Shakeſpear gave not the leaſt occaſion for
ſuch reflexions.

If any applications are made, which I did not
deſign; I ought not to be anſwerable for them:
if this is done by Mr. Warburton's friends, they
pay him an ill complement; if by himſelf, he
muſt have reaſon from ſome unlucky co-inci-
dences, which ſhould have made him more
cautious of touching ſome points; and he
ought to have remembered, that a man, whoſe
house

house is made of glass, should never begin throwing stones.

But I have been told; that, whatever was my design, my pamphlet has in fact done an injury both to Mr. Warburton, and his bookseller. I hope, I am not guilty of this charge: to do *him* an injury in this case, I must have taken away from him, or hindered him from enjoying, something which he had a right to; if I have proved, that he had no real right to something which he clamed; this is not injuring *him*, but doing justice to Shakespear, to the public, and to himself. I am just in the case of a friend of mine, who going to visit an acquaintance, upon entering his room met a person going out of it: Prithee Jack, says he, what do you do with that fellow? Why, 'tis *Don Pedro di Mondongo* my Spanish master. Spanish master! replies my friend, why he's an errant Teague: I know the fellow well enough, 'tis *Rory Gahagan*; I have seen him abroad, where he waited on some gentlemen; he may possibly have been in Spain, but he knows little or nothing either of the language or pronunciation; and will sell you the Tipperary Brogue for pure Castilian. Now honest *Rory* had just the same reason of complaint against this Gentleman, as Mr. Warburton has against me; and I suppose abused him as heartily for it: but nevertheless, the gentleman did both parties justice. In short, if a man will put himself off in the world for what he is not; he may be sorry for being discovered,

but

but he has no right to be angry with the person who discovers him.

As to his booksellers; it must be acknowleged, that those gentlemen paid very dear for the aukward complement he made them in his preface; of their being, " *not the worst judges,* " *or rewarders of merit;*" but, as to my hindering the sale of the book, the supplement did not come-out till a twelvemonth after the publication of Mr. Warburton's Shakespear; and in all that time it had so little made its way, that I could meet with no-body, even among his admirers, who had read it over; nor would people easily believe, that the passages produced as examples to the Canons were really there; so that if it had merit, it was of the same kind with that of Falstaff's; it was *too thick to shine,* and *too heavy to mount;* for people had not found it out : only they took it for granted, that an edition by Mr. Pope and Mr. Warburton must be a good one.

But the publication of the supplement has prevented the sale, since that time. If it has, it must be because the objections it contains against that performance are well grounded; otherwife, a little twelve-penny pamphlet could never stop the progress of eight large octavo volumes: the impartial public would have condemned the pamphlet, and bought-up the book. If then those objections are just, what have I done; but discovered the faultiness of a commodity, which Mr. Warburton had put-off

upon

upon them ; and they were, though innocently, putting-off upon the public, for good ware? In this cafe, therefore, Mr. Warburton ought to make them amends ; though I doubt he will plead *caveat emptor*, and the complement in his preface, against refunding.

I thought it proper to haften this new edition, which Mr. Warburton's ungentleman-like attack made neceffary for my defenfe, as much as poffible ; and am proud to acknowlege, that I have received confiderable affiftance in it from a gentleman ; who in a very friendly manner refented the ill ufage I have met with, as much as if it had been done to himfelf. I have added a few new Canons ; and given a great many more examples to the others; though, becaufe I would neither tire my reader and myfelf, nor too much incroach upon Mr. Tonfon's property; I have left abundant gleanings for any body, who will give himfelf the trouble of gathering them. This, I hope, will anfwer one objection I have heard ; that I had felected the only exceptionable paffages, a few faults out of great numbers of beauties, of which the eight volumes are full. This will never be faid by any perfon, who has read the eight volumes; and they, who do not care to give themfelves that trouble, ought not to pafs too hafty a judgment: whether it be true or no, will appear to thofe who fhall perufe thefe fheets. That there are good notes in his edition of Shakefpear, I never did deny ; but as he has had the plundering of two

dead

dead men, it will be difficult to know which
are his own ; some of them, I suppose, may be ;
and hard indeed would be his luck, if among so
many bold throws, he should have never a winning cast ; but I do insist, that there are great
numbers of such shameful blunders, as disparage
the rest ; if they do not discredit his title to
them, and make them look rather like lucky-
hits, than the result of judgment.

Thus I have, for the sake of the public, at
my own very great hasard, though not of life
and limb, yet of reputation, ventured to attack
this giant critic ; who seemed to me like his
brother *Orgoglio*, of whom Spenser says,

Book. I. Canto. 7. St. 9.

The greatest Earth his uncouth Mother was,
And blust'ring Æolus his boasted Sire ;
And she, after a hard labour,
Brought forth this monstrous Masse of earthly
Slime,
Puff'd up with empty wind, and fill'd with
sinful Crime.

I have endeavoured to take him in hand, as
prince *Arthur* did *Orgoglio* ; and the public must
judge, whether the event has been like what hap-
pened to his brother on the same experiment :

But soon as breath out of his breast did passe,
The huge great body which the Giant bore
Was vanish'd quite ; and of that monstrous Masse
Was nothing left, but like an empty bladder was.

Canto 8. St. 24.
The

The world will not long be impofed-on by ungrounded pretenfes to learning, or any other qualification ; nor does the knowledge of words alone, if it be really attained, make a man learned : every true judge will fubfcribe to Scaliger's opinion ; " If, fays he, a perfon's learn-" ing is to be judged-of by his reading, no-body " can deny Eufebius the character of a learned, " man ; but if he is to be efteemed learned, " who has fhewn judgment together with his " reading, Eufebius is not fuch."

I fhall conclude, in the words of a celebrated author on a like occafion ; * " It was " not the purpofe of thefe remarks, to caft a ble-" mifh on his envied fame; but to do a piece of " juftice to the real merit both of the *work*, and " its *author* ; by that beft and gentleft method " of correction, which nature has ordained in " fuch a cafe; of laughing him down to his pro-" per rank and character."

* Remarks on the *Jefuit* Cabal, p. 57, 58.

S O N N E T.

TONGUE-doughty Pedant; whose ambitious
    mind
  Prompts thee beyond thy native pitch to soar;
    And, imp'd with borrow'd plumes of Index-lore,
Range through the Vast of Science unconfin'd!

Not for Thy wing was such a flight design'd:
  Know thy own strength, and wise attempt no more;
    But lowly skim round Error's winding shore,
In quest of Paradox from Sense refin'd.

Much hast thou written—more than will be read;
  Then cease from *Shakespear* thy unhallow'd rage;
Nor by a fond o'erweening pride mis-led,
Hope fame by injuring the sacred Dead:
  Know, who would comment well his godlike page,
Critic, must have a Heart as well as Head.

CANONS

CANONS

OF

CRITICISM.

I.

A Profeſſed Critic has a right to declare, tha this Author wrote whatever He thinks be ought to have written; with as much poſitiveneſs, as if He had been at his Elbow.

II.

He has a right to alter any paſſage, which He does not underſtand.

III.

Theſe alterations He may make, in ſpite of the exactneſs of meaſure.

IV.

Where he does not like an expreſſion, and yet cannot mend it; He may abuſe his Author for it.

V.

Or He may condemn it, as a fooliſh interpolation.

VI.

As every Author is to be corrected into all poſſible perfection, and of that perfection the Profeſſed Critic is the ſole judge; He may alter any word or phraſe, which does not want amend-

B 2   *ment,*

ment, or which will do; provided He can think
of any thing, which he imagines will do better.

VII.

He may find-out obsolete words, or coin new
ones; and put them in the place of such, as He
does not like, or does not understand.

VIII.

He may prove a reading, or support an explanation, by any sort of reasons; no matter
whether good or bad.

IX.

He may interpret his Author so; as to make
him mean directly contrary to what He says.

X.

He should not allow any poetical licences,
which He does not understand.

XI.

He may make foolish amendments or explana-
tions, and refute them; only to enhance the value of his critical skill.

XII.

He may find out a bawdy or immoral meaning
in his author; where there does not appear to be
any hint that way.

XIII.

He needs not attend to the low accuracy of orthography, or pointing; but may ridicule such
trivial criticisms in others.

XIV.

Yet, when He pleases to condescend to such
work, He may value himself upon it; and not
only restore lost puns, but point-out such quaint-
nesses,

nesses, where, perhaps, the Author never thought of them.

XV.

He may explane a difficult passage, by words absolutely unintelligible.

XVI.

He may contradict himself; for the sake of shewing his critical skill on both sides of the question.

XVII.

It will be necessary for the Professed Critic to have by him a good number of pedantic and abusive expressions, to throw-about upon proper occasions.

XVIII.

He may explane his Author, or any former Editor of him; by supplying such words, or pieces of words, or marks, as he thinks fit for that purpose.

XIX.

He may use the very same reasons, for confirming his own observations; which He has disallowed in his adversary.

XX.

As the design of writing notes is not so much to explane the Author's meaning, as to display the Critic's knowlege; it may be proper, to shew his universal learning, that He minutely point out, from whence every metaphor and allusion is taken.

XXI.

It will be proper, in order to shew his wit; especially, if the Critic be a married Man; to take every opportunity of sneering at the Fair Sex.

XXII.

CANONS of CRITICISM.

XXII.

He may misquote himself, or any body else; in order to make an occasion of writing Notes, when He cannot otherwise find one.

XXIII.

The Profess'd Critic, in order to furnish his Quota to the Bookseller, may write NOTES *of Nothing; that is to say, Notes, which either explane things which do not want explanation; or such as do not explane matters at all, but merely fill-up so much paper.*

XXIV.

He may dispense with truth; in order to give the world a higher idea of his parts, or of the value of his work.

XXV.

He may alter any Passage of his author, without reason and against the Copies; and then quote the passage so altered, as an authority for altering any other.

I N T R O-

INTRODUCTION

To the First Edition.

SHAKESPEAR, an author of the greatest
genius that our, or perhaps any other,
country ever afforded; has had the misfortune
to suffer more from the carelessness or ignorance
of his editors, than any author ever did.

The first editions were, as Mr. Pope [a] observes, " printed from the prompter's book, or
" the piece-meal parts written-out for the
" players;" and are very much disfigured by
their blunders and interpolations.

[b] " At length, says Mr. Warburton, he had
" his appointment of an editor in form. But the
" bookseller, whose dealing was with wits, hav-
" ing learnt of them I know not what silly
" maxim, that none but a poet should presume
" to meddle with a poet; engaged the ingenious
" Mr. Rowe to undertake this employment. A
" wit indeed he was; but so utterly unacquaint-
" ed with the whole business of criticism; that
" he did not even collate or consult the first edi-
" tions of the work he undertook to publish:"
[I wish this does not appear to be the fault of
other editors, beside Mr. Rowe] " but contented

---

[a] Mr. Pope's *Pref.* p. 41.   [b] Mr. W.'s *Pref.* p. 8.

" himself

" himself with giving us a meagre account of
" the author's life, interlarded with some com-
" mon-place scraps from his writings." The
leaner Mr. Rowe's account was, it certainly
stood the more in need of larding; but, meagre
as it is, it helps a little to swell-out Mr. Warburton's edition.

The bookfellers however, who from employ-
ing Mr. Rowe are henceforth grown to be ' proprietors; " not difcouraged by their firft unfuc-
" cefsful effort, in due time, made a fecond;
" and (though they ftill " [foolifhly] " ftuck to
" their poets) with infinitely more fuccefs, in
" the choice of Mr. Pope." And what did He
do? Why, " by the mere force of an uncommon
" genius, without any particular ftudy or pro-
" feffion of this art," he—told us which plays he
thought genuine, and which fpurious; and degraded as interpolations fuch fcenes as he did
not like, in thofe plays which he allowed. He
then (that is, after he had by his own judgment determined what was worth mending)
" confulted the old editions;" and from them
mended a great number of faulty places.

" Thus far Mr, Pope;" which, it fhould
feem, was as far as a poet could go.   But alas !
" there was a great deal more to be done, before
" Shakefpear could be reftored to himfelf."

Sanctius his animal, mentifque capacius altæ
Deerat adhuc; et quod dominari in cætera poffit,
The poets were to clear-away the rubbifh; and
then to make way for a more mafterly workman,

' Mr. W.'s Pref. p. 9.

" This

" This therefore Mr. Pope,[d] with great mo-
" defty and prudence, left to the critic by profef-
" fion:" and, to give the utmoft poffible perfection to an edition of Shakefpear, he with equal
judgment and fuccefs pitched-on Mr. Warburton, to fupply his deficiency.

Here then is the foundation of the *Alliance
between poet and critic*; which has this advantage
over the famous one *between church and ftate*,
that here are evidently two diftinct contracting
parties: it is formed, not between Mr. Pope the
critic, and Mr. Pope the poet; but between Mr.
Warburton the critic, and Mr. Pope the poet;
and the produce of this alliance is a fort of *Act of
Uniformity*; which is to put a ftop to, by being
the laft inftance [e] of, " the prevailing folly of
" altering the text of celebrated authors with-
" out talents or judgment;" and to [*] fettle and
eftablifh the text of Shakefpear, fo as none fhall
hereafter dare difpute it.

Let us paufe a little; and admire the profound
judgment and happy fuccefs of the projecter of
this alliance. The reafons hinted-at for Mr.
Pope's not undertaking this work alone, are his
great modefty and prudence; the one made him
judge himfelf unfit for this arduous tafk; the
other prevented his undertaking it, as he was unfit. Now, if his co-adjutor had had the fame
qualities, what were we the nearer? How fhould
one be able to make-up the deficiences of the
other? There muft be a boldnefs of conjecture,

[d] Mr. W.'s *Pref.* p. 10.   [e] *ib.* p. 19.   [*] See the title.

3   a har-

a hardinefs in maintaining whatever is once af-
ferted, and a profound contempt of all other
editors, in a profefs'd critic; which are incom-
patible with the qualities beforementioned, but
which you will fee the advantages of in many
inftances; in Mr. Warburton's edition.

To return. Here was work to be done in
publifhing Shakefpear, which poets were not fit
for. Though you might believe this on Mr.
Warburton's word, or collect it from the bad
fuccefs of the poetical editors, and from the
" 'crude and fuperficial judgments on books and
" things" made by another great poet; " which
" has given rife to a deluge of the worft fort of
" critical jargon:" yet I fhall give you undeni-
able proof of it by one or two inftances, out of
many which are to be met-with in Mr. Warburton's edition.

In *King Lear* [g], Act III. Sc. 3. the fool fays,
    I'll fpeak a prophecy, *or* e'er I go.
which Mr. Warburton alters to
    I'll fpeak a proph'cy, *or two*, e'er I go,
where the word *prophecy* is, with great judgment,
I cannot fay melted, but hammer'd into a diffyl-
lable, to make room for the word *two*; and you
have the additional beauty of the open vowels,
fo much commended by Mr. Pope in his *Art of
Criticifm*; which make a fine contraft to the
agreeable roughnefs of the former part of the
line.

[f] Mr. W.'s *Pref.* p. 18, 19.   [g] Vol. 6. p. 26.

I fhall

I fhall not difpute the genuinenefs of this prophecy; which is not, as Mr. Pope fays, in the old edition; nor whether it is neceffary to make the fool divide his difcourfe with the method and regularity of a fermon: but what I admire in this emendation, even above the harmony of the numbers, is the reafon given for it; becaufe *or e'er I go* is not Englifh. On the contrary, if we examine, I believe it will be found; that *e'er*, which is a contraction of *ever*, is never ufed, as it is here, in the fenfe of *before*; without *or* being either exprefs'd or underftood. I may fay, there is hardly a more common expreffion in our language; and, not to mention the Dictionaries, which render *or ever* by *antequam, prius-quam*; Mr. Warburton, as Dr. Caius fays, " has * pray " his pible well;" to fay an expreffion is not Englifh, which he may meet with frequently there; OR EVER *your pots can feel the thorns,—* Pfal. lviii. 8. OR EVER *the filver cord be loofed*, Ecclef. xii. 6. OR EVER *they came at the bottom of the den*, Dan. vi. 24. *We*, OR EVER *he come near, are ready to kill him*; Acts xxiii. 15. Nay Shakefpear himfelf ufes it, uncorrected by Mr. Warburton, in *Cymbeline*; Vol. 7. P. 241.

or e'er I could
Give him that parting kifs.
And elfewhere.
Though Mr. Warburton, when it makes for his purpofe, [b] interprets *a thing of no vowels* by *i. e. without fenfe*; yet on other occafions he

* *Merry Wives of Windfor*, Vol. 1. p. 290.   [b] Vol. 7. p. 398.

feems

feems very fond of thefe elifions, fo much avoided by the ill-judging poets. In 1 *Hen.* VI. Vol. 4. P. 489. where the vulgar editions, that is, all but his own, have,

—'tis prefent death.

He affures us, that Shakefpear wrote;

—i'th' prefence 't's death.

a line, which feems penned for Cadmus when in the ftate of a ferpent.

Once more. In *Othello*, Act III. Sc. 7. the common editions read,

Farewel the neighing fteed, and the fhrill trump, The fpirit-ftirring drum, th' *ear-piercing* fife.

This epithet of *ear-piercing* a poet would have thought not only an harmonious word, but very properly applied to that martial inftrument of mufic; but Mr. Warburton fays, I would [y] read,

th' fear-fperfing fife.

which is fuch a word, as no poet, nor indeed any man who had half an ear, would have thought of; for which he gives this reafon, which none but a Profeffed Critic could have thought of; that piercing the ear is not [z] *an effect on the hearers.*

Mr. Pope has been blamed by fome people for the very fault, which Mr. Warburton charges

[y] To do Mr. W. juftice, I would fufpect this is a falfe print; it fhould be, I would *write*; for no man living can *read* fuch a clufter of confonants.
[z] Vol. 8. p. 345.

on

on the other poetical editor, Mr. Rowe; not attending enough to the bufinefs he pretended to undertake: it has been faid, that he rather yielded to the hafty publication of fome notes, which he had made *obiter* in reading of Shakefpear; than performed the real work of an editor. If this be not fo, what a prodigious genius muft Mr. Warburton be; who can fupply what Mr. Pope, "by the force of an un-" common genius," and in his matureft age, could not perform; merely by giving us obfervations and notes, which, though they " *take " in the whole compafs of criticifm, yet (to " ufe his own words) ᵇ fuch as they are, were " among his younger amufements; when ma-" ny years ago he ufed to turn-over thefe fort " of writers, to unbend himfelf from more feri-" ous applications!" And here I muft do Mr. Warburton the juftice to fay; that, however he may be flandered by the ignorant or malicious Tartufes, it is very apparent that he has not interrupted his more ferious ftudies by giving much of his time and attention to a playbook.

Mr. Pope's however, I fuppofe, was as good an edition as a mere poet could produce; and nothing, as Mr. Warburton juftly obferves, " ᶜ will give the common reader a better idea " of the value of Mr. Pope's edition; than the

---

" two

" two attempts which have been fince made
" by Mr. Theobald, and Sir Thomas Hanmer,
" in oppofition to it; who——left their author
" in ten times a worfe condition than they
" found him." And this will plainly appear to
any one, who compares Mr. Pope's firft edition
with Mr. Theobald's; before the bookfellers had
an opportunity of tranfplanting the blunders of
the latter into the text of the former: as indeed
no fmall number of readings, from both thofe
condemned editions, have unluckily crept into
Mr. Warburton's alfo.

Mr. Pope ambitioufly wifhed, ' that his edition fhould be *melted-down* into Mr. Warburton's; as it would afford him a fit opportunity
of *confeffing* his miftakes: but this Mr. Warburton with prudence refufed; it was not fit,
that the poet's and the critic's performances
fhould be confounded; and though they are, as
we may fay, rivetted together; particular care is
taken, that they fhould never run the one into
the other: they are kept entirely diftinct, and
poor Mr. Pope is left

      ' difappointed, unanneal'd,
With all his imperfections on his head.

To conclude. Nothing feems wanting to
this moft perfect edition of Shakefpear, but the
CANONS or RULES *for Criticifm*, and the GLOS-

' Mr. W.'s *Pref.* p. 19.   ' That is the reading of the old
Editions.

sary; which Mr. Warburton * left to be collected out of his Notes: both which I have endeavoured in some measure to supply; and have given examples, to confirm and illustrate each Rule. And I hope, when Mr. Warburton's edition is thus completed, by the addition of what his want of leisure only hindered him from giving the public; it will fully answer the ends he proposed in it: which are, " ᶠ First, " to give the *unlearned reader* a just idea, and " consequently a better opinion, of the art of " criticism; now sunk very low in the popular " esteem, by the attempts of some; who would " needs exercise it without either natural or ac-, " quired talents: and by the ill success of others; " who seem to have lost both, when they come " to try them upon English authors. And se- " condly, to deter the ᵉ *unlearned writer* from " wantonly trifling with an art he is a stranger " to; at the expence of his own reputation, " and the integrity of the text of established " authors:" which, if this example will not do, I know not what will.

* *Pref.* p. 14, 15. " I once designed to have given the reader a body of Canons for literal Criticism, drawn out in form: — but these uses may be well supplied by what is occasionally said upon the subject in the course of the following remarks." See also p. 16. lin. 25. as to the Glossary.

ᵉ *N. B.* A writer may properly be called *unlearned*; who, notwithstanding all his other knowledge, does not understand the subject which he writes upon.

ᶠ Mr. W.'s *Pref.* p. 14, 15.

CANONS

THE
CANONS or RULES
FOR
CRITICISM.

Extracted out of

Mr. Warburton's *Notes on Shakespear.*

CANON I.

A Profeffed *Critic has a right to declare, that his Author* wrote *whatever he thinks he* fhould *have written; with as much pofitivenefs, as if he had been at his Elbow.*

EXAMPLE I. Vol. 4. P. 330.

" Never went with his forces into France."

" Shakefpear wrote the line thus;
" Ne'er went with his *full* forces into France."

EXAMP. II. Ib. " Shakefpear wrote, " as rich
" with prize."

C

EXAMP.

EXAMP. III. Vol. 8. P. 163. " Shakespear " wrote, "*see too*."——

EXAMP. IV.——P. 339. " Shakespear wrote—— " *make* more virtuous," &c.

EXAMP. V. Vol. 4. P. 333.
" So many thousand actions *once* a foot"
" Shakespear *must have* wrote," *Anglicè* written ;
" *'t once* a foot," i. e. at once." WARB.

Yet I doubt, Mr. Warburton cannot shew an in-stance, where *at* has suffered this apostrophe ; before his Edition in 1747.

EXAMP. VI. Vol. 2. P. 444. We must read, as Shakespear *without question* wrote ;
" And *thyself*, fellow Curtis." WARB.

EXAMP. VII. Vol. 5. P. 8. 2 HENRY VI.
Certainly Shakespear wrote, *East.*

EXAMP. VIII. Vol. 2. P. 250. LOVE'S LABOR'S LOST.
" It insinuateth me of *infamy*."

Mr. Theobald had corrected this to *insanie :* (from *insania*) Mr. Warburton's note is, " There is no " need to make the Pedant worse than Shakespear " made him ; who *without doubt* wrote insanity." WARB.

But why, without doubt ? Shakespear understood the Characters he drew ; and why might not this Pe-dant, as well as others, choose to coin a new word ; when there was an old one as good ? In short, why
might

might not Holofernes take the same liberty, as Mr. Warburton so frequently does?

" ——————————I do perceive,
" Those poor *informal* women are no more
" But instruments of some more mightier member
" That sets them on.————"

i. e. " women who have ill concerted their story.
" *Formal* signifies frequently, in our Author, a
" thing put into form or method : so *informal,*
" out of method, ill concerted. How easy is it
" to say, that Shakespear might better have wrote
" *informing*; i. e. *accusing!* But he; who (as the
" *Oxford Editor*) thinks he did write so, knows
" nothing of the character of his stile." WARB.

Whatever Shakespear *wrote,* he certainly *meant* (with the *Oxford* Editor) informing. He could not mean, that the story was *ill concerted*, because in the very next line *Angelo* supposes, that it was concerted by some *mighty* person concealed ; to whom these women were only *instruments :* and it is treated throughout the scene, by *Angelo* and the Duke too, not as folly ; but as malicious wickedness.

——many a man's tongue *shakes* out his master's undoing.
" We should read—*speaks* out."—WARB.

But Why ? To *speak out his undoing* is awkward, if it be English at all. To *shake out* is more expressive ; as it gives us the idea of rash and unadvised speaking : *temere et leviter effutire.*

EXAMP. XI. Vol. 8. P. 45.   ROMEO and JULIET.

" *Laura* to his lady was but a kitchen-wench——
" *Dido* a dowdy—*Thisbe* a grey-eye or so, but not to
" the purpose.

" We should read and point it thus,

" *Thisbe* a grey-eye, or so : But *now* to the purpose.

" He here turns, from his discourse on the
" effects of love, to enquire after *Romeo*. WARB.

Mercutio's (the speaker) next words are——Signior
Romeo, bonjour ; there's a French salutation to
your French slop.

➤ Very much *to the purpose*, truly !

EXAMP. XII. Vol. 8. P. 51.   ROMEO and JU-
LIET.

" ——Though his face be better than any man's,
" yet his legs exceed all men's—&c.

" We should read—be *no* better than *another*
man's.——WARB.

In order, I suppose to set the old Nurse's *thoughs*
and *yets* into a little better form ; not considering,
that she confounds them again, in the very next
Sentence—*though they may not be talk'd-on, yet are*
they past compare.

EXAMP. XIII. Vol. 8. P. 282.   OTHELLO.

" ————————————————Gone she is :
" And what's to come of my *despised* time
" Is nought but bitterness—"

" Why *despised* time ? We should read—*de-*
" *spited*, i. e. vexatious.   WARB.

Why

Why defpifed? Why, becaufe he would defpife it himfelf: or perhaps, becaufe this marriage was confidered by him as cafting fuch a reflexion on his family; as would render it, and him, contemptible for the reft of his life: as he fays afterwards of his daughter to Othello, that fhe

——— " t' incur a *general mock,*
" Run from her guardage to the footy arms.
" Of *fuch* a *Thing* as *Thou.* ———

To produce all the examples Mr. Warburton has furnifhed us with to this Canon, would be to make an extract from a great part of his Notes; however, I cannot help adding one more, which fhews the true fpirit of a Profeffed Critic:

EXAMP. XIV. Vol. 4. P. 129. 1 HENRY IV. where lady Kate fays to Hotfpur,
- ———" and thou haft talk'd
* * * * * *
. . " Of palifadoes, *frontiers,* parapets," &c. .

In the fpecimen of Mr. Warburton's performance, which was given us in the General Dictionary, under the article of Shakefpear, note Q, his words on this paffage are as follows;

" All here is an exact recapitulation of the appa-
" ratus of a fiege and defence; but the impertinent
" word *frontiers,* which has nothing to do in the
" bufinefs, has crept in amongft them. SH KE-
" SPEAR WROTE, *Rondeurs*; an old French word for
" the round towers in the walls of ancient fortifi-
" cations. The Poet ufes the fame word englifhed
" in K. JOHN, Vol. 3. P. 408.

" 'Tis not the *rounders* of your old fac'd walls"

" This

" This word was *extremely proper* here, and exactly
" in place too, between the Palisadoes and Para-
" pets ; for first is the palisade, then the bastion,
" and then the parapet of the bastion : for the old
" bastion was first a round tower, afterwards it was
" reduced to a section of only the exterior face, as
" may be seen in the plans of old fortified places ;
" at length it received the improvement of its pre-
" sent form, with an angle, flanks, and shoulders."
WARB.

Yet, notwithstanding the *extreme propriety* of this
word, and the *exact order of place too* in which it
stands; all this parade of military skill is silently
dropped in Mr. Warburton's edition, and we are
directed to read, after the *Oxford Editor*,

—FORTINS.

I do not think it a matter of very great consequence, which of the words is retained; because it
seems not at all requisite, that what a man talks in
his sleep, and is repeted by a Lady, who is not supposed to be deeply skilled in such matters ; should
have all the precisenefs of terms and method, which
would be expected in a treatife on fortification :
However, it would have been candid in Mr. Warburton, to have owned his miftake ; and to have
acknowledged the correction of it, though it came
from a gentleman, " who had been recommended
" to him as a * poor Critic ;" and whofe neceffities
he boafts to have fupplied : but to give-up at once
what SHAKESPEAR WROTE, and Mr. Warburton
had fupported with fuch a pompous fhew of learning, merely on an hint from fo defpifed an Editor ;

---

* See Mr. *W*'s Preface, p. 10.

looks,

leoks, as if he had a mind to be thought the advifer of the emendation.

CANON II.

He has a right to alter any paſſage, which he does not underſtand.

EXAMP. I. K. HENRY VIII. Vol. 5. P. 400.

" Which of the peers
" Have uncontemn'd gone by him ; or, at leſt,
" *Strangely* neglected ?"
" The plain ſenſe requires to read
" *Stood not* neglected." WARB.'

The plain ſenſe, to any one who attends to Shake-ſpear's manner of expreſſing himſelf, is ; Which of the Peers has gone by him not contemned, or, at leſt, not ſtrangely neglected ; He leaves the particle *not*, which is included in the compound *un-contemn'd*, to be ſupplied before the latter clauſe.

There is an inſtance of a like manner of expreſſion in P. 404.

" I know her for
" A ſpleeny Lutheran ; and not wholeſome to
" Our cauſe, that ſhe ſhould lie i'th' boſom of
" Our hard-rul'd king.
where we muſt ſupply " *that it is not* whole-" ſome."

And there is the like Ellipſis in this paſſage ;
——— " What friend of mine,
" That had to him deriv'd your anger, did I
" Continue in my liking ? Nay, gave notice
" He was from thence diſcharged ?" P. 386.

But

But there are more than *two* editors of Shake-fpear, who have " regarded Shakefpear's anomalies " (as we may call them) amongft the corruptions of " his text ; which therefore they have cafhier'd to " make room for a jargon of their own :" as Mr. Warburton obferves in his *Preface*, P. 16.

EXAMP. II. Vol. 8. P. 88. ROMEO AND JULIET.

" Now afore God, this rev'rend holy friar
" All our whole city is much bound *to him.*

" *to him.*] For the fake of the grammar I would " fufpect Shakefpear wrote,

— " much bound to *hymn.*"

" *i. e.* praife, celebrate." WARB.

And I, for the fake of Mr. Warburton, would fufpect ; that he was not thoroughly awake, when he made this Amendment.   It is a place, that wants no tinkering ; Shakefpear ufes the nominative cafe ab-folute, or rather elliptical, as he does in HAMLET ;

" Your Majefty and we that have free fouls,
" It touches us not." Vol. 8. P. 196.

" But yefternight, my Lord, fhe and that Friar
" I faw them at the prifon."

MEASURE FOR MEASURE, Vol. 1. P. 444.

" The trumpery in my houfe, go bring it hither."

Vol. 1. P. 70. TEMPEST.

And this is a frequent way of fpeaking, even in profe.

EXAMP. III. Vol. 3. P. 64. ALL'S WELL THAT
ENDS WELL.

" *Diana.*——Think you 'tis fo ;
" *Helden.* Ay furely, *weer* the truth.

" We

" We fhould read *meerlye* truth ; *i. e.* certainly. So
" Sir Thomas Moore,

" That we may *merelye* meet in heaven." WARB.

Why fhould we not keep to Shakefpear's words ;
and fay, he ufes the adjective adverbially ; as he
does in many other places ? " *equal* ravenous, as he
" fubtil." V. 350. HEN. VIII. " I am myfelf *in-*
" *different* honeft." VIII. 184. HAMLET. Nor needed
Mr. Warburton to quote Sir Thomas Moore here ;
except for the obfolete way of fpelling *meerlye*, which
he has judicioufly followed : for *meer* the truth, fignifies, *fimply, purely* truth, not *certainly* ; which is a
needlefs repetition of *furely*.

EXAMP. IV. Vol. 6. P. 84. K. LEAR.

" But mice, and rats, and fuch fmall *deer*,
" Have been Tom's food for feven long year."

For *deer*, venifon, Mr. Warburton, after Sir T.
Hanmer, choofes to read *geer*, drefs or harnefs.

EXAMP. V. Vol. 5. P. 303.

— " The *adulterate* Haftings."

adulterate Shakefpear ufes for *adulterous* : but Mr.
Warburton, becaufe he would be correcting, alters
it to *adulterer* ; yet he left the word untouched in
that line in HAMLET, Vol. 8. P. 147.

" Ay, that inceftuous, that *adulterate* beaft."

EXAMP. VI. Vol. 3. P. 382. The WINTER'S
TALE.

" The *Fixure* of her eye has motion in't."

" This is fad nonfenfe. We fhould read,
" The *Fiffure* of her eye,"—
" *i. e.* the Socket, the place where the eye is." WARB.

The meaning of the line in the original is, Though the eye be fixed, (as the eye of a statue always is) yet it seems to have motion in it; that tremulous motion, which is perceptible in the eye of a living person; how much soever one endeavours to fix it.

Shakespear uses the word in the MERRY WIVES OF WINDSOR, Vol. 1. P. 305.

—— " The firm *Fixure* of thy foot would give an " excellent motion to thy gate," &c.

And in TROILUS and CRESSIDA. Vol. VII. P. 386.

deracinate

" The unity and married calm of states,
" Quite from their *fixure*.

Fissure, Mr. Warburton's word, never signifies a socket; but a slit.

EXAMP. VII. Vol. 5. P. 446. K. HENRY VIII.

—" These are but switches to *'em*."
" To what, or whom? ——
" We should point it thus,
" These are but switches —— *To 'em.*
" i. e. *Have at you*; as we now say. He says this, " as he turns upon the mob." WARB.

To whom? says Mr. Warburton —— why, to the mob. *to them,* is equivalent to, *in their account*; nor is there a more common expression in the English language; such a thing is nothing *to them,* a trifle *to them,* a flea-bite *to them,* &c.

It is however something new, that *to* THEM signifies *Have at* YOU.

Ex-

EXAMP. VIII. Vol. 8. P. 82. ROMEO AND
JULIET.
" Your firſt is dead, or 'twere as good he were,
" As living *here*, and you no uſe of him."

Here, ſignifies *in this world* ; not *in Verona*. Sir
Thomas Hanmer and Mr. Warburton, not under-
ſtanding this, alter it to, living *hence*.

EXAMP. IX. Vol. 8. P. 265. HAMLET.
" And flights of angels *ſing* thee to thy reſt."
" What language is this, of *flights ſinging?* We
" ſhould certainly read,
" And flights of angels *wing* thee to *thy reſt.*
" i. e. carry thee to heaven." WARB.

What language is this? why Engliſh certainly,
if he underſtood it. A *flight* is a flock, and is a very
common expreſſion ; as a *flight* of woodcocks, &c.
If it had not been beneath a *profeſs'd critic*, to conſult
a Dictionary ; he might have found it rendered,
Grex avium, in Littleton ; *Une volée*, in Boyer ; and
why a *flight* of angels may not *ſing*, as well as a
flight of larks, reſts upon Mr. Warburton to ſhew.

EXAMP. X. Vol. 8. P. 299. OTHELLO.
" If virtue no *delighted* beauty lack."
" This is a ſenſeleſs epithet. We ſhould read,
" *belighted* beauty ;" i. e. white and fair. WARB.

It would have been but *fair* for Mr. Warburton to
have given us ſome authority, beſides his own, for
the word *belighted*; at leſt, in that ſignification : but
till he does, we may ſafely think, that Shakeſpear
uſed *delighted*, either for *delightful*, or *which is delighted in.* We may reckon it among his anomalies
abovemention'd ; and juſtify ourſelves by an obſervation

tion of Mr. Warburton's in CYMBELINE, Vol. VII. P. 316. note 6. on the words *invifible inftinct:* " The " poet here transfers the term belonging to the ob- " ject upon the fubject; unlefs we will rather fuppofe " it was his intention to give *invifible* (which has a " paffive) an active fignification."—If Mr. W. had remembered this obfervation, and had only changed the places of the words *object, fubject, paffive,* and *active;* he needed not to have coined the word *belighted* for *fair.*

EXAMP. XI. Vol. 8. P. 301.— OTHELLO.

" *defeat* thy favour with an ufurped beard"

" This is not Englifh. We fhould read, *diffeat* thy " favour; i. e. turn it out of its feat, change it for " another." WARB.

Defeat fignifies, among other things, to *alter,* to *undo*; as the word *defaire,* from whence it comes, does: *Defeafance* has the fame fignification. But Mr. Warburton gives a pleafant reafon for his cor-, rection: " The word *ufurped* directs to this reading." For you know, *ufurpation* neceffarily implies the *diffeating* or dethroning the former king.

I afk Mr. Warburton's pardon, for having in the former edition fufpected him of making that word; I find, it is ufed by good authority: neverthelefs, there is neither reafon nor authority for bringing it in here.

EXAMP. XII. Vol. 4. P. 104. HENRY IV.

" Thou haft the moft unfavoury fimilies; and art, " indeed, the moft *incomparative,* rafcallieft, fweet, " young prince."

" *incomparative,* Oxford editor.—Vulg. *comparative.*" WARB.

This

This emendation of *incomparative* (I fuppofe, in the fenfe of *incomparable*) Mr. Warburton adopts for the fame reafon, which put Sir Thomas upon making it; becaufe he did not underftand the common reading; *comparative:* which Shakefpear ufes here in the fenfe of *dealing in comparifons*; or, if we may fay fo, a *fimile-monger.* In this place he ufes it as an adjective; but he has given us the fame word as a fubftantive, in the fame fenfe, in this very play; P. 160.

" And gave his countenance, againft his name,
" To laugh with gybing boys, and ftand the pufh
" Of every beardlefs, vain *comparative.*"

I think thefe gentlemen had the fame reafon for altering *iteration* for *attraction*, a few lines lower; where, after Prince Harry had ludicroufly quoted a text of Scripture, Falftaff fays; " O, thou haft damnable *iteration.*"—which, I fuppofe, means a way of *repeting* or quoting Scripture. In TROILUS and CRESSIDA (VII. 426.) *iteration* is applied to the *repeting*, or, as it is there called, *citing* of old hackney'd fimilies.

EXAMP. XIII. Vol. 4. P. 152. Firft Part of
HENRY IV.

" Methinks, my *moiety*, north from Burton here,
" In quantity equals not one of yours ."

" *Methinks, my moiety,*—] Hotfpur is here juft
" fuch another divider as the Irifhman, who made
" *three halves:* Therefore, for the honour of Shake-
" fpear, I will fuppofe, with the Oxford editor,
" that he wrote *portion.*" WARB.

If it were not for lofing that foolifh book-jeft about the Irifhman, thefe two editors might as well
have

have fuppofed, that Shakefpear ufed *moiety* for *portion, fhare,* in general; for fo he has ufed it in KING LEAR, Vol. 6. P. 3.

—" equalities are fo weigh'd, that curiofity in
" neither can make ufe of either's *moiety.*"

Now thefe *moietys* were only third parts or fhares of the kingdom, in the one place as well as the other.

EXAMP. XIV. Vol. 1. P. 104. MIDSUMMER
NIGHT'S DREAM.

—" my chief humour is for a tyrant; I could play
" Ercles rarely, or a part to tear a *cat* in."

" We fhould read, A part to tear a *cap* in; for
" as a ranting whore was called a *tear-fheet,* [2d
" part of HEN. IV.] fo a ranting bully was called
" a *tear-cap.*"   WARB.

Nic. Bottom's being called *Bully* Bottom, feems to have given rife to this judicious conjecture; but it is much more likely that Shakefpear wrote, as all the editions give it, " a part to *tear a cat*
" *in*;" which is a burlefque upon Hercules's killing a lion.

EXAMP. XV. Vol. 2. P. 60.   MUCH ADO ABOUT
NOTHING.

" Out on thy feeming—I will *write* againft it."

" What? a libel? Nonfenfe. We fhould read, I
" will *rate* againft it; i. e. *rail* or *revile.*" WARB.

Does Mr. Warburton then find it impoffible to write, unlefs he writes a libel? However that be, this

this emendation makes the matter worse; for we cannot say, I will *rate* against a thing, or *revile* against it, tho' *rail* we may; but that is not much better than *libelling*.

EXAMP. XVI. Vol. 3. P. 431. KING JOHN.

——" this day grows wondrous hot:
" Some *airy* devil hovers in the sky,
" And pours down mischief "——

" We must read, *fiery* devil; if we will have the
" cause equal to the effect." WARB.

Airy devil seems an allusion to the Prince of the power of the air; but the effect described is *pouring down* mischief, which would suit a *watery* devil better than a *fiery* one.

EXAMP. XVII. Vol. 4. P. 110. First part of HENRY IV.

" I then all smarting with my wounds; being gal'd
" To be so pester'd with a popinjay,
" Out of my grief, and my impatience
" Answer'd, neglectingly, I know not what, &c.

" in the former editions it was,
" I then all smarting with my wounds being *cold,*
" To be so pester'd," &c.

" But in the beginning of the speech, he repre-
" sents himself at *this* time not as *cold,* but *hot,* and
" inflamed with rage and labour.

" When I was dry with rage and extreme toil," &c.

C 1

   " I am perſuaded therefore, that Shakeſpear
" wrote and pointed it thus,

" I then all ſmarting with my wounds; being *gal'd*
" To be ſo peſter'd with a popinjay," &c. Warb.

   Mr. Warburton, in order to make a contradiction
in the common reading, and ſo make way for his
emendation; miſrepreſents Hotſpur, as at *this time*
[when he gave this anſwer] *not told, but hot.* It is
true, that at the beginning of his ſpeech, he de-
ſcribes himſelf as

——" dry with rage and extreme toil,
   " Breathleſs and faint, leaning upon his ſword."

Then comes-in this gay gentleman, and holds him
in an idle diſcourſe, the heads of which Hotſpur
gives us; and it is plain by the context, it muſt have
laſted a conſiderable while. Now, the more he had
heated himſelf in the action, the more, when he
came to ſtand ſtill for any time, would the cold air
affect his wounds: But though this imagined contradiction be the reaſon aſſigned for changing *cold*
into *gal'd* or *galed*; (for ſo he miſ-ſpells it, both in
text and notes; to bring it nearer, I ſuppoſe, to the
traces of the original) it is probable, the real reaſon
for this emendation was, becauſe otherwiſe he could
not make it join with the following line,

" To be ſo peſter'd with a popinjay."

   But this objection will be removed, if we allow,
what is undeniably the caſe in ſome other places †,

† Ex. gr. in Hen. V. Vol. 4. P. 73. Theob. 1ſt Edit. and in
2. Hen. VI. P. 190, by Mr. W's advice: ſo probably in Hen.
VIII. Act 3. Sc. 1. Wolſey's ſpeech, beginning, Noble Lady;
where the ſecond line ſhould follow the third. Vol. 5. P. 395.
Mr. W's Edit.

that

that the lines have been tranfpofed; and read them thus,

" I then all fmarting with my wounds being cold,
" Out of my grief, and my impatience
" To be fo pefter'd with a popinjay,
" Anfwer'd neglectingly," &c.

EXAMP. XVII. Vol. 2. P. 336. As you like it.

Clown. " You have faid; but whether wifely or
" no, let the *foreft* judge."

We fhould read, *Forefter*; i. e. the Shepherd, who was there prefent. WARB.

It would have been kind in Mr. Warburton to tell us, *why* we fhould read *forefter*; when the other word is better. . Nothing is more ufual than to fay, the *town* talks, the whole *kingdom* knows of fuch a thing; and one would imagine, Mr. Warburton could not have had a relation to one of the Inns of Court fo long; and not hear of a Man's being tried by his *Country.*

EXAMP. XVIII. Vol. 2. P. 22. . MUCH ADO ABOUT NOTHING.

" Therefore all hearts in love ufe *their* own tongues;
" Let every eye negotiate for itfelf," &c.

Mr. Warburton, after the Oxford Editor, reads *your* own tongues : but there is no need of mending the old reading, by an aukward change of the perfons; *Let,* which is expreffed in the fecond line, is underftood in the firft. See Ex. XXI.

D   EXAMP.

Examp. XIX. Vol. 2. P. 47.

" —And for your writing and reading, let them
" appear when there is *no* need of such vanity—]
" Dogberry is only absurd; not absolutely out of
" his senses. We should therefore read, *more* need."
Warb.

What Mr. Warburton says of Dogberry, is as
much as can fairly be said of himself; when he corrects only this one contradictory blunder of his,
among an hundred, of which his speeches are full;
and which make the humour of his Character. He
is perpetually making these *qui-pro-quos*; as Mr.
Warburton's friends the French call them.

Examp. XX. Ibid. P. 61.

" Who hath indeed most like a *liberal* villain
" Confess'd the vile encounters they have had.

" most like a *liberal* villain] We should read, like
" an *illiberal* villain."   Warb.

This is what Mr. Warburton calls *the rage of
correcting*; for if he had given to the word *liberal*,
the same explanation as he does in Othello, Vol.
8. P. 310. *liberal* for *licentious*; or even taken it
for *free, unreserved*; he needed not have altered
Shakespear's words.

Examp. XXI. Ibid. P. 63.

" But mine—*and* mine I lov'd,—*and* mine I prais'd,
" *And* mine that I was proud on—mine so much,
" That I myself was to myself not mine,
" Valuing of her—why she—O she is fallen," &c.

" The sense requires, that we should read AS in
" these three places." WARB.

And he goes-on to give us what he imagines to
be the reasoning of the speaker. But this correction
is owing to want of attention; and, if I am not mistaken, makes it little better than nonsense; he takes
mine to be the accusative case, which is the nominative, in apposition with *she*. If these lines are
read with proper pauses, here is a fine climax; which
is spoil'd by his emendation: perhaps he did not
know, that *whom* or *that* is to be understood after
mine in the two first places; as it is expressed in the
third.

EXAMP. XXII. Vol 2. P. 113. MERCHANT OF
VENICE.

" See to my house, left in the FEARFUL guard
" Of an unthrifty knave——

" But surely *fearful* was the most trusty guard for
" a house-keeper, in a populous city— I *suppose*
" therefore, that Shakespear wrote—

" FEARLESS guard, i. e. *careless*, &c." WARB.
And upon this *supposition* he alters the text, without giving any authority for using *fearless* for *careless*; forgetting in the mean time, that if Launcelot
was *fearful*, he might run away. But there is no
need either of that construction, or Mr. Warburton's alteration. *Fearful* guard here means, a
guard of which he has reason to be *afraid*; which
he cannot *trust* or *rely* on.

EXAMP. XXIII. Vol. 2. P. 286. LOVE'S
LABOR'S LOST.

" And cuckow buds of yellow hue
" Do paint the meadows *with delight.*

" I

— " I would read thus,
" Do paint the meadows *much bedight*,"
    " i. e. much *bedecked* or *adorned* ; as they are in
" fpring time." WARB.

But if they are much *bedight* already, they little need painting.

EXAMP. XXIV. Vol. 2. P. 337. AS YOU LIKE IT.
" O moft gentle *Jupiter!*

    " We fhould read, *Juniper*—alluding to the
" proverbial term of a Juniper lecture : a fharp
" or unpleafing one ; *Juniper* being a rough prick-
" ly plant." WARB.

Not to take notice of this *gentle, rough, prickly* plant, which Mr. Warburton has found-out ; I believe no body but he would have dreamed of a Juniper lecture here, any more than above ; where the fame Rofalind fays,

" O *Jupiter !* how weary are my fpirits !

EXAMP. XXV. Vol 5. P. 8. 2 HENRY VI.
" And all the wealthy kingdoms of the *weft*."
    " Certainly Shakefpear wrote, *eaft*." WARB.

Why fo certainly ? Has Mr. Warburton forgotten, what he feems defirous of making Shakefpear allude-to in fome places, the difcovery of the Weft-Indies ; and the hopes of immenfe gain from that new country ?

EXAMP. XXVI. Vol. 3. P. 309. WINTER'S TALE.
" I fay, good Queen ;
" And would by combat make her good, fo were I
" A man, *the worft* about you.
                                    —" Surely

—" Surely she [*Paulina*] could not say, that were
" she a man the worst of these [*the courtiers about the*
" *King*] she would vindicate her mistress's honor
" against the King's suspicions in single combat.
" Shakespear, I am persuaded, wrote,

A man on th' *worst* about you.

" i. e. were I a man, I would vindicate her honor on
" the worst of these sycophants about you." Warb.

But *surely* this emendation is for want of understanding English. If the text had been, a man the *best*
about you, there would have been a necessity for some
alteration; but the worst man here, does not signify
the *wickedest*; but the *weakest*, or *least warlike:* so a
better man, the *best* man in company, frequently refer
to courage and skill in fighting; not to moral goodness.

Examp. XXVII. Vol. 4. P. 430. Henry V.

" Thus far with rough and all unable pen
" Our *bending* author hath pursu'd the story.

" We should read, " *Blending* author"—

" So he says of him just afterwards, *mangling* by
" starts." Warb.

I believe, we shall hardly meet with the word
blending, thus neutrally used, in any good author;
and I am sure, we shall not meet with such a reason,
in any good critic; because *he says just afterwards,*
mangling; a reason, which deserves to be ranked under Canon VIII: but I doubt, Mr. Warburton took
mangling for *mingling*; and had a mind to introduce
a beautiful tautology.

　　　Bending

Bending may either signify *unequal to the task*, or *suppliant*, as Shakespear expresses it in HAMLET, Vol. 8. P. 193.

—" *stooping* to your clemency."

This is plain enough; " but (as Mr. Warburton " says, P. 481. of this volume) what will not a " puzzling critic obscure?"

EXAMP. XXVIII. Vol. 2. P. 410. TAMING OF THE SHREW.

————" farther than at home,
" Where small experience grows but in a few."

" *Where small experience grows but in a few*] This " nonsense should be read thus,

" Where small experience grows but in a *mew*."

" i. e. a confinement at home. And the mean- " ing is; that no improvement is to be expected of " those, who never look out of doors." WARB.

And he supports his use of the word by a line of Fairfax,

　　　She hated chambers, closets, secret mews.

So, because Fairfax calls a *chamber*, or a *closet*, a *mew*, Mr. Warburton will call a *whole country* so.

Mr. Theobald explanes it, *except in a few*; i. e. instances are uncommon; which is not nonsense; but perhaps the place should be pointed thus,

————" at home,
" Where small experience grows.——But, in a few, " Signior Hortensio, thus it stands with me;" &c. i. e. in short, in a few words.

So in HEN. VIII. Act II. Scene I. " I'll tell you " *in a little.*"

　　　　　　　　　　　　　Second

Second Part of HEN. IV. Act I. Vol. III. P. 445.
Theobald's I. Edition.

" *In few* ; his death, whose spirit lent a fire
" Even to the dullest peasant in his camp," &c.

HEN. V. Vol. 4. P. 334. " Thus then *in few*."

MEASURE FOR MEASURE, Act I. Scene the last,
Vol. I. P. 324. Theob. I. Edit.

" Do not believe it. *Fewness*, and truth, 'tis thus."

There are many more instances of this short expression applied to speech ; and in the TEMPEST,
Vol. 1. P. 73. a similar one applied to Time :

————" for *a little* (i. e. a little while)
" Follow, and do me service?"

EXAMP. XXIX. Vol. 5. P. 400. HENRY VIII.

————" when did he regard
" The stamp of nobleness in any person
" Out *of* himself ?"

" The expression is bad ; and the thought false :
" For it supposes Wolsey to be *noble* ; which was
" not so : we should read and point,

————" when did he regard
" The stamp of nobleness in any person ;
" Out *of't* himself ?

" I. e. When did he regard nobleness of blood in
" another ; having none of his own to value him-
" self upon ?" WARB.

Mr. Warburton's delicate ear seems formed for
the harmony of these sort of elisions, *out of't, on th'*
worst, thou split'st, 'tonce a foot, ang'shing a dissyllable, &c. for, unless it be to improve the sound, there
is no need of this amendment ; which, if another
had made it, he might perhaps have called the *pal-*
try clipt jargon of a modern fop. Vol. 6. P. 469.

Though

Though Wolsey was not nobly born, yet he had the *stamp of nobleness* impressed on him; both by the King and the Pope. And as to the expression— *out of himself*, in the sense of, *except in* himself—it has the genuine air of Shakespear: and is used in the same sense, in this very play; P. 357. The complement made to Shakespear in the beginning of this note, should be referred to Canon IV.

EXAMP. XXX. Vol. 7. P. 315. CYMBELINE.

" I'd let a *parish* of such Clotens blood.]

" This nonsense should be corrected thus,

" I'd let a *marish* of such Clotens blood.

" i. e. a marsh or lake. WARB.

The sense of the passage is, I would let blood (or bleed) a whole parish, or any number of such fellows as Cloten; not that I would let out a parish of blood: so that Mr. Warburton may keep his marish to be inhabited, as he says Venice was, by poor fishermen; without letting it blood: which might make it aguish. But if the reader approves his *correction*, it will lead us to another in Page 355. of this volume; where we may read,

———" and hath
" More of thee merited, than a *pond* of Clotens
" Had ever shore for"———

instead ———" than a *band* of Clotens
" Had ever *scar* for"———

EXAMP. XXXI. Vol. 1. P. 411. MEASURE FOR
MEASURE.

" *Is't* not *drown'd* in the last *rain?*] " This
" strange nonsense should be thus corrected, *It's not*
" *down*

" *down* i'th' laſt *reign* ; i. e. *theſe* are ſeverities un-
" known to the old Duke's time. *And this is to the*
" *purpoſe.*" WARB.

To what *purpoſe* it is, I cannot tell; except it be
to make a paſſage abſolute nonſenſe, which at leſt
was ſenſe; before he meddled with it. Though it
may be difficult to explane all that Lucio ſays in
this ſcene ; Mr. Warburton has had the luck to
make matters harder than he found them.

Lucio ſays, " How now, noble Pompey ? What,
" at the wheels of Cæſar ? &c.——What reply ? ha ?
" What ſayeſt thou to this tune, matter, and me-
" thod ? [i. e. *what anſwer have you to make me ?*]
" Is IT [*his reply or anſwer*] not drown'd in the laſt
" rain ?" A proverbial phraſe, to expreſs a thing
which is loſt.

This explication ſeems eaſier, than that *it* ſhould
ſignify *theſe* ſeverities ; and *down in the laſt reign,*
unknown to the old Duke's time; as much as Mr.
Warburton aſſures us, that it *is to the purpoſe.*

In his very next note, he has, by arbitrarily altering the pointing, obſcured a paſſage ; which was
clear before : loſt the real jeſt, in hunting for humor ; where none was deſigned : and attributed a
ſentiment to one of the ſpeakers, which there is not
the leſt foundation for : while he ſupports this only
by a——*This is in character.*

Note 8. " Go, ſay I ſent thee thither. For
" debt, Pompey, or how ?"] It ſhould be pointed
thus, " Go, ſay, I ſent thee thither for debt, Pom-
" pey ; or how"——i. e. to hide the ignominy of
" thy caſe, ſay I ſent thee to priſon for debt, or
" whatever pretence thou fancieſt better." The
other humorouſly replies, " For being a bawd,
" for

" for being a bawd; i. e. The true cause is the most
" *honourable.*   This is in character." Warb.

Pompey, as he is going to prison, on seeing Lucio,
cries, ' I spy comfort; I cry bail:' &c. hoping, that
Lucio would stand his friend : but he all along, instead of comforting, aggravates his distress, by ban-
tering him.   After several other questions, he asks,
" Art thou going to prison, Pompey?"

Clown. " Yes, faith, Sir.

Lucio. " Why 'tis not amiss, Pompey: farewel,
" Go, say I sent thee thither."

After this jest he resumes his questions, and asks
the cause of his commitment— " For debt, Pom-
" pey, or how?" to which the Clown gives the
true answer; that he was committed for being a
bawd.

Where now is there the left foundation for this
conceit, of *hiding the ignominy of his punishment?* or
the humor of that reply, for being a bawd ; i. e.
the true cause is the most honourable ; which is a reflexion, that deserves to be ranked under Canon
XII.

EXAMP. XXXII. Vol. 1. P. 412. MEASURE FOR MEASURE.

" *It is too* GENERAL *a vice*] The occasion of the
" observation was, Lucio's saying, That it ought
" to be treated *with a little more lenity;* and his an-
" swer to it is—*The vice is of great kindred.* No-
" thing can be more absurd than all this. From
" the occasion and the answer therefore it appears,
" that Shakespear wrote,

" It is too *gentle* a vice.

" which

" which fignifying both indulgent and well-bred,
" Lucio humoroufly takes it in the latter fenfe."
WARB.

Read either, *it is too indulgent* a vice, or *too well-bred* a vice, in anfwer to what Lucio fays; and you will find, they are both nonfenfe. The word *gentle*, therefore, if Shakefpear did write it, muft have a third fenfe; which Mr Warburton unkindly keeps to himfelf.

But the truth is, the old reading is right; and the dialogue, before Mr. Warburton interrupted it, went on very well. " A little more lenity to " leachery (fays Lucio) would do no harm in him;" the Duke anfwers, " It is *too general* a vice." " Yes " (replies Lucio)—the Vice is of great kindred, " — it is well allied," &c. As much as to fay, Yes truly, it is general; for the greateft men have it, as well as we little folks. And, a little lower, he taxes the Duke perfonally with it. Nothing can be more natural than all this.

EXAM. XXXIII. Vol. 3. P. 150. TWELFTH NIGHT.

——————" it is filly footh;
" And *dallies* with the innocence of love,
" Like the old age."

Speaking of a fong. It is a plain old fong, fays he, has the fimplicity of the ancients, and *dallies* with the innocence of love; i. e. fports and plays innocently with a love fubject, as they did in old times.

But Mr. Warburton, who is here out of his Element, and on a fubject not dreamt of in his Philofophy; pronounces peremptorily,

" *Dallies* has *no fenfe*; we fhould read *tallies*."
WARB.

Spoken

Spoken more like a baker or milkman, than a lover.

Examp. XXXIV. Vol. 1. P. 77. Tempest.

" I'll break my ftaff;
" Bury it *certain fadoms* in the earth, &c.

" Certain, in it's *prefent* fignification, is predicated
" of a precife determinate number : but this fenfe
" would make the thought flat and ridiculous. We
" muft confider the word *certain* therefore, as ufed
" in its *old* fignification of *a many* indefinitely. So
" *Bale* in his Acts of Englifh Votaries fays, *but*
" *he took with him* a certen *of his idle compa-*
" *nions:* for *a many*. So that Shakefpear, I fup-
" pofe, wrote the line thus; *Bury't* a certain *fa-*
" *dom in the earth.* Warb."

Certain has *now,* as it.alfo had *of old,* two fenfes :
it may either be ufed indefinitely; or elfe (as Mr. W.
choofes to exprefs himfelf) may be " predicated of a
precife determinate number." But how it came into
our Critic's head, that in it's indefinite ufe it muft
fignify a great number, or (as he *elegantly* calls it)
a many; I am at a lofs to guefs. Nor can I conceive, what bulky Grammarian fell from the fhelves
upon his head; that he takes fuch bitter revenge
on poor Prifcian, as to change *fadoms* plur. for *fa-*
dom fing. at the inftant he is telling you, Shakefpear
meant *many fadoms :* unlefs perhaps he did it for
the fake of uniformity of ftyle. Then indeed, to
fay—two, three, twenty *fadom*, inftead of *fadoms*,
is juft fuch a piece of vulgarity in fpeech; as to fay
—*a many* for a great many.

One may fay, that Mr. W. has written *certain*
obferva-

obfervations and emendations on Shakefpear: but nobody, that ever read them, except ONE, would imagine; that it was, or could be intended hereby to *predicate*, that the obfervations were *precife* and *determinate*; or the emendations *certain*.

I fuppofe, Shakefpear intended by this expreffion to fignify; that there was a *certain precife determinate* number of *fadoms*, which Profpero by his art knew of; at which depth if he buried his ftaff, it would never more be difcovered, fo as to be ufed in enchantments.

EXAMP. XXXV. Vol. 1. P. 356. MEASURE FOR MEASURE.

" —We have with fpecial *Soul*
" Elected Him, Our abfence to fupply."
" This nonfenfe muft be corrected thus; *with fpe-*
" *cial roll:* i. e. by a fpecial commiffion." WARB.

With fpecial *Soul*, may fairly be interpreted to mean, with great thought, upon mature deliberation; but *with* fpecial *roll*, for—*by* fpecial *commiffion*, is hard and awkward: and to *elect* a man by a commiffion, inftead of—*appoint* him, is flat *nonfenfe*; which muft be re-corrected thus—with fpecial SOUL.

EXAMP. XXXVI. Vol. 1. P. 217. TWO GENTLE-MEN, &c.

" I am but a Fool, look you; and yet I have the
" wit to think, my mafter is a kind of knave: but
" that's all one, if he be but one knave.] Where is
" the *fenfe*, or, if you wont allow the fpeaker that,
" where is the *humour* of this fpeech? Nothing had
" given the fool occafion to fufpect, that his mafter
was

" was become *double* ; like *Antipholis* in the Come-
" dy of Errors.　The laſt word is corrupt.　We
" ſhould read—if he but one *kind*.　He thought his
" maſter was a *kind* of Knave : however, he keeps
" himſelf in countenance with this reflexion ; that,
" if he was a knave but of *one kind*, he might paſs
" well enough among his neighbours." WARB.

Mr. W. aſks, " Where is the *ſenſe*, or *humour*
" of this ſpeech?" If he would have ſtopp'd there
for an anſwer, it might perhaps have been found
for him.　But after he has Led the reader away,
by that wild reaſoning about his maſter becoming
double ; Corrupted the text, by way of mending
it ; and laſtly, Explaned his own corruption ; it is
no eaſy matter to recover either ſenſe or humour to
the paſſage.　The plain ſenſe of it however ſeems
to be this.

Launce, from what has paſſed in the preceding
part of the play between *Protheus,* his maſter, and
Valentine, reflects ; that though *He* is a *Fool,* his
Maſter is a *Knave.*　But that's all one, ſays He ; if
he be *but one* knave, i. e. if he *only* be a knave ; if
I too be not found myſelf to be *an other*, viz. a hypo-
critical knave : for he goes-on ſaying—" He lives
" not, that *knows* I am in love ; yet I *am* in love, &c."
It is not his Maſter's honeſty, but his *own,* that
Launce is endeavouring to defend ; as it is not *Shakeſpear's* meaning, but his *own,* that Mr. W. is endeavouring to account-for : and then he confounds
and overbears his more diffident reader, by adding
here, as in many other places, a peremtory ——

" This is truely humourous."

EXAMP.

" —— Thou haft nor Youth, nor Age :
" But as it were an after-dinner's fleep,
" Dreaming on both : for all thy bleffed Youth
" Becomes as aged, and doth beg the Alms
" Of palfied Eld ; and when thou'rt old and rich,
" Thou' haft neither Heat, Affection, Limb, nor
" Beauty ;
" To make thy riches pleafant——"

" The drift of this period is to prove, that nei-
" ther Youth nor Age can be faid to be really en-
" joyed :—— which conclufion he that can deduce,
" has a better knack at logic than I have. I fup-
" pofe the poet wrote,

" —— for *pall'd* thy *blazed* youth
" Becomes *affuaged* ; and doth beg —— &c.

" i. e. When thy youthful appetite becomes palled,
" as it will be in the very enjoyment, the blaze of
" youth is at once affuaged"—— &c. WARB.

Which is as much as to fay, When thy youthful
appetite becomes palled, why then —— it becomes
palled. This is Mr. W's knack at Logic ; and
this he fupports with his ufual trick of—— " This is
" to the purpofe."

Now becaufe one may, without over much confidence, pretend to as good a knack at Logic as this ;
let us fee what may be made of the paffage, without
Mr. W's corruptions of it. And it may be thus explained.

' In your Youth you are in as bad a condition as
' an old man ; for tho' you have Appetites to enjoy
' the pleafures of life, yet you are unable to enjoy
' them for want of the Means to purchafe them, *viz.*
' Riches ;

' Riches ; not being come to your eſtate, being de-
' pendent on your Elders for ſubſiſtence.   And be-
' cauſe you are advanced in years, before you come
' to your Inheritance ; therefore by that time you
' get riches to purchaſe the pleaſures of life, your
' appetites and ſtrength forſake you ; and you are
' incapable of enjoying them, *on that account.* Ap-
' petite, in Shakeſpear's looſe manner, is ſignified
' by two words, *viz.* heat, affection ; and Strength
' by two others, limb, beauty.   This laſt Mr W.
does not like ; and therefore pronounces,

   " We ſhould read, bounty ; which compleats the
" ſenſe, and is this ; Thou haſt neither the pleaſure
" of enjoying riches thy-ſelf, for thou wanteſt vi-
" gour ; nor of ſeeing it enjoyed by others, for thou
" wanteſt bounty.   Where the making the want of
" bounty as inſeparable from old age as the want
" of health, is extremely *ſatyrical* ; though not al-
" together *juſt.*" WARB.

   This reaſon for the alteration is worthy of the
critic by profeſſion ; who not finding in his author
what to cenſure, firſt corrupts under pretence of a-
mending him ; and then abuſes him for the impu-
ted ſentiment.

CANON III.

*Theſe 'alterations be may make, in ſpite of the
exactneſs of meaſure.*

EXAMPLE I. Vol. 5. P. 383. HENRY VIII.
      " I do not know,
" What kind of my obedience I ſhould tender ;
" More than my All is nothing ; nor my prayers," *&c.*

   * See this ſentiment well expreſſed in LEAR, Vol. 6. P. 8.
                                          Where

Where the obvious fenfe is, If my All were more than it is, it would be Nothing (of no value): fo that I cannot poffibly make any fit return to the king for his favour.

There is a like expreffion in MACBETH,

" More is thy due, than more than all can pay."
Theob. 1ft Ed. Vol. 5. P. 399.

But Mr. Warburton pronounces, *ex cathedra*,

" *More than my all is nothing*] No figure can
" free this expreffion from nonfenfe. *In fpite of*
" *the exactnefs of meafure*, we fhould read ;

More than my All, *which is* Nothing :
" i. e. which All is Nothing."

Where, inftead of correcting Shakefpear, he fhould have corrected his own underftanding ; for, if her All might be Nothing, why might not a little more than her All be fo ?

By the fame figure (a very common one) Phædria in the Phormio fays, his All is lefs than Nothing—unde ego nunc tam fubito huic argentum inveniam mifer, Cui *minus nihilo* eft — Act III. Sc. 3.

EXAMP. II. Vol. 1. P. 119. MIDSUMMER NIGHT'S DREAM.

——" And fome keep back
" The clamorous owl, that nightly hoots and
" wonders
" At our queint *fpirits*. Sing me now afleep," &c.

" *At our queint fpirits*] We fhould read *fports.*"
WARB.

The perfons of the fairies feem a properer object
E
of

of wonder to the owl, than their sports; for which reason, as well as for the sake of the measure, the old reading, *spirits,* is preferable.

If Mr. Warburton stole this emendation from Sir Thomas Hanmer, for it occurs in his Edition also, he should have done him the justice to take the whole of it; and so have preserved the measure of the verse.

" At our quaint *sports.* Come, sing me now asleep."

EXAMP. III. Vol. 4, P. 8. KING RICHARD II.

" This we prescribe, though no Physician," &c.

" I must make one remark in general on the
" rhymes throughout this whole play; they are so
" much inferior to the rest of the writing, that they
" appear to me of a different hand. What con-
" firms this, is; that the context does *every where*
" *exactly* (and frequently much better) *connect* with-
" out the inserted rhymes, except in a very few
" places; and just there too, the rhyming verses are
" of a much better taste than all the others; which
" rather strengthens my conjecture." Mr. POPE.

The professed critic might have seen, that this observation of Mr. Pope's happens to be very unluckily placed here; because the context, without the inserted rhymes, will not *connect* at all. For example; let us read the passage, as it would stand corrected by this rule—

K. *Richard.* " Wrath-kindled Gentlemen, be
" rul'd by me;
" Let's purge this choler without letting blood.
*   *   *   *   *   *   *   *   *
" We were not born to sue, but to command;
" Which since we cannot do to make you friends,
" Be

" Be ready, as your lives fhall anfwer it,
" At Coventry, upon St. Lambert's day ;
" There fhall your fwords and lances arbitrate," &c.

Here we fee ; that, when the rhyming part of this dialogue is left-out, King Richard begins with dif-fuading them from the duel ; and in the very next fentence, abfurdly enough, appoints the time and place of their combat. Nor are thefe rhyming verfes in fo defpicable a tafte, as they are repre-fented ; on the contrary, what both of the perfons fay about the value of their good name and honor, contains fentiments by no means unworthy of their birth and nobility.

But Mr. Warburton feizes on this licence of his friend, to nibble at the rhyming part of the play ; and in Page 15, makes a needlefs alteration, in defi-ance of the rhyme ; and, as it feems, merely in de-fiance.

" As gentle and as jocund as to *jeft*,
" Go I to fight : Truth hath a quiet breaft."

" Not fo neither : we fhould read, to *juft*, i. e. to
" tilt or tourny ; which was a kind of fport too."
WARB.

By the pertnefs of his " *Not fo neither*," one would imagine, he had fome fmart reafon to give againft that expreffion to *jeft* : yet his remark, " *which was a kind of fport too*," brings it as near as poffible to the idea of *jefting* ; and feems to have been fuggeft-ed to him by his evil Genius, merely to weaken the force of his own emendation.

EXAMP. IV. Vol. 5. P. 320. RICHARD III.

" This, this, All-fouls day to my fearful foul
" Is the determin'd *refpite* of my wrongs."

" This

" This is nonsense : we should read, *respect* of my
" wrongs ; i. e. requital." WARB.

The whole tenor of the speech plainly shews ; that
the sense is, " This day is the utmost respite of the
" punishment, which heaven has determined to in-
" flict on me for the wrongs I have done." There
was therefore no reason, except for the harmonie's
sake, to change *respite* into *respect*.

EXAMP. V. Vol. 6. P. 98. KING LEAR.

Ang'ring itself and others—] Here Mr. Warburton, after the Oxford editor, would, if he could,
read *anguishing* ; but, imagining the measure would
not bear this word, they slip out the *u* by a clean
conveyance, and write *ang'ishing* ; which, as it still
has three syllables, does not mend the matter. They
should have given us boldly *ang'shing*, a dissyllable.

EXAMP. VI. Vol. 6. P. 401. MACBETH.

" To fright you thus, methinks, I am too savage ;
" To do *worse* to you were fell cruelty."

" Who can doubt it ?　But this is not what he
" would say.　A stranger of ordinary condition ac-
" costs a woman of quality without ceremony, and
" tells her abruptly, that her life, and her children's
" lives, are in imminent danger ; but, seeing the effect
" this had upon her, he adds, as we should read it,

" To do *worship* to you were fell cruelty.

" that is, but at this juncture to waste my time in
" the gradual observances due to your rank, would
" be the exposing your life to immediate destruction.
" *To do worship*, signified, in the phrase of that time,
" to *pay observance*." WARB.

Our

Our critic is strangely punctilious, and mannerly, all of a sudden ; the times he is talking of were not so ceremonious, and Shakespear makes messengers accost even crowned heads as abruptly, as this does Lady Macduff. He does her worship, as Mr. Warburton interprets it, in those words. " Bless you, " fair Dame !" And why may not, *to do worse to you* signify to fright you more, by relating all the circumstances of your danger ; which would detain you so long, that you could not avoid it ?

I remember another fit of mannerliness, which took him very unluckily. In Vol. 4. P. 113. he had sneer'd Sir Thomas Hanmer, for changing Sirrah into Sir. Ist part of HENRY IV.

—" *but,* Sirrah, *from this hour.*] The Oxford " editor (says he) is a deal more courtly, than his old " plain Elizabeth author. He changes *Sirrah* there- " fore to *Sir.*" But Mr. Warburton, three pages off, is no less courtly ; where he makes Eteocles in Euripides say, " I will not, *Madam,* disguise my thoughts," &c. Ib. P. 116.

EXAMP. VII. Vol. 6. P. 419.   MACBETH.

" We learn no other, but the *confident* tyrant
" Keeps still in Dunsinane.—

" The Editors have here spoiled the measure ; " in order to give a tyrant an * epithet, which does " not belong to him : (namely *confidence,* or repo- " sing himself securely in any thing or person :) " while they rejected the true one, expressive of a " tyrant's jealousy and suspicion, and declarative of " the fact.   We must surely read,
"   ——— the *confin'd* tyrant."   WARB.

* He should have said, a *quality* ; for a substantive, namely *Confidence,* is improperly called an *Epithet.*

The

The verfe, which ever reading we take, is not very harmonious; but the new one is certainly worfe than the old. Four fhort fyllables to gether,

[We learn no other but the confined tyrant] is worfe than only three; and the laft fyllable but one of the meafure being long (as in *confined*) always gives a roughnefs in Englifh metre.

So much for the form. As for the matter; furely *Macbeth* had very extraordinary *things* and *perfons* to repofe *confidence* in; when his Life and his Kingdom both depended upon the coming to pafs of two Events, each of which was, as He himfelf thought, impoffible; i. e. the moving of Birnam wood, and the oppofition of a man not born of woman. Nor will it avail Mr. W. to fay, that the Speaker here is not fuppofed to know of thefe grounds of *Macbeth*'s confidence; for though he was ignorant of the facts, the confidence of *Macbeth*, which was the refult of thofe facts, could not but be publicly known.

CANON IV.

Where he does not like an expreffion, and yet cannot mend it; He may abufe his Author for it.

EXAMP. I. Vol. 5. P. 353. HENRY VIII.

" My life itfelf, and the *beft heart* of it."

" *and the beft heart of it.*] The expreffion is mon-
" ftrous. The heart is fuppofed the feat of life: But
" as if he had many lives, and to each of them a
" heart, he fays, his *beft heart*. A way of fpeak-
" ing, that would have become a cat rather than a
" king." WARB.

Poor

Poor Shakefpear! your anomalies will do you no fervice, when once you go beyond Mr. Warburton's apprehenfion ; and you will find, a profefs'd critic is a terrible adverfary ; when he is thoroughly provoked : " you muft then fpeak by the card ; or e-" quivocation will undo you." How happy is it, that Mr. Warburton was either not fo attentive, or not fo angry, when he read thofe lines in HAMLET ;

" Give me that man,

" That is not paffion's flave, and I will wear him
" In my heart's core ; ay, in my heart of heart"——

We fhould then perhaps have heard, that this was a way of fpeaking, that would have rather become a pippin than a prince.

EXAMP. II. Vol. 8. P. 337. OTHELLO.
" *Keep leets and law-days*——] i. e. *govern.* A me-" taphor wretchedly forced and quaint." WARB.

EXAMP. III. Vol. 3. P. 104. ALL'S WELL
THAT ENDS WELL.

——" then if you know
" That you are well acquainted with yourfelf]
" i. e. then if you be wife. A ftrange way of ex-" preffing fo trivial a thought." WARB.

Strange indeed, if that were the thought ; but the true fenfe of the paffage is, Confefs the ring was hers ; *for you know it as well as you know that you are yourfelf.*

EXAMP. IV. Vol. 6. P. 172. TIMON OF ATHENS.

Note 2. " Nothing can be worfe or more ob-" fcurely expreffed ; and all for the fake of a " wretched rhyme." WARB.

E 4

EXAMP.

EXAMP. V. Vol. 6. P. 402. MACBETH.

"   " each new morn
" New widows howl, new orphans cry, new forrows
" Strike heaven on the face; that it refounds
" As if it felt with Scotland, and yell'd out
" Like fyllables of dolor."

——— " *and yell'd out*
" *Like fyllables of dolor.*] This prefents a ridiculous image." WARB.

I cannot conceive, what fort of notion Mr. Warburton has of ridicule; if he thinks this, and the *
virginal palms of the young Roman ladies in Coriolanus, to be ridiculous images.

EXAMP. VI. Vol. 7. P. 150. ANTONY AND
CLEOPATRA.

—" That, without which
" A Soldier and his fword *grant* fcarce diftinc-
" tion] Grant for afford. It is badly and ob-
" fcurely expreffed." WARB.

EXAMP. VII. Vol. 8. P. 355. OTHELLO.
———" *number'd*———
" *The Sun to courfe*—] i. e. number'd the Sun's
" courfes. Badly exprefs'd." WARB.

EXAMP. VIII. Vol. 4. P. 442. HENRY VI.
Firft Part.

" nine *Sibyls* of old *Rome*] There were no nine
" *Sibyls* of *Rome*. But he confounds things; and

* See Canon VII. Example 9.

" miftakes

" miftakes this for the nine books of *Sibylline O-*
" *racles,* brought to one of the *Tarquins.*" WARB.

And why will not the expreffion ferve to fignify juft thus much, and no more? But there is
fome little fhew of Learning in the Note; though
not enough to let us know, *which* of the *Tarquins*
it was.

EXAM. IX. We may not improperly add, by
way of Supplement to the Examples of this
Canon, the *Character* of Shakefpear; as drawn by
Mr. Warburton in his Notes, while he is pretending to explane him.

He was, it feems,

	Vol.	Pag.
Selfifh and ungenerous	1.	398
Envious of others' happinefs	4.	4
Unjuftly fatyrical, on mankind	1.	400
Very juftly fo, on his own countrymen	1.	43
A Hobbift, in his notion of Allegiance	4.	18
A Flatterer of King James	4. 6.	323 396 408
An Abufer of Him	8.	353
An Abufer of firft Minifters	5.	350
A cunning Shaver, and very dextrous Trimmer between very oppofite Parties	1.	113
A Judge of Statuary	7.	349
Ignorant of it	3.	377
Inventer of a fine fort of Solder	7.	157

Let any one read this fhort fummary of Mr.
W's character of our Poet; and then judge, whether

ther of the two has been retained in the cause of
Dulness against Shakespear; the Gentleman, or
the Preacher, of Lincoln's-Inn. Especially, when
it is farther considered; that, in most of the passages here refer'd-to, the remark is a mere conundrum of the Editor; without any ground or foundation in the Author's either words or sense!

CANON V.

*Or He may condemn it, as a foolish interpo-
lation.*

EXAMPLE I. Vol. 8. P. 188.————

So Mr. Warburton does this passage in HAMLET.

" neither having the accent of Christian, nor the
" gate of Christian, Pagan, nor Man:"

though there is a manifest reference to it, in the
words immediately following; " have so strutted
" and bellowed."

EXAMP. II. Vol. 3. P. 397.   KING JOHN.

" And so am I, whether I smack or no.

" A nonsensical line of the players."   WARB.

EXAMP. III. Vol. 4. P. 353.   HENRY V.

" Up in the air crown'd with the golden sun."

" A nonsensical line of some player."   WARB.

EXAMP.

EXAMP. IV. Vol. 4. P. 130.   1 HENRY IV.

——" *and took't away again,* &c.] This ftupi-
" dity between the hooks is the players." WARB.

EXAMP. V. Vol. 6. P. 72.   KING LEAR.

" You fulphurous and thought-executing fires,
" Vaunt-couriers of oak-cleaving thunderbolts,
" Singe my white head——

" The fecond of thefe lines muft needs be the play-
" ers' fpurious iffue.   The reafon is *demonftrative.*
" Shakefpear tells us, in the firft and third lines, tru-
" ly, that the flafh does the execution ; but in the
" fecond he talks of an imaginary thunderbolt, (dif-
" tinct from the flafh or fire, which fire he calls only
" the *vaunt-couriers* or fore-runners of it) which he
" falfely fays does it.   This is fo glaring a contra-
" diction, as makes it impoffible to be all of one
" hand."   WARB.

The latter part of this note I fubfcribe-to.   It appears to be fo in fact ; for the contradiction is of Mr.
Warburton's hand ; and, if there be any fpurious
iffue, it muft call him Father ; Shakefpear's fenfe is
as plain, as words can make it.

" O lightning, thou fore-runner of thunder,
" finge me," &c.

What is there here, that can poffibly miflead Mr.
Warburton to think of thunder fing'ing him ? The
lightning and the thunder have two diftinct offices
allotted them by the fpeaker.   He calls on the former, to *finge his white bead* ; and on the latter, to
ftrike flat the thick rotundity of the world.   And thus

I   the

the fentiment rifes properly throughout the fpeech, and the line in queftion is a very fine part of it ; for, however abfurd thunderbolts may be in true philofophy, their poetical exiftence is unqueftionable ; and their actual exiftence is ftill univerfally believed by the common people in the country : who every day gather up flints of a particular form, which they call by that name. But Mr. Warburton will make his *writing and reading* appear ; *when*, as honeft *Dogberry* fays, *there is no need of fuch vanity.* He had better have given a truce to his Philofophy, and minded his Grammar a little better ; and then he would not have fet the numbers a tilting at each other in the manner he has done above.

——*Fire* (fingular) I S the *vaunt-couriers* (plural) but the low care of Grammar is beneath a Profefs'd Critic.

See Canon II. Example 30.

Examp. VI. Vol. 3. P. 139.   Twelfth Night.

" *with fuch eftimable wonder.*] An interpolation of " the players." **Warb.**

Examp. VII. Vol. 8. P. 126.   Hamlet.

————" your father loft a father ; " That father his ;————

" Thus Mr. *Pope* judicioufly corrected the faul- " ty copies. On which the Editor, Mr. *Theo-* " *bald*, thus *difcants.*" ' This fuppofed refinement ' is from Mr. Pope ; but all the editions elfe, that ' I have met with, old and new, read——That fa- ' ther loft, loft his ;——the reduplication of which ' word here gives us an energy and elegance, which ' is much eafier to be conceived, than explained in " terms.'

" terms.' " I believe so. For, when *explained in*
" *terms,* it comes to this: That father, after he
" had lost himself, lost his father. But the read-
" ing is *ex fide Codicis*; and that is enough." W A R B.

Mr. W's reason for believing, that the beauty
of redoubling the word—*lost*—is easier to be conceived than explained, is; because, when it is explained, according to Him, it amounts to Nonsense. An odd reason this, why it should be easily conceived! Most people, when they talk nonsense, do it without conceiving at all: But Mr. W.
it seems, has both parts of the Midwife's Blessing;
A quick conception, as well as an easy delivery.
When the passage, as Mr. *Theobald* gives it, is
rightly explained, it comes to this. That father,
who is now lost (not *after*, but *before* he was lost
himself) lost *his* father. But Mr. W. † ' in spite
' of that extreme negligence in Numbers, which
' distinguishes the first Dramatic writers;' is here
misled by his *dear* Mr. *Pope,* into " all the finical
' exactness of a modern measurer of syllables.'

† Pref. P. XII.

C A N O N VI.

*As every Author is to be corrected into all
possible perfection, and of that perfection the
Professed Critic is the sole judge; He may alter
any word or phrase, which does not want amendment, or which will do; provided He can think
of any thing, which he imagines will do better.*

EXAMP.

EXAMP. I. Vol. 5. P. 220. RICHARD III.

" *where* no blood *dwells*] This may be right.
" But probably Shakespear wrote, *whence no blood*
" *wells*." WARB.

i. e. (adds he) whence no blood has its spring or
course. This round-about explication of *well*, may
be necessary to mislead an ignorant reader to approve of the emendation : but he that knows that
to *well* means neither more nor less than to *flow*,
will see the monstrous impropriety of Mr. W's
conjecture—*whence* no blood *wells*—when the very
circumstance described is, the *flowing*, or *welling*
of the blood from K. Henry's wounds, at the approach of his murderer, the Duke of Glocester.

EXAMP. II. Vol. 6. P. 63. K. LEAR.

" All's not offence, that indiscretion *finds*,
" And dotage terms so."

" I am almost persuaded, that Shakespear wrote
" *fines*, i. e. *censures*; the common reading being
" scarce sense." WARB.

This fine or censure proceeds from Mr. Warburton's not understanding the common reading. *Finds*
is an allusion to a Jury's verdict; and the word *so* relates to *finds*, as well as to *terms*. We meet with the
very same expression in HAMLET, Vol. 8. P. 241.

" Why, 'tis *found so*.

Shakespear uses the word in this sense in other places;
" The crowner hath sat on her, and *finds it* Christian
" burial." *ib.*

As

As you like it, Vol. 2. P. 360. " Leander—was " drown'd ; and the foolish chroniclers [*perhaps* co- " roners] of that age *found it was*—Hero of Sestos."

Examp. III. Vol. 6. P. 75. King Lear.
" That under *covert and convenient* seeming"—

" This may be right. And if so, *convenient* is " used for commodious or friendly. But I rather " think, the poet wrote
" That under *cover of convivial* seeming."—Warb.

Were not Mr. W. known to be of a different cha- racter, one might imagine him very fond of convi- vial doings ; from this note, and one in All's well that ends well ; where on the words,

" And pleasure drown the brim ;"

his observation is, " Metaphor taken from an over- " flowing cup. It is one of the *boldest* and *noblest* " expressions in all Shakespear." Vol. 3. P. 50.

Examp. IV. Vol. 4. P. 332. King Henry V.
" The civil citizens *kneading* up the honey.

" This may possibly be right ; but I rather think, " that Shakespear wrote *heading* up the honey." Warb.

Examp. V. Vol. 7. P. 323. Cymbeline.
—" The very Gods—

" The *very* Gods may indeed signify the Gods " themselves, immediately, and not by the interven- " tion of other agents or instruments ; yet I am per- " suaded, the reading is corrupt ; and that Shake- " spear wrote ;

—" the *warey* Gods—

" *warey*

" *warey* here fignifying, *animadverting, forewarning,*
" and *ready to give notice* ; not, as in its more ufual
" meaning, *cautious, referved.*" WARB.

Here again it were to be wifhed, that Mr. Warburton had given fome authority for ufing the word
in this fenfe ; which if he had looked for, he might
have found at left how to fpell it.

EXAMP. VI. Vol. 5. P. 205.   K. HENRY VI.
Third Part.

For " devil-butcher" Mr. Warburton reads *devil's
butcher* (i. e. kill-devil.)

EXAMP. VII. Vol. 8. P. 99. ROMEO AND
JULIET.

" A *beggarly* account of empty boxes."

 " I fufpect, that Shakefpear wrote,

" A *braggartly* account of empty boxes.

" Not but *account* may fignify *number* as well as
" *contents* ; if the firft, the common reading is right."
WARB.

Qu. What are the contents of empty boxes ?

EXAMP. VIII. Vol. 7. P. 398. TROILUS AND
CRESSIDA.

—" If thou ufe to beat me, I will begin at thy
" heel, and tell what thou art by inches, thou thing
" of no *bowels,* thou !

—" *thou thing of no bowels*] Though this be fenfe,
" yet I believe it is not the poet's—I fhould imagine,
" the true reading was ; Thou thing of no *vowels,*
" i. e. without fenfe ; as a word without vowels is
" jargon, and contains no idea." WARB.

EXAMP.

EXAMP. IX. Vol. 5. P. 213. KING RICHARD III.

" To fright the *fouls* of fearful adverfaries."

" This may be right. But I rather think, Shake-
" fpear wrote the *faule*, French, the *croud*, or *mul-*
" *titude*." WARB.

EXAMP. X. Vol. 2. P. 294. AS YOU LIKE IT.

—" Albeit I confefs your coming before me is
" nearer to his *reverence*."

Mr. Warburton owns, *this is fenfe*; and gives it
the proper interpretation: but prudently prefers
revenue to *reverence*; and has alter'd the text accordingly.

EXAMP. XI. Vol. 2. P. 155. MERCHANT OF
VENICE.

" I thank you for your wifh; and am well *pleas'd*
" To wifh it back on you"——] I fhould rather think,
" Shakefpear wrote,

———" and am well *pris'd*;

" from the French *appris*, taught, inftructed," &c.
WARB.

Why Mr. Warburton fhould rather think fo, I
cannot imagine; except for the fake of introducing
a word of his dear French *origine*: but he takes a
large fine for his *donum civitatis*; as he elfewhere
calls it. Shakefpear neither ufes French words fo
needlefsly, nor does he hack and mangle his words
at this rate, to fit them for a place they were not
defigned for——" am well pleafed to wifh it back,"
&c. is the fame with——" wifh it back to you with
" a great deal of pleafure." And now the reader

may

may pay Mr. Warburton the fame complement for
his emendation, as Portia does to Jeſſica for her
good wiſhes ; and be *well 'pris'd*, and *well pleaſed*
likewiſe, to wiſh it him back again.

EXAMP. XII. Vol. 4. P. 332. KING HENRY V.

" Others, like merchants, *venture* trade abroad]
" What is the venturing trade ? I am perſuaded,
" that we ſhould read and point it thus ;
" Others, like *merchant-venturers*, trade abroad."
WARB.

When Mr. Warburton underſtands what merchant-venturers are, he will know what it is to venture trade : till then he might leave Shakeſpear as
he found him.

Mr W. himſelf ſpeaks of *Ventures* in this ſenſe,
Vol. 1. P. 58. and 'tis ſtrange he ſhould underſtand
the *Subſtantive*, and yet be at ſuch a loſs about the
Verb.

EXAMP. XIII. Vol. 5. P. 39, 2 HENRY VI.

" So cares and joys *abound*, as ſeaſons fleet] I
" imagine, Shakeſpear might write ;
" So cares and joys *go round*"——WARB.

Any one elſe would imagine, that Shakeſpear
needed no amendment here ; but I fancy, Mr. Warburton might borrow his emendation from a Tetra-
ſtich he contemplated at the top of an Almanack.

" War begets poverty, poverty peace,
" Peace makes riches flow, time ne'er doth ceaſe,
" Riches produceth pride, pride is war's ground,
" War begets poverty—*ſo the world goes round.*

He

He seems also to have had his eye upon the Almanack in another place; which properly belongs to CAN. XXIII.

" Time and the hour runs through the rougheſt " day. MACBETH. Vol. 6. P. 343.] Time is " painted with an hour-glaſs in his hand. This " occaſioned the expreſſion." WARB.

EXAMP. XIV. Vol. 3. P. 145. TWELFTH NIGHT.

" Do ye make an alehouſe of my Lady's houſe; " that ye ſqueak out your *coziers* catches, without " any mitigation or remorſe of voice;" &c.

"*Coziers* catches] Cottiers, ruſtic, clowniſh." WARB.

I ſuppoſe, the reaſon of Mr. Warburton's amendment was, becauſe he could not find Shakeſpear's word in Skinner; who told him, that *Cottyer* is *ruſticus, villanus*: but, had he looked into that part of his Dictionary, which contains the old Engliſh words; he would have found *Coſier, ſartor veſtiarius;* or Minſhew would have told him, it was a botcher or cobler.

EXAMP. XV. Vol. 2. P. 120. MERCHANT OF VENICE.

Laun. " The old proverb is very well parted be- " tween my maſter Shylock and you, Sir; You have " the grace of God, and He has enough."
Baſſ. " Thou *ſpeak'ſt* it well;—] I ſhould chooſe " to read, Thou *ſplit'ſt* it well;" WARB.

I ſuppoſe, becauſe the diviſion put him in mind of ſplitting a text; or becauſe ſplit'ſt was more muſical and harmonious to Mr. Warburton's ear.

EXAMP.

Examp. XVI. Vol. 6. P. 4. K. Lear.

—" exprefs our *darker* purpofe] *Darker,* for
" more *fecret.* Warb."

I am at a lofs to find, where is the neceffity of this
doughty explication ; unlefs it be to introduce the
next note, p. 5. where Mr. Warburton has difcovered a fecret ; which, had it not been for his *ufual fa-
gacity,* might have lien in the dark for ever.

—" and 'tis our *faft* intent, &c.] This is an in-
" terpolation of Mr. Lewis Theobald ; for want of
" knowing the meaning of the old reading in the
" Quarto of 1608, and the firft Folio of 1623 ;
" where we find it,

——" and 'tis our *firft* intent,

" which *is as* Shakefpear *wrote it* ; who makes Lear
" declare his purpofe with a dignity becoming his
" character : That the *firft* reafon of his abdication
" was *the love of his people* ; that they might be pro-
" tected by fuch, as were better able to difcharge the
" truft : and his *natural affection for his daughters*
" only the fecond." Warb.

Had Mr. Warburton, as he pretends, collated
all the former editions, he muft have known, that
fast *intent* is not an interpolation of Mr. Lewis
Theobald * : and, if He kept the reading of the fecond folio, for *want* of knowing the meaning of the
other; Mr. Warburton would have done well to have
followed him : for *our* first *intent* can never fignify
the first reason of our intent ; though he fophifti-
cally fhuffles them upon us, as expreffions of the
fame import ; and upon this change of the terms

* See Canon XXIV. Example 3.

founds

founds all his cobweb refinements about the dignity of Lear's character, his patriotism, and natural affection, his *first* and *second* reasons ; not a word of which appears in the text, which seems to allude only to King Lear's age and infirmities.

——" and 'tis our fast intent
" To shake all cares and business from our AGE ;
" Conferring them on younger strengths, while we
" UNBURTHEN'D crawl tow'rd earth."——

Fast intent means *determin'd resolution* ; which I think is the best reading : *First* must here signify *chief*; but neither of the readings affects the general sense of the passage.

EXAMP. XVII. Vol. 6. P. 407. MACBETH.

" All ready at A POINT] At a point may mean,
" all ready at a *time* ; but Shakespear meant more,
" and certainly wrote,
" All ready at APPOINT,—i. e. at the place appointed." WARB.

EXAMP. XVIII. P. 412. Ibid.

" That, Sir, which I will not *report* after her]
" I think, it should rather be *repeat*." WARB.

EXAMP. XIX. Vol. 6. P. 87. K. LEAR.

Fool. " He's mad, that trusts in the tameness of a
" wolf, the health of a horse, the love of a boy, or
" the oath of a whore."

——" *the* HEALTH *of a horse*,] Without doubt, we
" should read HEELS ; i. e. to stand behind him."
WARB.

Shake-

Shakefpear intends to mention four things; all of which have a fpecious appearance, but are not to be confided in : *tamenefs*, *love*, and an *oath* are of this fort ; but how do the *heels* of an horfe tally with the reft ? It is probable, that he alludes to the tricks of jockeys ; in making up unfound horfes for fale : however, I cannot but wonder, that Mr. Warburton fhould not be fatisfied of the precarioufnefs of a horfe's health ; who has difcovered *one* diftemper incident to thofe animals, (I mean, the OATS) which neither *Markham*, *Newcaftle*, *Soleyfel*, nor *Bracken* ever dreamt of.

EXAMP. XX. Vol. 4. P. 212.   2. HEN. IV.

—— and doth *enlarge* his Rifing) *i. e.* encreafe his army.   But this won't go down with Mr. W.'s queazy palate, without a flice of bacon to relifh it. And therefore he fays,

   " It is probable, Shakefpear wrote, *enlard*; i. e. " fatten and encourage his Caufe."   WARB.

Admirable Thought ! which no words can fhew the beauty of !   Here therefore, as in CAN. XV. Ex. 12. we muft fubmit to the emendation ; and only read the whole paffage fo, as to preferve the ' *integrity* of the *metaphor*.'

And doth *enlard* his Rifing with the blood
Of *fat* King *Richard*, fcrape'd from *Pomfret* ftones.

inftead of—*fair* King *Richard*.   And this receives no fmall confirmation from Shakefpear himfelf; who joins the two words together in TROILUS and CRESSIDA : Act 2. Sc. 8. where Ulyffes, fpeaking of Achilles, faith—— Vol. 7. P. 414.

That were to' *enlard* his Pride, already *fat*.

C A N O N

CANON VII.

He may find-out obfolete words, or coin new ones; and put them in the place of fuch, as he does not like, or does not underftand.

EXAMPLE I. Vol. 6. P. 368. MACBETH.

" their daggers

" Unmanly *breech'd* with gore,——

Breech'd with gore has, I believe, been generally underftood to mean cover'd, as a man is by his breeches; and, though the expreffion be none of the beft, yet methinks it might pafs in a fpeech; which, as Mr. Warburton obferves in his note on a line juft before, is an unnatural mixture of far-fetched and common-place thoughts: efpecially, fince he urges this very circumftance as a proof of Macbeth's guilt.

But this is not fufficient; and therefore he fays,
" This nonfenfical account of the ftate, in which
" the daggers were found, muft furely be read thus;

" Unmanly *reech'd* with gore——

" *Reech'd, foil'd with a dark yellow*; which is the
" colour of any *reechy* fubftance, and muft be fo
" of fteel ftain'd with blood. He ufes the word
" very often; as *reechy* hangings, *reechy* neck, &c.
" fo that the fenfe is, they were *unmanly* ftained
" with blood; and that circumftance added, becaufe
" often fuch ftains are moft honorable." WARB.

Mr. Warburton fhould have fhewed, by fome better authority than his own, that there is fuch a word as *reech'd*; which I believe he will not find it

F 4

eafy

eafy to do. *Reechy* comes from *pecan,* A. S. *fumare*; (from whence our *reak* and *reaking.*) and fignifies with Shakefpear, *fweaty*; as *reechy* neck, *reechy* kiffes; or, by a metaphor perhaps, *greafy*; but does not mark any color: however, the verb, being neuter, has no paffive voice; and therefore, there is no fuch participle as *reech'd.*

Nor is it true, that a dark yellow is the color of all reechy fubftances. As to the * cook-maid's neck; that I fuppofe may be fo, or not, according as her complexion happens to be fo. As to the hangings; if they hung a great while in London, they had, it is probable, a great deal more of the footy than the yellow in their tinct. If I were to afk Mr. Warburton, whether *reechy* kiffes were of a dark yellow; he would tell me, that they are not fubftances; and therefore are not within his rule: but, if the kiffes were *reechy,* the lips, that gave them, muft be fo too; and I hope, Mr. Warburton will not pay the king of Denmark fo ill a complement, though he was a ufurper; as to fay, that his lips were foil'd with a dark yellow, when he kiffed his queen.

I cannot but add; that it is far from being generally agreed, that thefe fame *dark yellow* ftains are often moft honorable. I know but one authority for it, which it would have been but fair in Mr. Warburton to have produced; as it is evident, that his whole criticifm is founded on it. The paffage is in the *Tragedy of Tragedies*; where Tom Thumb is reprefented as

> " Stain'd with the *yellow* blood of flaughter'd
>   giants.

* ———The kitchen malkin pins
Her richeft lockram 'bout her reechy neck;
Clamb'ring the walls to eye him. Vol. 6. P. 469. *Coriolanus.*
                                                    EXAMP.

EXAMP. II. IN RICHARD III. Vol. 5. P. 226.

" My dukedom to a beggarly *denier*."
" This may be right; but perhaps Shakefpear
" wrote *taniere*, French, a hut or cave." WARB.

It is more than *perhaps*, that Shakefpear never
thought of *taniere*; which is a den; *caverne, où les
betes fauvages fe retirent:* and when it is ufed figuratively for the habitation of a man, it is confidering
him as living, not like a poor man, in a cottage, but
like a beaft; *retraite*, fays Furetiere, *d'un bomme
fauvage et folitaire*. What put Mr. Warburton upon
this emendation, I fuppofe, was; that he thought a
dukedom to a penny was no fair bett: and that the
wager would be more equal, if the beggar were to
impone, as Ofric fays, his cottage. Upon the fame
principle we fhould correct that line of Biron's fpeech
in LOVE'S LABOR'S LOST, Vol. 2. P. 199.

" I'll lay my head to any good man's *hat*."

read *heart*; for a head to a hat is too unequal a
wager.

EXAMP. III. Vol. 6. P. 214. TIMON OF ATHENS.

" With all th' abhorred births below *crifp* heaven.
" We fhould read *cript*, i. e. vaulted; from the
" latin *crypfa*, a vault." WARB.

Mr. Warburton fhould have fhewed by fome authority, that there is fuch a word as *cript*, for vaulted; which he feems to have coined for the purpofe:
but, if there is, it fhould be fpelt *crypt*, not *cript*;
and comes from *crypta*, not *crypfa*; which indeed
would

would give *cryps*, and that might eafily be miftaken for *crifp*; as Mrs. Mincing fays, " fo pure and fo " *crips.*"

EXAMP. IV. Vol. 4. P. 97.   1 HENRY IV.

" No more the thirfty entrance of this foil
" Shall *damp* her lips with her own childrens blood."

" *Shall* damp *her lips*] This nonfenfe fhould be " read, fhall *trempe*, i. e. moiften; and refers to " thirfty in the preceding line."   WARB.

Why muft this be nonfenfe? And why muft Shakefpear thus continually be made to ufe improper French words, againft the authority of the copies, inftead of proper Englifh? To *damp*, fignifies to wet, to moiften; which is the precife fenfe Mr. Warburton and the context require.   *Tremper* fignifies fomething more; to dip, to foak, or fteep: *je fuis tout trempé*, I am foaked through.

But, fays Mr. Warburton, *trempe* from the French *tremper* properly fignifies the moiftnefs made by rain. If he fpeaks of *trempe* as an Englifh word; fince he coined it, he may perhaps have a right to give it what fignification he pleafes; but the French *tremper* fignifies to dip, or foak, in any liquor whatfoever. *Tremper fes mains dans le fang: tremper les yeux de larmes: tremper du fer dans l'eau*; and figuratively, *tremper dans un crime*.

EXAMP. V. Vol. 2. P. 62. MUCH ADO ABOUT
NOTHING.
" Griev'd I, I had but one?
" Chid I for this at frugal nature's *frame?*

The obvious fenfe feems to be, Did I repine, that nature had framed me and my wife fo; that we
fhould

should have but one child ? But this Mr. Warburton either did not see, or did not like ; and therefore he coins a substantive from a verb, cuts-off one syllable to fit it for the place, (for here he does not mend, *in spite of the versification* ;) and then says, without any authority but his own, " We must cer-" tainly read——

" Chid I for this at frugal nature's *'fraine?*
" i. e. *refraine.*"

EXAMP. VI. Vol. 3. P. 95. ALL'S WELL THAT ENDS WELL.

——" but is it your *carbonado'd* face?] Mr. Pope
" read it *carbinado'd*; which is right. The joke,
" such as it is, consists in the allusion to a wound
" made by a carabine; arms, which Hen. IV. had
" made famous by bringing into use among his
" horse." WARB.

This joke, and the amendment for the sake of it, *such as it is*, is entirely Mr. Pope's. Shakespear used *carbonado* for *flash, scotch.* In K. LEAR, Vol. 6. P. 49. " I'll so *carbonado* your shanks." And in Coriolanus, Vol. 6. P. 527.
He *scotcht* him, and *notcht* him, like a *carbonado.* See *the Glossary.*

EXAMP. VII. Vol. 2. P. 243. LOVE'S LABOR'S LOST.

" And beauty's *crest* becomes the Heavens well."

Mr. Warburton says, we should read *beauty's crete*; i. e. beauty's *white*, from Creta.

This

This word is, I suppose, from his own mint. I wonder, he did not rather give us *craye*; which is French for chalk.

EXAMP. VIII. Vol. 6. P. 541. CORIOLANUS.

" For I have ever *verified* my friends,
" (Of whom he's chief) with all the size, that verity
" Would without lapsing suffer.

Verified here is certainly wrong; as Mr. Warburton in a long note has shewn. To mend it, he gives us a word; which, if it is not his own, I doubt he can find no better authority for, than the Dictionary of N. Bailey, Philolog. who has taken care to preserve all the cant words he could pick-up. However, he gives the honor of it to Shakespear; and says, " without doubt he wrote——

" For I have ever *narrified* my friends,

" *i. e.* made their encomium. This too agrees with
" the foregoing metaphors of *book*, *read*; and con-
" stitutes an uniformity among them." WARB.

I suppose, Menenius read his encomiums out of a book, or at least learned them there; and then *narrified* by rote. But though Mr. Warburton makes no doubt of Shakespear's writing *narrified*, I must own I do; and if it were lawful for one, who is not a critic by profession, to make a conjecture after him, which yet I would not venture to thrust into the text without authority; I should imagine, that possibly Shakespear might have written;

" For I have ever *varnished* my friends
        "——with all the size, that verity
" Would without lapsing suffer."

                                        that

that is, I have laid-on as much praise, as would stick.
It is an allusion either to painting or white-washing:
and the word *varnish* (or *vernish*, as it is sometimes
spelt) agrees with the following metaphor of *size*;
at left as well as *narrify* does with *book* before. The
only misfortune is, that the uniformity is broken:
but that is of the less consequence, because otherwise it would be knocked to pieces by the bowls,
which come-in in the very next line.

   ——" nay sometimes,
 " Like to a bowl upon a subtle ground,
 " Have tumbled past the throw"——

 Whether this be right or no, I doubt *narrifying*
with *size* will pass on nobody but a Professed Critic.

 EXAMP. IX. Vol. 6. P. 542. CORIOLANUS.
——" The virginal *palms* of your daughters."
 " by virginal palms may indeed be understood, the
 " holding-up of hands in supplication. Therefore
 " I have altered nothing. But, as this sense is *cold*,
 " and gives us even a *ridiculous idea*—I suspect,
 " Shakespear might write *pesmes* or *pâmes*, i. e.
 " swooning fits; from the French *pasmer*, or *pâ-
 " mer*." WARB.

 Mr. Warburton must sure have a very hard heart:
if the idea of virgins holding-up their hands in supplication for their lives and honor, can seem to him
either *cold or ridiculous*; and nothing will satisfy him,
but making them swoon; that he may have an opportunity of bringing-in a French word.

            EXAMP.

EXAMP. X. Vol. 7. P. 378.   TROILUS AND
CRESSIDA.

" If he do, the *rich* shall have more."

" It should be read thus,

"—the *mich* shall have more.

" *i. e.* much. He that has much folly already,
" shall then have more. This was a proverbial
" speech; implying that benefits fall upon the
" rich." WARB.

Here, because *to be rich in* any thing does not
signify *to* have *much* of it; Mr. Warburton has
happily invented a word, the *mich* or *much*, to bear
that signification.

EXAMP. XI. Vol. 7. P. 267.   CYMBELINE.

" One of your great knowing
" Should learn, being *taught*, forbearance,
That is, I suppose, " one of so much knowledge,
" as you pretend to, should learn to leave-off an
" unsuccessful suit; when you are so often desired
" to do so."

But this will not satisfy Mr. Warburton : he insists; that a man, who is taught, has no more need of
learning; not remembering, that some are so heedless and forgetful, as to need being taught the same
things again and again. Not to misrepresent him,
I will give his whole note :

" Sure whoever is taught, necessarily learns.
" Learning is not the fit and reasonable consequence
" of

" of being taught; but is the thing itself.† As it is
" superfluous in the expression, so (which is the
" common condition of nonsense) it is deficient in
" the sentiment. It is no mark of a knowing per-
" son, that he has learnt forbearance simply. For
" forbearance becomes a virtue, or point of civil
" prudence, *only* as it respects a *forbidden* object.
" Shakespear, I am perfuaded, wrote;

" One of your great knowing
" Should learn (being *tort*) forbearance."

" *i. e.* one of your wisdom should learn (from a
" sense of your pursuing a forbidden object) for-
" bearance; which gives us a good and pertinent
" meaning in a correct expression.

" *Tort,* an old French word, signifying *the being in
" the wrong,* is much in use among our old English
" writers; which those, who have not read them,
" may collect from its being found in the *Etymolo-
" gicon* of the judicious Skinner. WARB.

" That *tort* is a French word, every one, who
knows any thing of that language, must know; but

---

† Shakespear himself seems to have diftinguished differently
from his Commentator; where (1 Hen. IV. Vol. 4. P. 190.) he
makes Vernon say, describing the P. of Wales's modefty to Hotspur.

He made a blushing cital of himself;
And chid his truant youth with such a grace,
As if he master'd there a double spirit,
Of *teaching,* and of *learning,* instantly.

and so again in MUCH ADO, &c. Vol. 2. P. 13.

My love is thine to teach; *teach* it but how;
And thou shalt see, how apt it is to *learn.*

that

that it is an *old* French word, in any other sense
than the rest of their words are old, is not true; for
it is as much in use as ever: and that it signifies *being* in the wrong, I cannot recollect to have found
in any *old English writer*; though I have read several. I was therefore obliged to go, as Mr. Warburton advises, to the judicious Skinner; whom I
hope he appealed-to without consulting, because he
gives him no manner of authority for what he asserts:

Tort (says he) exp. Extortion, a Fr. G. Tort *inju-
ria*, utr. a Lat. *torquere.*

In this he agrees with the French Dictionaries;
which give us *tort*, a substantive, *injury, wrong*, &c.
but no such adjective; which the sense here requires.
There is indeed an old English adjective formed
from hence, as Mr. Warburton's neighbours at
Lincoln's Inn would have told him; that is, *tortious*;
to which *tortionare* in the French answers: Shakespear also uses *tortive* in Troilus and Cressida,
Act 1. Sc. 5: but, if Mr. Warburton had brought
any one of these in, it must have been " in spite
" of the versification."

I hope, for the future, Mr. Warburton will apply Imogen's advice to this liberty he takes of coining words; and, according to his own reading,

" —learn (being Tort) forbearance."

EXAMP. XII. Vol. 1. P. 95. MIDSUMMER NIGHT'S
DREAM.

" One, that compos'd your beauties; yea, and one,
" To whom ye are but as a form in wax

I   " By

" By him imprinted ; and within his power
" To *leave* the figure, or disfigure it."
    " We fhould read,
" Te *'leve* the figure, &c.
" i. e. to *releve*, to *heighten*, or *add to the beauty of*
" the figure, which is faid to be imprinted by him.
" 'Tis from the French, *relever*," &c. WARB.

Why fhould we read, *'leve?* Mr. Warburton does not here pretend, that Shakefpear wrote it fo. He did not ufe to clip and coin at this rate. But it is from the French—Is it fo? Why then, to the French let it go again, till Mr. Warburton has learned the language better ; in the mean time, let him fuffer Shakefpear to fpeak fenfe and Englifh. A man may either *leave* a figure, which he has impreffed in wax with a feal or mold ; or he may *disfigure* it : but the *relief* of the figure depends upon the mold, and not on any thing that is done after the impreffion ; nor does the degree of the relief neceffarily add to the beauty of the figure ; fince a figure in *bas relief* may have more elegance and beauty, than another in *mezzo*, or even in *alto relievo*. But, fuppofing the word to be of good allowance, let us examine the fentiment. And is it in the power of a parent to heighten or add-to the beauty of a girl, who is not fo charming as one could wifh? Happy difcovery! I hope, Mr. Warburton's daughters will be all beauties ; whatever becomes of the boys : In the mean time, if he has this fecret, I will anfwer for it, that it will be more worth to him than all his critical fkill ; let him find ever fo good *judges and rewarders of merit* among the Bookfellers.

G

EXAMP.

EXAMP. XIII. Vol. 1. P. 239. TWO GENTLEMEN
OF VERONA.

" My fubftance fhould be *ftatue,* in thy ftead] It
" is evident this noun fhould be a participle, STA-
" TUED; i. e. placed on a pedeftal, or fixed in a
" fhrine to be ador'd." WARB.

I fuppofe, becaufe the miniature picture, *in the
ftead of* which her fubftance was to be *ftatued,* was
placed on a pedeftal. But Mr. Warburton fhould
have fhew'd, that we are in poffeffion of fuch a
verb as *to ftatue*; before he formed a participle from
it. The meaning of Shakefpear is plain enough, to
any but a profefs'd Critic. " He fhould have my
" fubftance as a *ftatue,* inftead of thee [*the picture*]
" who art a fenfelefs form.

EXAMP. XIV. Vol. 2. P. 133. MERCHANT OF
VENICE.

" And quicken his *embraced* heavinefs] This un-
" meaning epithet would make me choofe rather
" to read,

" *Enraced* heavinefs.

" from the French *enraciner,* accrefcere, invete-
" rafcere." WARB.

His *embraced* heavinefs plainly enough means, the
heavinefs which he indulges and is fond of. But
Mr. Warburton muft be correcting, where there is
no need; and therefore will have it *enraced.* I afk
pardon for laughing at him in the former Edition,
as the author of that word; fince I find, it is ufed
by Spenfer; though that perhaps is more than he
knew. However, the word's being made ufe of
by Spenfer (who took great liberty of coining, efpecially

3

cially when he wanted a rhyme) is no juftifiable
reafon for Mr. W.'s foifting it into Shakefpear,
without any authority but his own.

EXAMP. XV. Vol. 2. P. 329. AS YOU LIKE IT.
" Thy tooth is not fo keen,
" Becaufe thou art not *feen.*"

This paffage is certainly faulty ; and perhaps it
cannot be reftored, as Shakefpear gave it. Sir
Thomas Hanmer at left altered it into fenfe ;

Thou caufeft not that teen.

But this, it feems, will not do ; becaufe, in his *rage
of correction,* he forgot to leave the reafon, why the
winter wind was to be preferred to man's ingratitude.
So now Mr. Warburton comes with his emendation ; which he charitably communicated to Sir
Thomas, though he was fo gracelefs as not to make
ufe of it.

" *Without doubt,* Shakefpear wrote,
" Becaufe thou art not *fheen,*" &c. WARB.

Though this matter is fo clear with Mr. Warburton, every body who underftands Englifh will
doubt of it ; becaufe SHEEN fignifies *bright,* which
makes no better fenfe than SEEN ; nor does he produce any authority for its fignifying SMILING, which
is the fenfe he here puts upon it ; and to make it pafs
the better, he lugs-in a parcel of " *fmiling, fhining,*
" *court fervants, who flatter while they wound* ;" of
whom there is not the leaft hint in the fong, or in
the whole fcene.

He fays " *fheen,* i. e. fmiling, fhining ;" &c. Let
us examine his authoritys. " So, in the MIDSUM-
" MER NIGHT'S DREAM ;

" Spangled

" Spangléd ftarlight *fheen*."

" Chaucer ufes it in this fenfe,

" Your blifsful fufter Lucina the *fhene* ;"

" And Fairfax,

" The facred angel took his target *fhene*."

Thefe are the examples he produces ; *whether wifely or not, let the foreft judge :* but the conceit of a *fmiling target* is entirely his own ; and, if he will allow me a pun, *invitâ Minervâ* ; for it feems in direct oppofition to the famed Ægis of Pallas. But this is hardly a laughing matter ; for with what face can he fay *fmiling, fhining*—So Shakefpear— Chaucer ufes it in THIS fenfe—And Fairfax—when, if he knows any thing of the language, he muft know ; that not one of them, in thefe inftances, ufes *fheen* in the fenfe of SMILING ; and that, in its true fenfe of BRIGHT or *fhining*, it would make the paffage worfe than he found it ?

If Sir Thomas Hanmer, as he fays, took occafion, from having *this emendation communicated to him*, to alter the whole line ; he fhewed more judgment, than if he had inferted fuch a falfe and nonfenfical note. But " in his rage of correction, he " forgot to leave the reafon, why the *winter wind* " was to be preferred to *man's ingratitude*." If *fheen* does not fignify *fmiling*, I doubt Mr. Warburton will be in the fame cafe. However Shakefpear has equally forgotten, in the next ftanza, to leave the reafon, why a *freezing fky* is to be preferred to a *forgetful friend* ; which, perhaps, may give a reafonable fufpicion, that the word *becaufe* in the firft ftanza may be corrupt.

EXAMP.

EXAMP. XVI. Vol. 3. P. 11. ALL'S WELL THAT
ENDS WELL.

  —" the composition, that your valor and fear
" makes in you, is a virtue of a good *wing*; and I
" like the wear well]　The integrity of the meta-
" phor directs us to Shakespear's true reading;
" which doubtless was, *a good* MING; i. e. *mixture*,
" *composition*; a word common to Shakespear, and
" the writers of this age; * and taken from the
" texture of cloth.　The M was turned the wrong
" way at the *press*; and from thence came the
" blunder." WARB.

  I suppose, Mr. Warburton, who has collated *all*
the editions, can, from some or other of them, produce a proof of what he so positively asserts; that
the M was turned the wrong way at the press: if
it be so, it will be easily distinguished from a W,
especially in the old printing; where the W was
generally unconnected, thus, VV †.

  If it were not for preserving the integrity of the
metaphor, which Mr. Warburton is generally more
concerned about than Shakespear is; I see no reason, why " a virtue of a good wing" may not
refer to his nimbleness or fleetness in running away.
But Mr. Warburton says, " *Ming* for *mixture, com-
" position*, is a word common to Shakespear and
" the writers of this age;" I desire him to produce
his authorities both for the word, and the use of

                                              it;

  * *Ming*, a verb, tho' not very common to the *writers* of *this*
age; yet is still very common to the *talkers*, in some parts; is used
in the sense of *knead*; and is plainly a contraction of *mingle*. But,
what the texture of cloth has to do here, I know not; nor is it worth
inquiring: as Shakespear probably never us'd nor heard the word.

  † Mr. Warburton is so fond of this conceit, of an M being set
upon it's head at the press; that he has used it again in CYMBE-
LINE, Vol. 7. P. 290.

it ; for, confidering what we have feen in the laft example foregoing, it is too much to take on his bare affertion ; nor can I, till I fee it ufed by people of better credit, pay him the complement to fay ; *I like the wear well.*"

EXAMP. 17. Vol. 4. P. 287. 2 HENRY IV.

" Unlefs fome *dull and* favourable hand] Evi-
" dently corrupt. Shakefpear feems to have wrote,
" *doleing*; i. e. *a hand ufing foft melancholy airs.*"
WARB.

Why this is the very fenfe, which the true text exhibits. But the temptation of coining a new word is irrefiftible. It feems, however, not very luckily coin'd here ; fince *doleing*, if there were fuch a word, might perhaps rather fignify *giving-out largeffes*; in which fenfe, though Mr. Warburton might think a *doleing* hand a favourable one, other people perhaps would not judge it fo mufical, as the context requires.

If he gives us *doleing* for *condoling*, he may as well write *fternation* for *confternation.*

EXAMP. XVIII. Vol. 8. P. 375. OTHELLO.

———" O thou weed,
" Who art fo lovely fair, and fmell'ft fo fweet,"&c.
" The old quarto reads,
" O thou *blacke* weed, why art fo lovely fair, &c.
" which the editors not being able to fet right, al-
" tered as above. Shakefpear wrote,
" O thou *bale* weed, &c. Bale, i. e. *deadly poifonous.*"
WARB.

But

But till he produces such an adjective as *Bale*, which he cannot do from Shakespear, or any good author; he will not with all his dogmatical assertions convince us, that Shakespear wrote so; the adjective is *baleful.* This note being towards the end of his long work, we may make the same remark on him, as he has made on Sir Thomas Hanmer; " That " he did not understand his author's phraseology " any better when he had *ended,* than when he had " *begun* with him." See P. 396. Vol. 8.

EXAMP. XIX. Vol. 6. P. 392. MACBETH.

" Round about the cauldron go,
" In the poison'd *entrails* throw] Every thing
" thrown into the cauldron, is particularly enu-
" merated; and yet we find NO *poisoned entrails* a-
" mong them——I believe Shakespear wrote,
——" poison'd ENTREMES——
" an old word used for *ingredients,*" &c. WAR.

If Mr. Warburton means, there is no mention afterwards of the entrails being *poisoned*; what he says is true; but then it will affect his *entremes* too: but he is mistaken, if he affirms there are no *entrails* mentioned; for the word *entrails* signifies the inward parts, [*intestina, partes internæ,* Skinner.] in a larger sense than the viscera or guts; and so the maw of the shark, liver of the Jew, gall of the goat, and tyger's chawdron, are entrails: so that there is no need of Mr. Warburton's *entremes*; which, he indeed says, is an old word used for ingredients; but he should have produced some authority for it, since his own will not go far, with those who know how easily he affirms things of this sort.

EXAMP.

EXAMP. XX. Vol. 7. P. 238. CYMBELINE.

She's a good *sign*; but I have seen small reflection of her wit.]   "If *sign* be the true reading, "the poet means by it, *constellation*; and by *reflec-* "*tion* is meant, *influence.* But I rather think, from "the answer; that he wrote, *shine.* So, in his "Venus and Adonis,

"As if from thence they borrow'd all their *shine.*" WARB.

So, because *shine* signifies *brightness*, you may call a *bright* person — *a good shine!* The expression is monstrous. *Sign* is the true reading; without signifying *constellation*, or even a single *star.*

The sense is as plain, as words can make it. She has a fair outside, a specious appearance; but no wit. *O quanta species, cerebrum non habet!* Phædr.\

I wish, even *thus much* could be said of Mr. W.'s Note.

EXAMP. XXI. Vol. 1. P. 328. MERRY WIVES, &c.

They must *come-off*]   "This can never be our "Poet's or his Host's meaning: To *come-off* being "in other terms to *go scot-free.* We must read; "*compt*-off; i. e. clear their reckoning." WARB. Mr. W.'s explanation of to *come-off* by to *go scot-free*, is worthy of him; who saith, to *lay-by* means to *stand still*, *to 'em* means *have at you*, *I'll make a sop of the moon-shine of you* means *I'll make the sun shine through you*, &c. To *come-off* is to pay; and is so us'd frequently by Massinger: In one place * so plainly, as to admit no room for a doubt about the meaning, or for an essay after an emendation.

* See his *Unnatural Combat*, Act IV. Scene II.

CANON

CANON VIII.

He may prove a reading, or support an explanation, by any sort of reasons ; no matter whether good or bad.

EXAMPLE. I. Vol. 5. P. 413. K. HENRY VIII.

" This is the state of man ; to-day he puts-forth
" The tender leaves of hope, to-morrow blossoms;
" And bears his blushing honors thick upon him :
" The third day comes a frost, a killing frost;
" And when he thinks, good easy man, full surely
" His greatness is a rip'ning, nips his *root* ;
" And then he falls, as I do.

" *Nips his root*] As spring frosts are not injurious
" to the roots of fruit-trees ; I should imagine,
" the poet wrote *shoot* ; *i. e.* the tender shoot, on
" which are the young leaves and blossoms," &c.
WARB.

That is, because a *killing* frost will not *kill* trees in the *spring*. The conclusion of the speech evidently shews, that the death or destruction of the tree was the consequence of this nipping.

EXAMP. II. Vol. 8. P. 181. HAMLET.

" Madam, it' so fell out, that certain players
" We *o'ertook* on the way.

" The old Quarto reads *oer'raught*, corruptly for
" *o'er-rode*, which I think is the right reading ; for
" *o'ertook* has the idea of following with design, and
" accompanying. *O'er-rode* has neither : which was
" the case." WARB.

I know

I know not where Mr. Warburton found this idea ; but I believe no body but himself follows with defign, and accompanies, every one, whom he chances to overtake on the road. Nor is *o'er-raught*, which is the reading of the old Quarto, neceffarily a corruption of *over-rode :* it is the regular paft tenfe of *over-reach*, which was probably ufed formerly in the fenfe of overtake ; as *overgo*, *overpafs*, were ; but going out of ufe, the players might leave it for the more ufual word.

Shakefpear ufes the primitive in ANT. and CLEOP. The hand of death has *raught* him. Theobald's edition. Vol. 6. P. 302. and the fame form of the paft tenfe is ftill preferved in the verbs *teach*, *befeech*, *catch*, *fetch*, *feek*, *wreak*, &c. Indeed we now write *fought*, *befought* and *wrought* ; but Milton wrote *faught* and *befaught* : as may be feen in his own two editions of Paradife Loft. *Wrought* is fuppos'd to come from *work* ; which probably occafion'd it's being ufually fpell'd with *o* : but the other formation is more natural : *faught* from *fetch* is only us'd in common converfation, and that by vulgar people ; a word of the fame found, but fpell'd with *o*, being the paft tenfe of *fight* : for which the fame vulgar fay *fit*, as *'lit* from *'light*. In the 2d part of HEN. VI. Shakefpear feems to ufe *raught* for 'reft or taken-away. Act II. Sc. 5.

EXAMP. III. Vol. 7. P. 84. JULIUS CÆSAR.

" And, in their fteads, do *ravens*, crows, and kites,
" Fly o'er our heads."

" A raven and a crow is the fame bird of prey :
" the firft name taken from its nature ; the other
" from its voice. We fhould therefore read,

" *ravenous* crows and kites," WARB.

Though

Though Mr. Warburton cannot find it in the Dictionaries; yet every crow-keeper in the country will tell him, there is as real a difference between a raven and a crow; as there is between a crow and a rook, or a rook and a jack-daw. The carrion crow, or gor-crow [i. e. gore-crow] as it is called, is not the raven. Ben Johnson diftinguishes them in his Fox, Act I. Scene 2.

———" vulture, kite,
" Raven, and gor-crow, all my birds of prey"—

And Willoughby on birds would have told him; that there is this small difference between them, that one weighs almoft as much again as the other.

EXAMP. IV. Vol. 2. P. 350. AS YOU LIKE IT.

" But for his verity in love, I do think him as
" concave as a *cover'd* goblet, or a worm-eaten
" nut."

" Why a cover'd goblet ? Becaufe a goblet is *ne-*
" *ver* kept cover'd, but when empty. Shakefpear
" never throws-out his expreffions at random."
WARB.

If Shakefpear does not, I am afraid Mr. Warburton does; for he here afferts a thing, in which every young lady, who has been at a ball, can contradict him; that a goblet is *never* kept cover'd, but when *empty*. And, though Mr. Warburton does not frequent thofe affemblies; yet there are a great many other inftances, where it may be very proper to cover a cup, that is not empty; as if people are apt to preach over their liquor, or if there fhould be more than the company cares to drink at the prefent. In thefe, and other like cafes, it is lawful and ufual to put-on the cover to keep-out flies or duft; and to
prevent

prevent the bifhop, negus, or whatever liquor, from dying.

EXAMP. V. Vol. 8. P. 345. OTHELO.

    " Not poppy, nor mandragora,
" Nor all the drowfy fyrups of the world,
" Shall ever med'cine thee to that fweet fleep,
" Which thou *ow'dft* yefterday."

" *owedft*] This is right, and of much greater force
" than the common reading [*hadft* ;] not to fleep
" being finely called defrauding the *day* of a *debt*
" of nature." WARB.

If there be any fraud in the cafe, it is the *night* is cheated, and not the *day*; I would therefore propofe to read,

       which thou ow'dft *yefter-night.*

But, unluckily for Mr. Warburton's fine obfervation, and my improvement grafted upon it, *owedft* here is *ownedft*, fynonymous to *hadft*; and is frequently fo ufed by Shakefpear and the old authors. If Mr. Warburton will be contented with two inftances, they fhall be from his Bible :

    † *And he that oweth the houfe fhall come, and tell the prieft,* &c.

    ‖ *So fhall the Jews—bind the man, that* oweth *this girdle.*

EXAMP. VI. Vol. 1. P. 66. THE TEMPEST.

In the note on thefe lines,

" This is a moft majeftic vifion, and
" Harmonious charming *Lays*—

---

   * It is fo ufed in *Norfolk* to this day, in common converfation.
   † LEVIT. xiv. 35. ‖ ACTS xxi. 11.

               (where

(where by the way I would advise him to read *Lay*, because " *this is* charming *Lays*," is not so usual; in print at left) Mr. Warburton says, the word charming cannot *with propriety* be applied to any thing but *music* and *poetry*; because they were supposed to operate as *charms*. He here expresly excludes *Beauty*; which was ever supposed to have that operation in the highest degree. But this is not the only instance of the insensibility of our critic's heart.

Examp. VII. Vol. 4. P. 128. 1 Henry IV.

—" By this hand, if I were now by this rascal, I
" could brain him with his † ladie's fan."
" † The fans then in fashion had very long han-
" dles." Warb.

I do not know, where Mr. Warburton pick'd up this anecdote; of the size of the ladies' fans in the reign of Henry IV: but the observation is certainly very pertinent, and necessary; for, notwithstanding Hotspur was in such a passion, as to talk of dividing and going to buffets with himself; for moving such a dish of skimm'd milk with so honourable an action: yet it would be too much beyond probability to think of beating a lord's brains out with his lady's fan; had the fans then been such *slight toys*, as are now used.

This puts me in mind of an observation of John Bunyan's; that *great bowls and great spoons will hold more, than little bowls and little spoons.*

Yet, how unlucky would it be; if, after all, this learned criticism should be an ignorant mistake; and the humor of the passage should lie in alluding to the lightness, not the heaviness of the lady's fan? Both the paintings and the authors about Shakespear's

fpear's time prove, that the ladies wore feather fans;
there are, I think, feveral paffages in Ben Johnfon
to this purpofe; one I remember is in *Every man out
of his humour*, Act 2. Scene 2. where Faftidious
Brifke fays—" this *feather* grew in her fweet fan
" fometimes; though now it be my poor fortune to
" wear it, as you fee, Sir."

So in *Cynthia's revels.* Act 3. Scene 4.

" Will fpend his patrimony for a garter,
" Or the left *feather* in her bounteous fan."

EXAMP. VIII. Vol. 1. P. 45. THE TEMPEST.

—" how cam'ft thou to be the fiege of this *Moon-
" calf?*

—" *Moon-calf?*] It was imagined, that the moon
" had an ill influence on the infant's underftanding.
" Hence *idiots* were called *moon-calves.*" WARB.

I do not know what authority Mr. Warburton
has, for afferting, that *idiots* were called *moon-calves*;
but Shakefpear gives him none here. Stephano
was not yet enough acquainted with Caliban, to
judge what influence the moon might have on his
underftanding; but he gives him the name of moon-
calf from his ill-fhaped figure. Moon-calf, *Partus
Lunaris*—Datur et Teut. Monkalb—*Mola*, feu
Caro informis, &c. Skinner.

EXAMP. IX. Vol. 2. P. 301. AS YOU LIKE IT.

Rof. " With *bills* on their necks: Be it known to
" all men by thefe prefents"——

Rofalind here, to banter Le Beu, gives a ridiculous defcription of the men he was going to give
them an account of; fuppofing them to come with
bills

bills or *labels* on their necks, importing who they were; and there seems nothing here for a critic to stumble-at: but Mr. Warburton divides the speech, and gives the latter part to the Clown; "because "Rosalind and he are at cross purposes." Whether his division of this passage be right or no, his explication of it certainly is not. "She speaks of an in-"strument of *war*; and *He* turns it into an instru-"ment of *law* of the same name." Warb. Very acute! As if people carried such instruments of war as *bills* and *guns* on their *necks*, not on their shoulders; and as if Rosalind had any occasion to talk of instruments of *war*, when the conversation was only about a *wrestling*.

Examp. X. Ibid. P. 310.

"And thou wilt shew more bright, and *seem* "more virtuous, when she is gone] This implies "her to be some-how remarkably defective in vir-"tue; which was not the speaker's thought. The "poet doubtless wrote,

—————"and *shine* more virtuous;

"i. e. her virtues would *appear* more splendid, when "the lustre of her cousin's was away." Warb.

"This implies her to be some-how remarkably de-"fective in her virtue."]

How so, good Mr. Warburton? This would have been the case, had he said, *Thou wilt seem virtuous*; but the words, as they are, imply the direct contrary. Let us hear however, what is the meaning of the judicious amendment;

"*and shine more virtuous*:"

"i. e. her virtues would *appear* more splendid:"
which

which is juſt what he found in the text, *She would.*
ſeem more virtuous.

EXAMP. XI. Vol. 3. P. 382. WINTER'S TALE.

" I could *afflict* you further] If it had not been
" for the anſwer, one ſhould have concluded ; that
" the poet had wrote, *affect* you ; however he uſes
" *afflict* in the ſenſe of *affect*. This is only obſerved
" to ſhew, *that* when we find words, to which we
" muſt put an unuſual ſignification to make ſenſe ;
" *that* we ought to conclude, Shakeſpear took *that*
" liberty ; and *that* the text is not corrupted.   A'
" thing the Oxford editor ſhould have conſidered."
WARB.

Not to take notice of the peculiar ſpelling in
FURTHER, and the beautiful repetition of the THATS ;
This obſervation of Mr. Warburton's, however un-
accurately expreſſed, is a very juſt one ; and it
would have been much for his own reputation, and
the eaſe of his reader, if he had oftener conſidered
it : but the misfortune is, that the obſervation has
nothing to do here ; for *afflict* is uſed in the proper
ſenſe, for *grieve, trouble* ; nor can it be ſaid to be
uſed in the ſenſe of *affect*, any otherwiſe ; than as a
man cannot be *afflicted*, without being *affected* by
that which *afflicts* him ; which is no great diſcovery
to any body but Mr. Warburton.

EXAMP. XII. Vol. 3. P. 398. K. John.

" Knight, Knight, good mother—Baſiliſco like."
  Mr. Theobald has produced the paſſage at length,
to which this expreſſion undeniably alludes ; but this
will not do ; Mr. Warburton muſt refine upon it.

" But the beauty of the paſſage conſiſts in his al-
                                            " luding

" luding at the same time to his high original. His
" father, Richard the first, was furnamed *Cœur-de-*
" *lion.* And the *Cor Leonis*, a fix'd star of the first
" magnitude in the sign *Leo*, is called *Basilisco.*"
WARB.

He should have said, that the *Cor Leonis* is called
Basiliscus, or *Regulus*; for those are the names it goes
by: but then there would have been no foundation
for this, which is absolutely the conundrum of a
Hypercritic. The words, put out of verse, are
these; *I say, like Basilisco in the play, call me* (not
knave but) *knight, good mother*——What pretence is
here for any allusion to a star; which it does not appear, that Shakespear ever knew, or thought-of ?
Or how could the Bastard be in this instance like the
Cor Leonis; unless that star were *knighted ?* which
Mr. Warburton will as easily prove, as what he asserts of the allusion.

EXAMP. XIII. Vol. 1. P. 70. TEMPEST.

" The trumpery in my house, go bring it hither;
" For stale to catch these thieves."

" If it be asked, what necessity there was for this
" apparatus; I answer, that it was the superstitious
" fancy of the people, in our author's time; that
" witches, conjurers, &c. had no power over those,
" against whom they would employ their charms;
" till they had got them at this advantage, commit-
" ting some sin or other: as here of theft." WARB.

Very ingenious——but how then came Prospero's
charms to have power over Ferdinand, the HOLY *
Gonzalo, and Miranda ? How over these very fellows, as described in the speech immediately preceding ?

* P. 77.

H

Ex-

Examp. XIV. Vol. 1. P. 133. Midsummer Night's Dream.

" Her brother's noon-tide *with* th' Antipodes."

" She says, she would as soon believe, that the
" moon, then shining, could creep through the
" centre, and meet the Sun's light on the other side
" the globe.   It is plain therefore, we should read,

—" *i' th'* Antipodes ;

" i. e. *in* the *Antipodes, where* the Sun was then
" shining." Warb.

Excellent Grammarian, as well as Philosopher !
Why noontide *with* (i. e. *among*) the Antipodes, will
not mean on the other side the globe, (which is all
that the context and Mr. Warburton want it to
mean) is utterly unaccountable.

But *in* the Antipodes, is a very unaccurate expression; for *the Antipodes* means not *a place* on the globe,
as Mr. Warburton's explanation, *in* the Antipodes where, necessarily implies; but *the people*
inhabiting that place.

Examp. XV. Vol. 1. P. 402. Measure for
Measure.

" The princely Angelo—princely guards."

 Mr. Warburton, having unjustly abused all the
former editors ; and puzzled-out what every body
knew, as well as he could tell them ; " That the
" word *guards* in this passage does not mean *satellites*,
" but *lace* ;" proceeds to inform us, that " *priestly*
" *guards* means sanctity ; which is the sense required :
" But princely guards mean nothing but *rich*
" *lace*," &c.   Warb.

I   Now

Now, if this latter part be true, I should be glad to know; how *priestly guards* should come to signify any thing more than *black lace.*

EXAMP. XVI. Vol. 2. P. 138. MERCHANT OF VENICE.

—" a bankrupt, a prodigal] This is *spoke* (if he
" would write correctly, he should say *spoken*) of
" Antonio. But why *prodigal?* Bassanio indeed
" had been too liberal; and with this name the
" Jew honours him, when he is going to sup with
" him—

—" *I'll go in haste to feed upon*
" *The* prodigal *Christian*——

" But Antonio was a plain, *reserved, parsimonious*
" merchant. *Be assured therefore*, we should read,
" —*A bankrupt* FOR *a prodigal*; i. e. he is become
" a bankrupt, by supplying the extravagances of his
" friend Bassanio." WARB.

Surely his lending money without interest, was reason enough for the Jew to call him prodigal; and this Shylock upbraids him with immediately after: " *he* WAS WONT (not only he *did* in this instance, " but it was his *custom*) *to lend money for a Chri-* " *stian courtesy.*" But, in order to support this silly alteration, Mr. Warburton falsifies the character of Antonio; who, throughout, is represented not as *parsimonious*, but as the very perfection of *frankness* and *generosity*. He also seems to think it good logic to conclude; that, because the Jew calls one man a prodigal in one place, it is impossible he should call any body else so in another.

Ex-

EXAMP. XVII. Vol. 2. P. 135. MERCHANT OF VENICE.

—" How much honor
" Pick'd from the chaff and ruins of the times
" To be new *varniſh'd*] This confuſion and mix-
" ture of the metaphors, makes me *think* ; that
" Shakeſpear wrote,
" To be new *vanned*—

" i. e. winnow'd, purged," &c.   WARB.

Which is as much as to ſay, *pick'd from the chaff*, to be *pick'd from the chaff* ; for ſo his own expla-nation makes it : " *vanned* — from the French " word *vanner*, which is derived from the Latin, " *vannus, ventilabrum*," [mark that, I pray you ; for it ſerves to ſhew his learning in two languages at once] " the *fann* uſed for winnowing the chaff from " the corn." Why then might it not have been *fanned?*

This note he concludes with pronouncing, that " This alteration reſtores the metaphor to its inte-grity ;" and, by way of confirming his amendment, adds ; that " our poet frequently uſes the ſame thought." He does ſo ; but not ſo profuſely as our critic would have him, twice in the ſame ſentence.

If Mr Warburton thus puts into the text of Shakeſpear, without any authority, whatever he *thinks* he wrote ; he will abundantly convince the world of the propriety of that expreſſion, *of the laſt edition* ; to ſignify the worſt, or meaneſt ſort.

EXAMP. XVIII. Vol. 4. P. 42. RICHARD II.

—" the *abſent* time] For unprepared.   Not an " inelegant ſynecdoche."   WARB.

* See Dunciad, B. 4. P. 67.

Not

Not to enter into the elegance of the synecdoche, which seems but a hard and unnatural one ; Mr. Warburton might have seen, fifteen lines lower, if his towering genius would have suffered him to look downwards ; the true reason for this epithet : i. e. that *the King* was *absent*.

—" because th' anointed King is hence."

EXAMP. XIX. Vol. 4. P. 192. 1 HENRY IV.

" Here's *no* vanity !] In our author's time, the negative, in common speech, was used to design ironically the excess of a thing."—WARB.

Profound Critic ! as if it were not at all times so used ! But no matter for that ; the note is contrived so, as to make a careless reader believe, that he is particularly versed in the phraseology of his author's time ; and this looks well : though the discovery be much of the same kind, with that of the Fool in KING LEAR ;

" Then comes the time, who lives to see't,
" That going shall be us'd with feet."

But, perhaps, there was no Irony intended here : for Falstaffe might very naturally say, on seeing Sir W. B. dead ; Here's no vanity : i. e. This is past jesting ; This is a serious affair.

EXAMP. XX. Vol. 4. P. 283. 2 HENRY IV.

" As flaws congealed in the spring of day] Al-
" luding to the opinion of some philosophers ; that
" the vapors being congealed in the air by the cold,
" (which is most intense towards the morning) and
" being afterwards rarefied and let loose by the
" warmth of the sun, occasion those sudden im-

H 3 petuous

" petuous gufts of wind, which are called *flaws.*" WARB. after the Oxford editor.

The appearance of philofophical learning here mifled Mr. Warburton to adopt this note of the Oxford editor's, notwithftanding the abfurdity of *winds* being *congeled*; which feems borrowed from Sir John Mandeville, who tells us of fighs, oaths, and tunes being frozen up for fome time, and afterwards *let loofe by the warmth of the Sun:* but they neither of them underftood the meaning of the word in this place; which feems to be the fmall blades of ice, which are ftruck on the edges of the water in winter mornings; and which I have heard called by that name.

EXAMP. XXI. Vol. 4. P. 265. 2 HENRY IV.

" Philofopher's *two* ftones] One of which was an " univerfal medicine, and the other a tranfmuter of " bafer metals into gold." WARB.

But the *Panacea* was not a ftone, but a potable medicine; which therefore Mr. Warburton fhould have taken care to have *congeled,* as he did the *winds* above, before he gave it the denomination of a ftone. The meaning is, *twice the worth of* the philofopher's ftone.

EXAMP. XXII. Vol. 4. P. 303. 2 HENRY IV.

—" We will eat a laft year's pippin of my own " grafting, with a difh of carraways."

Who would imagine, that hiftory and literature fhould be brought-in by head and fhoulders, to explane the meaning of *a difh of carraways?* But what cannot a great critic do? Mr. Warburton having, with a becoming gravity, informed us, that carraways

are

are " a comfit or confection, fo called in our au-
" thor's time ;" (and I fuppofe, both before and
fince his time too) adds, that " a paffage in De
" Vigneul Marville's Melanges d'Hiftoire et de
" Litt. will explain this ODD TREAT :" and fo
quotes the paffage, which is not worth tranfcribing.
But why does he think it fo *odd a treat?* It is ftrange,
that Mr. Warburton's good mother fhould never
have treated mafter with fo common and excellent
a regale, as a roafted apple and carraways ; fure he
was a naughty boy, or has forgotten his mother's
kindnefs to him.

EXAMP. XXIII. Vol. 4. P. 381. HENRY V.
———" their gefture fad,
" *Invefting* lank lean cheeks, and war-worn coats,"
&c.

" A gefture *invefting* cheeks and coats, is nonfenfe.
" We fhould read,
" *Inveft in* lank lean cheeks,
" which is fenfe ; i. e. their fad gefture was cloathed,
" or fet-off, in lean cheeks, and worn coats. The
" image is ftrong and picturefque." WARB.

Whether geftures *invefting* cheeks and coats, or
geftures *inveft in* cheeks and coats, has the more
fenfe in it, not to mention *ftrength* and *painting* ; is a
queftion aworthy of our Profeffed Critic : but, in the
mean time, as he has determined in a like cafe,
Vol. 7. P. 180. " Nonfenfe for nonfenfe, the old
" fhould keep its ground ; as being in poffeffion."

EXAMP. XXIV. Vol. 5. P. 148. 3 HENRY VI.
" O boy! thy father gave thee life too foon."
" Becaufe, had he been born later, he would not now
" have been of years to engage in this quarrel.

H 4   " And

"And hath bereft thee of thy life too late] i. e.
"he should have *done it*, by not bringing thee into
"being; to make both father and son thus mi-
"serable. This is the sense; such as it is." —
WARB.

Such as it is, indeed! He should have taken away
life, before he had given it!

The father, having killed his son, is lamenting
those times of misery and confusion, occasioned by
the civil war: the general purport of those lines,
therefore, seems to be no more than this; That, in
such disastrous times, a short life is the most desira-
ble; and, the sooner one is out of them, the better.
There is a passage much of the same cast, in Tarquin and Lucrece. Stanz. 258.

O! quoth Lucretius, I did give that life;
Which she too early and too late hath spilled.

EXAMP. XXV. Vol. 5. P. 165. 3 HENRY VI.

"O but impatience *waiteth on true sorrow*.
"And see, where comes the breeder of my sorrow."

"How does impatience *more particularly* wait on
"true sorrow? On the contrary, such sorrows as
"the Queen's, which came gradually on through a
"long course of misfortunes, is generally less im-
"patient, than that of those, who have fallen into
"sudden miseries. The true reading seems to be,

"O but impatience WAITING RUES TO-MORROW,"
&c.

"i. e. when impatience waits and sollicits for re-
"dress, there is nothing she so much dreads, as be-
"ing put-off till to-morrow: (a proverbial expres-
"sion for procrastination)" &c. WARB.

And

And so—Face about, and as you were before; for it appears at last, that impatience *did* particularly wait on the Queen's sorrow. And we learn also; that putting-off till to-morrow, which is the English of procrastination, is a proverbial Expression for it.

EXAMP. XXVI. Vol. 1. P. 119. MIDSUMMER NIGHT'S DREAM.

" Then, for the third part of a *minute*, hence."

" We should read, the third part of the *midnight*. " The common reading is nonsense. Possibly " Shakespear might have used the French word " *minuit.*" WARB.

The common reading, says Mr. Warburton, is *nonsense*. And so, because he does not think the third part of a minute long enough, he would read *midnight*; i. e. for the third part of an instant, an indivisible point of time. But his *fatal* French led him into this blunder. " Possibly Shakespear " might have used the French word *minuit*." He seems to be very little acquainted with Shakespear; who could make such a nonsensical conjecture.

EXAMP. XXVII. Vol. 6. P. 116. KING LEAR.

" Whose face 'tween her forks presages snow," &c.

—" Whose face 'tween her forks] i. e. her hand " held before her face, in sign of modesty, with " the fingers spread-out, forky." WARB.

The construction is not, " whose face between her " forks," &c. but, " whose face presages snow," &c. the following expression, I believe, every body but
Mr.

Mr. Warburton understands; and He might, if he
had read a little farther; which would have saved
him this ingenious note.—See In *Timony.* Vol. 6.
P. 222.

" Whose blush doth thaw the consecrated snow,
" That lies on Dian's lap——

EXAMP. XXVIII. Vol. 2. P. 417. TAMING OF
THE SHREW.

" Please ye we may CONTRIVE this afternoon."

" Mr. Theobald asks, *what* they were to contrive?
" and then says, a foolish corruption possesses the
" place; and so alters it to *convive.*—But the com-
" mon reading is right; and the critic was only
" ignorant of the meaning of it. *Contrive* does not
" signify here to *project,* but to *spend* and *wear-out.*
" As in this passage of Spenser,

" *Three ages, such as mortal men* CONTRIVE."——
WARB.

I should think; there is no need either of Mr.
Theobald's *convive,* or of Mr. Warburton's new explication of *contrive;* if indeed it be not more properly a new word. If he had attended to the context, he might have answered his brother Critic's
question; *what* they were to contrive? They were
to *contrive* means jointly to gratify Petruchio, for
making room for their courtship, by taking-off the
elder sister Catherine.

" But, says Mr. Warburton, *contrive* does not
" signify here to *project;* but to *spend,* and *wear
" out.* As in this passage of Spenser,

" *Three ages, such as mortal men* CONTRIVE."

Con-

Contrive, Skinner fays, comes from *controuver* * ; and he renders it *excogitare, fingere.* In which fenfe, if I am not miftaken, Spenfer ufes it in the paffage quoted ; " Three ages, fuch as men gene-" rally *compute* or *reckon* them."

If it did fignify to *fpend* or *wear-out,* which will require more proof than this paffage ; it muft be formed from the verb *contero,* and from the preterperfect tenfe of that verb, *contrivi* ; and I do not at prefent recollect any Englifh verbs, formed from the preterperfect tenfe of the Latin ; except fuch as have come to us through French words fo formed, as *prepofe, impofe,* &c. But here is a difcovery, which if Mr. Warburton will make good, I will even forgive him all the injuries he has done to Shakefpear. This paffage is quoted from the ELEVENTH book of Spenfer ; fo that he has recovered, I hope, the fix books, which have been fo long lamented as loft in the Irifh fea: for thus he quotes it—" FAIRY QUEEN, Book xi. Chap. 9." Now, notwithftanding that unfortunate *chapter,* which fhocks one a little ; no body will imagine, that Mr. Warburton, who is fo accurate a *collater,* and makes ufe of *no indexes,* or *fecond hand* quotations ; though in an outlandifh Italian book he might take *Decade* and *Novel* for *December* and *No-vember :* yet in one of our own poets, whom he has fo much ftudied, could miftake B. II. C. 9. for BOOK the ELEVENTH, CHAPTER the NINTH. Perhaps, the latter books may be written in *Chapters,* not *Cantos,* as thofe printed are ; but he fhould have quoted VERSE 48 too.

* As *Retrieve* alfo, which he fpells *Retrive,* does from *Re-trouver.*

EXAMP. XXIX. Vol. 6. P. 62. K. LEAR.

———" if your fweet fway
" *Allow* obedience———]. Could it be a queftion,
" whether heaven *allowed* obedience? The poet
" wrote,

" *Hallow* obedience," &c. WARB.

But furely one may as well queftion, whether
heaven *allows* obedience; as whether it *hallows*, i. e.
fanctifies, it. It is ftrange, that a man of learning
fhould imagine; that the word IF here implies *doubting* or *queftioning.* The form of the expreffion is
elliptical; but, when the words left-out are fupplied,
it implies not *doubting*, but ftrong *affirmation.*

" If you do love old men—(which you furely do)
" If your fweet fway allow obedience (which it
" undoubtedly does; nay more, it commands it)
" If you yourfelves are old—(which you certain-
" ly are)
" Make it your caufe."

Does Mr. Warburton imagine; that, when Ni-
fus fays,
" Si qua tuis unquam pro me pater Hirtacus aris
" Dona tulit, fique ipfe meis venatibus auxi;"
when Calchas makes the fame fort of addrefs to
Apollo, in the firft book of Homer's Iliad;
Or, when Anchifes fays,
" Jupiter omnipotens, precibus fi flecteris ullis"——
That the one had the left doubt, whether Jupiter
was ever moved by prayer; or that the others que-
ftioned, whether or no they themfelves had ever fa-
crificed to Diana or Apollo?

EXAMP.

Examp. XXX. Ibid. p. 67.
—— " touch me with noble anger."

Here our Profess'd Critic, in order to introduce a supersubtle and forced explanation of his own, is searching after knots in a bulrush.

Can any thing be more intelligible, more pertinent, or finer, than this sentiment of Lear's?

" If you, ye gods, have stirred my daughters'
" hearts against me; at left let me not bear it with
" any unworthy tameness! but *touch me with noble*
" *anger*; let me resent it with such resolution, as
" becomes a man;
—" and let not *woman*'s weapons, water-drops,
" Stain my *man*'s cheeks."

What need is here for Mr. Warburton's recondite learning, about what the antient poets said concerning the misfortunes of particular families?

Examp. XXXI. Vol. 7. P. 117. Antony and
Cleopatra.

" And soberly did mount an † *arm-gaunt* steed]
" i. e. his steed worn *lean* and *thin* by much ser-
" vice in *war*. So Farefax,
" His *stall-worn* steed the champion stout be-
" strode." Warb.

Mr. Warburton here seems to have stolen Don Quixote's Rosinante, to mount the demy Atlas of *this* earth; as Cleopatra calls him just before. Where

† I have sometimes thought; that the meaning may possibly be, *thin-shouldered*; by a strange composition of Latin and English: —*gaunt* quoad *armos*—and I have been since told; that Mr. Seward makes the same conjecture occasionally, on a passage in Beaumont and Fletcher.

I

is

is the propriety of this; that a man, who command-
ed so large a part of the world, should have only a
lean, thin, worn-out horse, to carry him to a battle; which was to decide, whether he should be
master of the rest or not? However, he seems to
have matched him well; with one from *Farefax,*
who is *stall-worn.*

  " A different cause, says parson Sly,
   " The same effect may give."   PRIOR.

One is worn-out with too much action, the other
with standing still.   They seem neither of them to
have been troubled with the distemper called OATS*;
and one may reasonably suspect, that their grooms
gave them foul play.

  But Mr. Warburton, who made this match, has
played us a Yorkshire trick; and the odds are pro-
digiously on old Fairfax's side: for when I come to
look upon him in his stable, he is really not a *stall-
worn,* but a *stalworth* steed; now STALWORTH, or
STALWART, for it is written both ways, signifies
bold, courageous, strong.

  " Wherefore this worthy *stalwart* Hercules,"
  Gawin Douglas's Æneis, p. 249. l. 45. *& alibi*;
and in his Glossary he explanes it, *Chalybei animi,
stabilis et firmi animi, &c.*

  EXAMP. XXXII. Vol. 8. P. 191.   HAMLET.

  —" Nay, then let the Devil wear black; FOR I'll
 " have a suit of sables] The conceit of these words
 " is not taken. They are an ironical apology for
 " his mother's chearful looks: Two months were
 " long enough in conscience to make any dead hus-
 " band forgotten. But the editors, in their non-

  * See the Glossary, at the word *Oats.*

          " sensical

"	senfical blunder, have made Hamlet fay juft the
"	contrary. That the Devil and he would both go
"	into mourning; though his mother did not. The
"	true reading is this; *Nay, then let the Devil wear*
"	*black, 'FORE I'll have a fuit of fable.* As much as
"	to fay, *Let the Devil wear black for me; I'll have*
"	*none.* The Oxford editor defpifes an emendation
"	fo eafy, and reads it thus; *Nay, then let the Devil*
"	*wear black; for I'll have a fuit of* ermine. And you
"	could expect no lefs; when fuch a critic had the
"	dreffing of him. But the blunder was a pleafant
"	one. The *fenflefs* editors had wrote *fables*, the
"	*fur* fo called, for *fable, black*; and the critic only
"	changed this for that: by a like figure, the com-
"	mon people fay, *You rejoice the* COCKLES *of my*
"	*heart*, for MUSCLES *of my heart*; an unlucky mif-
"	take of one fhell-fifh for another." WARB.

This is, as Mr. Warburton fays of Sir Thomas
Hanmer, Vol. 2. p. 346. *amending with a vengeance.*
If every paffage, which our profeffed Critic does
not underftand, muft thus be altered; we fhall have,
indeed, a complete edition of Shakefpear. In this
note, which I have quoted at length, that the reader
may fee the whole ftrength of Mr. Warburton's
reafoning; I know not which to admire moft: the
confiftency of his argument, the decency of his
language, or the wit of his lenten jeft about fhell-
fifh, which makes fo proper a conclufion.

The original reading is,

—"*Nay, then let the Devil wear black*; for *I'll*
"	*have a fuit of* fables." Mr. Warburton acknow-
ledges, that the word *fables* fignifies a *fur* fo called;
and every body knows, that they are worn by way
of finery in that country. Nay, he himfelf, in this
very

very play, p. 236. speaking of these same *fables*, says;
" they import, that the wearers are rich burghers
" and magistrates." He says, moreover, that the
true reading (whatever it be) is " as much as to
" say, *Let the Devil wear black for me; I'll have
" none.*" Now I will leave it to any body to judge,
whether this true meaning be not expressed in the
common reading; and then to determine, *whose is
the nonsensical blunder*, and *who* is the *senseless editor*.

EXAMP. XXXIII. Vol. 3. P. 25.   ALL'S WELL
THAT ENDS WELL.

————" How shall they credit
" A poor unlearned virgin; when the schools,
" *Embowell'd* of their doctrine, have left-off
" The danger to itself?"

This plainly means, that the physicians had ex-
hausted all their skill.   But Mr. Warburton must
refine, as follows;

" *Embowell'd* of their doctrine] The expression
" is beautifully satirical; and implies, that the theo-
" ries of the school are spun out of the *bowels* of
" the professors; like the cobwebs of the spider."
WARB.

One would think, our critic's *brains* were in his
bowels; when he spun this note.

EXAMP. XXXIV. Vol. 1. P. 348.   MERRY
WIVES OF WINDSOR.

Falst. " Well, I am your theme; you have the
" start of me; I am dejected; I am not able to an-
" swer the *Welch flannel*," &c.
——" the *Welch flannel*] Shakespear possibly wrote
" *flamen.* As Sir Hugh was a *choleric* priest, and
" apt

" apt to táke fire, *flamen* was a very proper name;
" it being given to that order of Latin priests, from
" the *flame-coloured* habit." WARB.

Bene qui conjiciet, vatem hunc perhibebo optimum,
says Dr. Newton; in laud of that happy skill in di-
vination, which Mr. Warburton boasts of in his
motto *; and of which he gives us so extraordinary
a sample in this learned note.

Flannel is the chief manufacture of Wales, and
probably might make part of Sir Hugh's dress; and
it is in allusion to this, that Falstaff calls him *Welch
flannel.* But the reason Mr. Warburton gives for
his correction, is as good as the correction itself;
" the name *flamen* being given to that order of La-
" tin priests, from the *flame-coloured habit.*" But
Festus, *de verborum significatione,* would have told
him; " *Flamen* dialis dictus, quod *filo* assidue ve-
" letur; indeque appellatur *flamen,* quasi *filamen.*"
And Varro *De linguâ Latinâ* — " quòd — caput
" cinctum habebant *filo, flamines* dicti." The same
saith old Bishop Isidore, in his chapter of *Clerks.*

EXAMP. XXXV. Vol. 7. P. 51. JULIUS CÆSAR.

————" here thy hunters stand
" " Sign'd in thy spoil, and crimson'd in thy *lethe.*

" Mr. Theobald says, the Dictionaries acknowledge
" no such word as *lethe*——After all this pother,
" *lethe* was a *common* French word, signifying *death*
" or *destruction*; from the Latin *lethum.*" WARB.
A very *common* word indeed, which the Dictionaries do not acknowledge; for this Mr. Warbur-

*——— Quorum omnium interpretes, ut Grammatici, Poetarum
proxime ad eorum quos interpretantur divinationem videntur ac-
cedere. Cic. de Divin.

ton

ton does not deny. They give us indeed *leth*, a
laft of herrings; if that will ferve his turn. One
would expect; that he, who is only learning French,
fhould give us fome better authority than his own
for this *common* French word; and, to do him juftice fo he does; after his manner.

" So in ANTONY AND CLEOPATRA, he (Shake-
" fpear) fays,

———" Even to a *lethied* dulnefs;"

That is, becaufe Shakefpear has made an Englifh
word from the Latin *lethum*, death; or *Lethe*, the
river of oblivion; *therefore lethe* is a common
French word; which I think is a very mean, or,
as our critic explanes it in K. LEAR, Vol. 6. P. 97.
a very * *mediocre* argument.

EXAMP. XXXVI. Vol. 2. P. 5. MUCH ADO
ABOUT NOTHING.

——" If he have wit enough to keep himfelf *warm*,
" let him bear it for a difference between himfelf
" and his horfe.] But how would that make a
" difference between him and his horfe? We
" fhould read—keep himfelf *from harm*." WARB.

The reafon for this alteration is pleafant—" be-
" caufe it is the nature of *horfes*, when wounded,
" to run upon the point of the weapon." i. e. Becaufe horfes, when they have gotten harm, have
not wit enough to keep themfelves from harm.
It is a proverbial expreffion. Shakefpear alludes to it

* Our mean] i. e. moderate, mediocre condition.

again,

again, in The Taming of the Shrew. Vol. 3. P. 427.

" Catharine. Am I not wife ?
" Petruchio. Yes ; keep you warm."

EXAMP. XXXVII. Vol. 2. P. 34. MUCH ADO ABOUT NOTHING.

—paft the *infinite* of thought] " Human thought " cannot fure be called *infinite*, with any kind of " figurative propriety. I fuppofe, the true read- " ing was, *definite*." WARB.

Whatever the impropriety may be of applying this term to *finite*, and even *trifling* things ; the practife is fo common, that it is almoft a fhame to quote any proof of it : yet I cannot forbear giving One from Mr. W.'s own Preface, P. ix. where, fpeaking of the two poetical Editors of Shakefpear, he fays—

" The proprietors, not difcouraged by their firft " unfuccefsful Effort, in due time made a fecond ; " and, tho' they ftill ftuck-to their Poets, with " *infinitely* more fuccefs, in their choice of Mr. " Pope."

So that this, it feems, was only a fudden fit of humility in Mr. W ! And though Human Thought itfelf be unworthy of the term *infinite* ; yet the fuccefs of a *Bookfeller*, in his choice of a *Critic* for Shakefpear, may, without impropriety, be fo call- ed ; and That, (which makes it ftill more extra- ordinary) even before the choice fell on Mr. W.

EXAMP. XXXVIII. Vol. 2. P. 411. THE TAMING OF THE SHREW.

" Few words fuffice ; and therefore, if you know " One rich enough to be *Petruchio*'s wife ;

I 2

(As

" (As wealth is burden of my wooing dance)
" Be she as foul as was *Florentius'* Love,
" As old as *Sibyll,* and as curst and shrewd
" As *Socrates' Xantippe,* or a worse,
" She moves me not; or not removes, at left,
" Affection's *edge* in *me.*"———

" This man is a ftrange talker. He tells you,
" he wants *money* only : yet, after this, of *affection*'s
" *edge* being fo ftrong in him ; that nothing can a-
" bate it.——The true reading, I am perfuaded, is——

" Affection *fieg'd* in *coin*—i. e. feated, placed,
" fixed. This makes him fpeak to the purpofe ;
" that his *affection* is all love of *money.*" WARB.

And why may not this love of money. be *that*
affection ; whofe edge, he fays, nothing can abate?

There is but one thing wanting, to make us receive Mr. W's alteration. Let him but prove,
that this man is, as he calls him, a *ftrange talker* ;
and then no-body will deny, that the expreffion——
Affection fieg'd in coin, will very well fit his mouth.

EXAMP. XXXIX. Vol. 4. P. 124. 1 HENRY IV.

" If I travel but *four foot* by the *fquare* further
" on foot, I fhall break my wind.] The thought
" is humorous ; and alludes to his bulk : Infinu-
" ating, that his legs being *four foot* afunder, when
" he advanced *four foot,* this put-together made
" *four foot fquare.*" WARB.

According to this known rule, let us meafure
the leap of the dancer in the WINTER'S TALE,
Vol. 3. P. 347. who jumped twelve foot and a
half *by the fquare :* i. e. twelve foot and a half *for-
wards,* and as much *fideways.* But whether he did
this, by jumping in the diagonal ; or whether he
carried

carried his legs twelve foot and a half afunder; is not very eafily determined.

For want of attending to this menfuration, a very fine piece of humour, alfo, will be loft to the reader in 2 HEN. IV. Vol. 4. P. 279. where *Falstaff* fays to Prince *John* of *Lancafter*—‘ I fpeeded hither with the very extremeft inch of poffibility.’—Infinuating, without queftion, that on this occafion of the battle he travelled by the *inch fquare* ; (for, though *fquare* be not expreffed here, I am perfuaded it is underftood :) and carried his legs not above an inch afunder. An extremely natural pofture for a coward in a battle !

By the *fquare* in both places, it is evident that Shakefpear means nothing more than a common Meafure, or Foot-Rule. Milton has ufed the word *fquare* in the fame manner, for meafure *fimpliciter.* Comus, l. 339.

Eye me, bleft Providence, and *fquare* my trial
To my proportioned ftrength——

EXAMP. XL. Vol. 6. P. 334. MACBETH.

“ As, whence the Sun *gives* his reflection) Here
“ are two readings in the copies, *gives*, and *’gins* ;
“ i. e. begins. But the latter, I think, is right—
“ &c.” WARB.

Mr. W. in many of his notes, is fond of giving us a tafte of his knowledge in his philofophy : how happily, the reader may judge, in fome meafure, from the very long note on this paffage ; Some particulars of which are worth examining. e. g.

“ That ftorms generally come from the *Eaft,*
“ is founded on obfervation. The natural and
“ conftant motion of the Ocean is from Eaft to

I 3 “ Weft ,

" Weſt; and the Wind has the ſame direction.
" Varen. Geograph. lib. i. cap. 14. prop. 10. See
" alſo Dr. Halley's account of the Trade-winds
" and Monſoons." WARB.

The Captain, who is the ſpeaker here, if he had
been a ſea captain, would have known, that neither of theſe aſſertions are true; except between
the Tropics. See Dr. Halley's account of the
Trade-winds and Monſoons. The moſt frequent
and moſt violent ſtorms, in theſe parts of the world,
are from the South-Weſt, not from the Eaſt.

" It is no wonder, that ſtorms ſhould come
" moſt frequently from that quarter [the Eaſt];
" or that they ſhould be moſt violent: becauſe
" there is a concurrence of the natural motions of
" Wind and Wave." WARB.

The exact *contrary* of this is the truth. The
moſt violent agitations being cauſed by the oppo-
ſition of Wind and Wave : i. e. when the Wind
blows one way, and the Tide moves the other.

" The Sun may *give* its reflection, in *any* part of
" its courſe above the horizon; but it can *begin*
" it, only in *one*." WARB.

It were to be wiſhed, that Mr. W. would inform us; Where that *one* part above the horizon
is, in which the Sun may *begin* his courſe.

" The Rainbow is no more a reflection of the
" Sun, than a Tune is a Fiddle." WARB.

There is, I ſuppoſe, (as Mr. W. ſays of Sir
T. H. Vol. 3. P. 157) ſome conceit in this ſimile
of the Fiddle; but it lies ſo deep, that the reader
has reaſon to wiſh he could have explained his own
meaning. As for the aſſertion itſelf, it ſhews
great

great ignorance; for the Rainbow is really nothing elfe, but the reflected image of the Sun, optically deformed. But that Mr. W. fhould have no notion how this can be, will be no matter of wonder to any one; who reads that notable note (in Richard II. Vol. 4. P. 35.) concerning a certain mathematical recreation in Optics; where he gives us all He knows about figures optically deformed.

All this deluge of philofophy is poured-in upon us, only to fupport a *wrong* reading; and thereby obfcure and confound a very beautiful and a very appofite fimilitude. The whole paffage, with what I doubt not is the true meaning of it, is thus.

As, whence the Sun *gives* his reflection,
Shipwrecking ftorms and direful thunders break;
So from that Spring, whence Comfort feem'd to
      come,
Difcomfort well'd. ——— i. e. Difcomfort and Comfort came from the fame Spring; juft as thofe dreadful accidents of Storms and Thunder come from the fame place, from whence procedes, the greateft of earthly bleffings, the Light of the Sun : viz. from the heavens, the Sky.

EXAMP. XLI. Vol. 6. P. 351. MACBETH.

" *King.* This caftle hath a pleafant Seat; the Air
" Nimbly and fweetly recommends itfelf
" Unto our *gentle fenfes.*———

" *Banq.*———This gueft of fummer,
" The temple-haunting martlet, does approve,
" By his lov'd manfionry, that heaven's breath
" *Smells* wooingly here———] How odd a cha-
" racter is this of the Air, that it could recom-

" mend

" mend itfelf to *all* the fenfes ; not excepting the
" *Sight* and *Hearing*? Without doubt we fhould
" read,
    " Unto our *general fenfe*——meaning *touch* or
" *feeling*: which, not being confined to one part,
" like the reft of the fenfes, but extended over the
" whole body ; the poet, by a *fine* periphrafis, calls
" the *general fenfe*." WARB.

Here the fenfe of *feeling* is become a *general*
Senfe ; which in King *Lear* he feems to think was
entirely *confined to one part*. See P. 98. Unlefs perhaps he may there allude-to the diftich of *Mat.
Prior*,

      The bully beat, and happy lover
      Confefs, that feeling lies all over.   *Alma.*

But to the paffage.   Why will Mr. W. needs
have it, that—*fenfes*—neceffarily implies—*all* the
fenfes ? and again, fuppofing it does mean fo, How
came the difficulty about Sight and Hearing particularly, into his head ? as if a man could not *fee,*
whether it was a fine day or no ; or *bear*, whether
the wind blows! There's two, the moft defperate,
of his five fenfes, which have the Air for their Object.   Mr. W. himfelf allows *feeling* ; and talks a-
bout—*recreating the fibres*—very much in the ftile
of a Quack-Doctor's bill.   *Banquo*'s Martlet will
ftand-up for *Smelling*.   And fo at laft we may apply to Mr. W. what *Beatrice* (in MUCH ADO ABOUT
NOTHING, Vol. 2. P. 5.) fays of Signior *Benedick* ;
—' in this conflict four (at left) of his five wits
' go halting off ; and now muft the whole man be
' governed with one'——. And unluckily too,
that *one* is—his *Tafte!*

EXAMP.

EXAMP. XLII. Vol. 7. P. 253. CYMBELINE.

" ——————————the twinn'd ftones
" Upon *th' unnumber'd* beach"————

The beach is called unnumber'd, from the ftones upon it being numberlefs. Shakefpear very probably had in his eye his own beautiful defcription of Dover cliff in KING LEAR; where he fpeaks of

" ——————————the murmuring furge,
" That on *th' unnumber'd* idle pebbles chafes."

which line is indeed a comment on this before us. Yet our profeffed Critic will needs call it Nonfenfe; and fays, " Senfe and Antithefis oblige us to read;

" upon the *bumbled* beach————i. e. becaufe in-
" fulted with the flow of the tide." WARB.

EXAMP. XLIII. Vol. 8. P. 334. OTHELLO.

" 'Tis as I fhould entreat you wear your *gloves*]
" Abfurd. We fhould read, *cloths*." WARB.

How rarely our bafhful Defdemona is come-on, fince P. 298; where our mealy-mouthed Critic feems to imagine that it would be an * indecorum in her to think that Othello ever pulled-off his cloths: whereas here it is a matter of indifference to her modefty, whether he ever puts them on.

The fenfe requires, that the circumftance fhe mentions fhould be extremely trivial; therefore the old reading is preferable, and not abfurd.

EXAMP. XLIV. Ibid. P. 298.

" My downright violence *and ftorm of* fortunes]

———————

* See CAN. XII. Ex. IV.

" But

" But what violence was it that drove her to run
" away with the Moor? We should read—

" My down-right violence *to forms, my* fortunes."
WARB.

A critic by profeſſion is, I ſuppoſe, a character
too grave and pompous ever to be violently in love.

Downright violence means the unbridled impe-
tuoſity, with which her paſſion hurried her on to
this unlawful marriage; and *ſtorm of fortunes* may
ſignify the hazard ſhe thereby run, of making ſhip-
wrack of her worldly intereſt. Both very agreeable
to what ſhe ſays a little lower.

———To his honours and his valiant parts
Did I my ſoul and fortunes conſecrate.

EXAMP. XLV. Ibid. P. 278.

As when by night and negligence the fire
Is *ſpied* in populous cities.———]

" This is not ſenſe; take it which way you will.
" If *night* and *negligence* relate to *ſpied*, it is abſurd
" to ſay—the fire was *ſpied* by *negligence*. If *night*
" and *negligence* refer only to the time and occaſion,
" it ſhould then be *by* night, and *thro'* negligence:
" otherwiſe the particle *by* would be made to ſig-
" nify *time,* applied to one word; and *cauſe,* ap-
" plied to the other. We ſhould read therefore—
" is *ſpred*—; by which all theſe faults are avoided."
WARB.

The plain meaning is, not—the fire was ſpied
by negligence; but—the fire, which came by night
and negligence, was ſpied.— And this double
meaning to the ſame word, is common to Shakeſpear with all other writers; eſpecially where the
word

word is fo familiar a one, as this in queftion. *Ovid*
feems even to have thought it a beauty, inftead of
a defect.

EXAMP. XLVI. Ibid. P. 277.

"——Muft be *led* and calm'd.——] Thus the old
" Quarto. The 1ft Folio reads *belee'd* : but that
" fpoils the meafure. I read *let*, hindered." WARB.

Belee'd is by far the beft reading of the three.
But it fpoils the meafure ! fays Mr. W.

" Chriftian and heath'n muft be belee'd and
" calm'd."

'Tis ftrange that Mr. W, after having fo often
jumbled together fuch throngs of confonants, as
are enough to throttle a Hottentot ; fhould at laft
be fo very nice, as not to endure the word *heath'n*
in one fyllable.

EXAMP. XLVII. Vol. 8. P. 75. ROMEO AND JULIET.

Oh now I *would* they *had* chang'd voices too.]

" The *toad* having very fine eyes, and the *lark*
" very ugly ones, was the occafion of a common
" faying among the people, that the toad and lark
" had chang'd eyes. To this the fpeaker alludes.
" But fure fhe need not have *wifhed*, that they had
" changed *voices* too. The lark appeared to her
" untunable enough in all confcience : As appears
" by what fhe faid juft before,

" It is the lark that fings fo *out of tune* ;
" Straining *harfh difcords*, and *unpleafing fharps*.
" This directs us to the right reading. For how
" natural was it for her after this to add,

" Some

" Some fay, the lark and loathed toad change eyes :
" O, now I *wot* they *have* chang'd voices too.

" i. e. the lark fings fo harfhly, that I now per-
" ceive the toad and fhe have chang'd *voices* as well
" as *eyes*." WARB.

Mr. W. feems to have no great notion of what
fhe was *wifhing* for. The lark had given her lover
notice of the Morning ; fo fhe wifhes, that the toad
and lark had chang'd voices ; becaufe the toad's
croaking is a fign of Night, and the lark's finging
of the Morning.

EXAMP. XLVIII. Vol. 8. P. 288. OTHELLO.

" As in thefe cafes, where *they aim* reports.] Thefe
" Venetians feem to have had a very *odd* fort of
" perfons in employment ; who did all by *hazard,*
" as to what and how they fhould report ; for this
" is the fenfe of man's *aiming reports.* The true
" reading without queftion is,

———Where *the Aim* reports.

" i. e. where there is no better ground for infor-
" mation, than *conjecture*." WARB.

Mr. W. may puzzle his own head, as much as
he pleafes, with calling the *fame* thing, *conjecture*
in one place, and *hazard* in another ; but the fenfible reader will think a profeffed critic as *odd* a fort
of perfon in employment, as any Venetian of them
all ; unlefs he tells us, why *an Aim* (fubft.) may
fignify *a* conjecture, when *to aim* (verb.) wont fignify *to* conjecture.

* See P. 191.

EXAMP.

EXAMP. XLIX. Vol. 8. P. 248. HAMLET.

" Yet here she is allow'd her *virgin rites,*
" Her *maiden strewments* —] The old Quarto
" reads, virgin *Crants,* evidently corrupted from
" *Chants*; which is the true word. A *specific* ra-
" ther than a *generic* term being here required, to
" answer to *maiden strewments.*" WARB.

I suppose, because *generic* comes from *genus*; and
that from *gigno*; a word, improper to be us'd on
so *maidenly* an occasion: For else, her *maiden strewments,* seems only to be specifying what is meant
by her *virgin rites* in general. But, however that
be, Mr. W. is certainly very unlucky, in taking
the word *chants.* He had better have pitched upon
grants, wants, pants, or any other, provided it
rhymes to *chants*; because it should seem by the
very next speech of the Priest, that these same
chants were the only things that were deny'd her.

We should profane the service of the dead,
To *sing* a *requiem,* and such rest to her,
As to peace-parted souls.———

If Mr. W's reading be approved, we should, to
restore *integrity,* make a slight alteration in the latter line; and read

Her maiden *'struments*———

for *instruments.* Music, not only vocal, but in-
strumental also.

CANON

CANON IX.

He may interpret his Author so; as to make him mean directly contrary to what He says.

EXAMPLE I. Vol. 3. P. 331. WINTER'S TALE.

" 'Fore the RED blood reins in the winters PALE.
" i. e.. Before the PALE winter reins in the RED or
" *youthful* blood." WARB.

EXAMP. II. Ibid. P. 347.

—" three swineheards, that have made them—
" selves all *men of hair*; they call themselves *saltiers.*"
that is, who have made themselves all over hairy,
(probably with goats skins;) they call themselves
satyrs.

But the servant's blunder in the name occasioned
Mr. Warburton's making one in the sense. I suppose, *Saltiers* put him in mind of *saltare*; that, of
skipping and *bounding*; and *bounding*, of *tennis-balls*;
which produce this learned note:

" *all men of hair*] i. e. nimble; that leap, as if they
" rebounded. The phrase is taken from tennis-
" balls, which were stuff'd with hair." WARB.

EXAMP. III. Vol. 3. P. 118. TWELFTH NIGHT.

" That breathes upon a bank of violets
" Stealing, and giving odor—] — It may al-
" lude to another property of music, where the
" *same strains* have a power to excite pain or plea-
" sure; as the state is, in which it finds the hearer.
" Hence Milton makes *the self-same* strains of Orpheus

" *pheus* proper to excite both the affections of mirth
" and melancholy, juft as the mind is then difpo-
" fed. If to mirth, he calls for fuch mufic;

> " That Orpheus' felf may heave his head,
> " From golden flumbers on a bed
> " Of heap'd Elyfian flow'rs, and hear
> " Such ftrains," &c.

" If to melancholy——

> " Or bid the foul of Orpheus fing
> " Such notes, as, warbled to the ftring,
> " Drew iron tears down Pluto's cheek," &c.
>   WARB.

Which *felf-fame* ftrains of *Orpheus* are, in the firft inftance, what are performed by another perfon, and Orpheus is only a hearer of; in the other, Orpheus fings himfelf.

EXAMP. IV. Vol. 4. P. 117. 1 HENRY IV.

" He apprehends a world of figures here] This,
" I fuppofe, alludes to what he had faid before, of
" unclafping a fecret book." WARB.

Then, *I fuppofe*, this fecret book muft be a book of accounts; fince it held a world of figures. But, be it what it will, Hotfpur's impatience had not fuffered his uncle Worcefter to unclafp or even to produce it as yet; fo that whatever he faw, it was nothing in that fecret book.

Thefe figures therefore mean fhapes created by Hotfpur's imagination; but not the form of what he fhould attend; viz. of what his uncle had, to propofe.

EXAMP. V. Vol. 5. P. 39. 2 HENRY VI.

" For by his *death* we do perceive his guilt]
"   *Death*

" *Death* for defeat.   Becaufe, by the laws of duel,
" he that was defeated, was executed in confe-
" quence of it." WARB.

Here Mr. Warburton is killing a dead man; for,
if this note means any thing, it means to inform
us; that the *armourer* was not killed, but only
conquered; knock'd-down indeed with the fand-
bag, but was to be hanged afterwards; yet, only
fix lines above, his own text declares that he *dies.*
Thus it ftands,

- " Sound trumpets; alarum to the combatants.

　　　　　[*They fight, and Peter ftrikes him down.*
ARM. " Hold, Peter, hold; I confefs, I confefs
　　 " treafon." [*dies.*

But our Profefs'd Critic feldom fees an inch beyond his nofe, in matters that lie plainly before
him; while he is hunting for refinements, which
his author never thought of.

　　EXAMP. VI. VOL. 3. P. 426. KING JOHN.

" *Conftance.* Lewis, ftand faft; the Devil tempts
　　 " thee here
" In likenefs of a new *untrimmed* bride."

- —" a new *untrimmed* bride] Mr. Theobald fays;
" that, as *untrimmed* cannot bear any fignification
" to fquare with the fenfe required, it muft be cor-
" rupt; therefore he will cafhier it, and read, *and*
" *trimmed*; in which he is followed by the Oxford
" editor: but they are both too hafty. It fquares ve-
" ry well with the fenfe; and fignifies *unfteady.* The
" term is taken from navigation. We fay, in a
" fimilar way of fpeaking, *not well manned.*" WARB.

　　　　　　　　　　　　　　　　　　　I am

I am afraid, Mr. Warburton, with all his gravity here, will be found to have made more hafte than good fpeed. *Unfteady,* which is no great recommendation of a bride, cannot *fquare well* with the fenfe; where the fpeaker defigns to exprefs a *ftrong* and *irrefiftible* temptation : but Mr. Warburton is perpetually out in his philofophy, upon this fubject. Nor, though the term fhould be taken from Navigation, (which I fee no reafon for in this place;) does the *trim* of a fhip fignify its ballaft ; but its fails, colors, and pendants : and fo he himfelf fays, in a note of his on the following paffage in the MERRY WIVES OF WINDSOR, Vol 1. P. 303.

— " that becomes the fhip-tire," &c.] " The
" *fhip-tire* was an open head-drefs; with a kind of
" fcarf depending from behind. Its name of *fhip-*
" *tire* was, I prefume, from its giving the wearer
" fome refemblance of a *fhip,* as Shakefpear * fays,
" *in all her trim :* with all her pennants out, and
" flags and ftreamers flying. Thus Milton, in
" Samfon Agoniftes, paints Dalila—

" Like a ftately fhip
" * * * * * *
" With all her brav'ry on, and tackle trim,
" Sails fill'd, and ftreamers waving,
" Courted by all the winds that hold them
       play." WARB.

Trim here, and in many other places, means finery : as in 1 HENRY IV. P. 109.

— " a certain lord, neat, *trimly* drefs'd,
" *Frefh* as a bridegroom"—

K   The

* TEMPEST, Vol. 1. P. 84.

The very same image as here, a *new* and *trimmed* bride. And from this common fignification, it is applied to a fhip, when fhe has all her *bravery* on.

And now let Mr. Warburton judge, whether Lady Blanch appeared before fuch an affembly, with or without her *trim*.

EXAMP. VII. Vol. 3. P. 369. WINTER's TALE.

——" fo muft thy *grave*
" Give way to what's feen now——] " *Grave* for
" *epitaph.*" WARB.

Thy grave here means, thy beauties, which are buried in the grave; the *continent* for the *contents*.

EXAMP. VIII. Vol. 6. P. 348. MACBETH.

——" The raven himfelf *is* hoarfe,
" That croaks the fatal entrance of Duncan
" Under my battlements."

Here Mr. Warburton, in order to introduce a tedious and impertinent refinement, *fuppofes* the text to be corrupt; and that we fhould read,

" The raven himfelf's *not* hoarfe." WARB.

The reafon he gives is fomewhat pleafant. " Had
" Shakefpear meant *this*, (that the raven is hoarfe
" with croaking) he would have expreffed his mean-
" ing *properly*; as he knew fo well how to do it."
Had Mr. Warburton looked but to the fpeech which this is in anfwer to, and which occafions this reflection; he would have feen this meffenger (whom the Queen calls the raven) defcribed as one,

" Who, almoft dead for breath, had fcarcely more
" Than would make up his meffage."

3   Well

Well then might fhe call this raven *boarfe*; and how Shakefpear could find more *proper* words for this, would puzzle Mr. Warburton from all his half learned languages to fhew.

Examp. IX. Vol. 1. P. 276. Merry Wives of Windsor.

Nym.—" I have a fword, and it fhall bite *upon* " *my* necessity;" i. e. when I find it *neceffary*; or, when I am reduced to *neceffity*.

But Mr. Warburton calls this " an *abfurd* paf- " fage ;" and, without any *neceffity* at all, makes an *abfurd* oath of it.

" This abfurd paffage, fays he, may be point- " ed into fenfe. I have a fword, and it fhall bite— " Upon my neceffity, he loves your wife" &c. For which he gives this judicious reafon ; " that Nym " meant, his fword fhould bite (not *upon his ne- ceffity*, but) *upon the highway.*" Warb.

Examp. X. Vol. 1. P. 43. Tempest.

—" any ftrange beaft there makes a man] I can- " not but think this fatire very juft upon our " countrymen; who have been always very ready " to make Denifons of the whole tribe of the *Pi-* " *theci*, and complement them with the *Donum* " *Civitatis*; as appears by the names in ufe. Thus " *monkey*; which, the Etymologifts tell us, comes " from *monkin, monikin,* homunculus. *Baboon*, " from *babe*, the termination denoting addition " and increment ; a large babe. *Mantygre* fpeaks " its original. And when they have brought their " *firnames* [he fhould have faid *furnames*] with them " from their native country, as *ape* ; the common

K 2 " people

" people have as it were *christen'd* them, by the ad-
" dition of *jack-an-ape*." WARB.

Notwithstanding all this parade of learning, I
believe, no body but Mr. Warburton would have
thought of this satire upon our countrymen; which
is a mere blundering conceit of his own: it is neither
just in itself, nor has he the left ground for it from
the text. Nay, I will undertake, that it may be
deduced as fairly from any passage in the *Divine
Legation*; as from this of Shakespear, rightly understood.

Trinculo says, " Were I in England now—and
" had but this FISH painted; not a holiday fool
" there, but would give me a piece of silver; there
" would this monster MAKE a man: (i. e. make his
" fortune *) any strange beast there MAKES a man;
" when they will not give a doit to a lame beggar,
" they will lay-out ten to see a dead Indian."
The satire, we see, is levelled at their extravagant
curiosity; not their *adopting the tribe of the pitheci*,
or *monkeys*: to which, moreover, this *fish* here mentioned could not very properly be referred.

As for his instances of the *donum civitatis*; as, in
order to shew his reading, he calls it; let *monkey* be
derived from the Teutonic, MO~: They are not the
English only, who derive the name of this animal
from thence; (if they indeed do:) the Italian *mona*,
and the Spanish *munneca*, are from the same foun-
tain; and it is probable, that our *monkey* is derived
from this last. If *baboon* comes (as Skinner says, it
perhaps may) from BABE; the French *babouin*, and
the Italian *babbuino* procede from thence too; and

---

* See instances of Shakespear's using the word in this sense,
towards the end of the third Act of THE WINTER'S TALE, Vol.
3. P. 112. Theobald's first edition.

3   ther

there is no reason for any reflection on the English, particularly, on that account.

As for his *mantygre*, which, he says, *speaks its original*; it does so, but in a language, which Mr. Warburton seems not to understand; MANTICORA (which we corruptly call *mantygre)* is an Indian word; whether original with them, or derived in part from the Arabic, as some, or the Teutonic, as others hold, does not concern the present question: the Greeks and Romans both adopted it; and whether we borrowed it from these or the Indians, we are not answerable for the propriety of its derivation.

I wonder Mr. Warburton, when his hand was in, did not complete his *donum civitatis*; and that, after he had CHRISTENED his *ape,* (a strange expression, by the way, for a clergyman!) he did not derive it from APA, as little children call it, before they can pronounce PAPA.

EXAMP. XI. Vol. 8. P. 141. HAMLET.

" This heavy-headed revel, east and west
" Makes us traduced".———

That is, This heavy-headed revel makes us traduced through the world; but Mr. Warburton says,

" This heavy-headed revel, *east and west*"] i. e.
" this revelling, which observes no hours, but con-
" tinues from *morning* to *night,*" &c. WARB.

Had this been the meaning, it should have been from west to east; or, from evening till morning. But common sense, and common English will not serve Mr. Warburton's turn, without refining away the meaning of his author; which is *from one end of the world to another.*

K 3

EXAMP. XII. In another paſſage of this play, he has altered the text; ſo as to make it point-out a diſtant place: where is neither occaſion nor authority for it.

Page 209.

———" Heav'n's face doth glow
" O'er this ſolidity and compound maſs
" With triſtful viſage; and, as 'gainſt the doom,
" Is thought-ſick at the act."

Queen. " Ay me! what act,
" That roars ſo loud, and thunders in the *index?*"

Where, I think, it is plain, that Shakeſpear has uſed *index*, for *title*, or *prologue* *. So he uſes it in K. RICHARD III. Vol. 5. P. 304. " The flatter-" ing *index* of a direful page;" or pageant, as others read. And again, in the ſame play P. 257. " I'll ſort occaſion, as *index* to the ſtory we late talk'd of." So alſo in Othello. Theob. Vol. 7. P. 412.

" Letchery, by this hand; an *index* and obſcure prologue to the hiſtory of luſt and foul thoughts."

But Mr. Warburton ſays, " This is a ſtrange " *anſwer:*" (I thought it had been a *queſtion*) " But " the old Quarto brings us nearer to the poet's ſenſe, " by dividing the lines thus:

Queen. " Ay me! what act?

Ham. " That roars ſo loud, and thunders in the " index."

" Here we find the Queen's *anſwer* very natural. " He had ſaid, the Sun was thought-ſick at the act. " She ſays,

* The Index uſed formerly to be placed at the beginning of a book; not at the end, as now.

" Ay

" Ay me ! what act ?"

" He replies (as we should read it)

" That roars so loud, *it* thunders *to* the *Indies.*"

" He had before said, heaven was shocked at it ;
" he now tells her, it resounded all the world over.
" This gives us a *very good* sense ; where *all* sense
" was wanting." WARB.

Here Mr. Warburton takes occasion, from what seems a mistaken division of the passage in the old Quarto, to represent an act as *thundering to the Indies* ; that is, *making a noise all over the world,* as he explanes it ; which was probably known only to the murderer himself, and to Hamlet ; to whom his father's ghost had reveled it. And, when he has made the mistake, he contrives, as he frequently does, to commend himself ; by commending Shakespear for what he never wrote, or thought of ; " This, says he, gives us a very good sense ; where " all sense was wanting." Modest enough for a Professed Critic !

EXAMP. XIII. Vol. 7. P. 70. JULIUS CÆSAR.

Caf. " Brutus, bay not me,
" I'll not endure it ; you forget yourself,
" To hedge me in ; I am a soldier, I,
" Older in practice, abler than yourself
" To make conditions."

Brut. " Go to, you are not, Cassius."

" We are not to understand this, as if Brutus had
" said, *you are not an abler soldier* ; which would be
" wrangling on a childish question, beneath the cha-
" racter of Brutus. On the contrary, when Cassius
" had made so unbecoming a boast, Brutus, in his

K 4

" reply,

" reply, only reproves him for degeneracy : And
" he could not do it in words more pathetic, than
" by faying, *you are not* Caffius ; i. e. you are no
" longer that brave difinterefted philofophic *Caffius,*
" whofe character was made-up of honor and pa-
" triotifm ; but are funk down into the impotency
" and corruption of the times." WARB.

One may juftly fay of our critic, as Worcefter
does of Hotfpur,

" He apprehends a world of figures here ;
" But not the form of what he fhould attend."

If Mr. Warburton had not been giddy with his
ideas of bravery, difinterestednefs, philofophy, honor, and patriotifm, which have nothing to do here ;
he would have feen, that *Caffius* is the vocative cafe,
not the nominative ; and that Brutus does not mean
to fay, *you are not an abler foldier* ; but he fays, *you are
not an abler than I* ; a point, which it was far from
being beneath his character to infift on.

If the words, *you are not* Caffius, meant a new
imputation on him of degeneracy ; his mere denial of
it is very flat : and Brutus' replying to that denial, by
a mere repetition of his former affertion, without
adding any reafon for it, is ftill worfe : whereas, if
the words mean only a denial of what Caffius had
juft faid, it is natural enough for each of them to
maintain his ground, by a confident affertion of the
truth of his opinion.

And, that the fuperiority of foldierfhip was the
point of their difpute ; is moft manifeftly evident,
by Brutus' refuming it a little lower ;

" You fay, you are a *better* foldier :
" Let it appear fo ; make your vaunting true ;
" And it fhall pleafe me well ;."

Upon

Upon which Caffius anfwers,

"You wrong me ev'ry way—you wrong me, Brutus;
"I faid, an *elder* foldier; not a *better*.
"Did I fay, *better?*"

EXAMP. XIV. Vol. 6. P. 19. KING LEAR.

" I will *convey* the bufinefs, as I fhall find means;
" and acquaint you withal.] *Convey*, for introduce:
" but *convey* is a fine word, as alluding to the prac-
" tife of clandeftine conveying goods, fo as not to
" be found upon the felon." WARB.

' This is not fuch * a fort of criticifm, as may
' be raifed mechanically on the rules, which *Dacier*,
' *Rapin*, and *Boffu* have collected from antiquity;'
but founded upon that † ' true Law and Principle
' of nature and common fenfe,' which leads us to interpret an Author by Himfelf. For the explanation
is evidently fuggefted, or, as fome would fpeak, ‡
excited, to Mr. W. by his old friend *Piftol*—' Convey
' the wife it call: *Steal?* foh, a fico for the phrafe.'
MERRY WIVES OF WINDSOR. Vol. 1. P 262.
The allufion is without doubt highly proper to
be addreffed to one of *Glocefter*'s great rank; efpecially, by his fon: and, if the old man, before his
eyes were put-out, was as fharp fighted as Mr. W.
to difcover it; it muft needs raife in him an equally
advantageous opinion both of *Edmund*'s politenefs
and honefty.

EXAMP. XV. Vol. 7. P. 386. TROILUS and CRESSID.

——————— " But when *Planets*
" In evil mixture to diforder wander, &c.] By
" *Planets*, Shakefpear here means *Comets*; which

* Pref. P. 18.   † Pref. P. 19.   ‡ Vol. 5. P. 350.
" by

" by some were supposed to be excentrical planets.
" The evil effects here recapitulated were those,
" which superstition gave to the appearance of
" Comets." WARB.

" If we can suppose any thing wanting to prove,
that one *means* Planets, when he *says* so; not only
the whole tenor of the passage, but the very line here
quoted may serve for a proof. The words—*in evil
mixture*—evidently alluding to the conjunctions of
the *Planets.* But indeed, no mortal could have
thought of this explanation, but he; who says, *
Moonshine signifies *Sunshine.*

EXAMP. XVI. Vol. 2. P. 4. MUCH ADO ABOUT NOTHING.

" joy could not show itself *modest* enough, with-
" out a badge of bitterness] This is *judiciously* ex-
" pressed. Of all the transports of joy, that which
" is attended with tears is least offensive; because
" carrying with it this mark of pain, it allays the
" envy, that usually attends another's happiness.
" This he *finely* calls a *modest* joy; such a one as did
" not insult the observer by an indication of happi-
" ness unmixt with pain." WARB.

Our honest hearted old Poet, who had nothing
of the *atrabilaire* in his make, (nay, I question whether he had ever heard the *word*;) never dreamed of
such stuff as, that it was *fine* to think ones self *insulted*
by the *indication* of *happiness* in another. How different are the reflexions he puts in the mouth of
good *Leonato* on this occasion.—' a kind overflow
' of kindness! There are no faces truer than those,
' that are so washed. How much better is it to
' weep at joy, than to joy at weeping!'

* Vol. 6, P. 48.

Ex-

EXAMP. XVII. Vol. 2. P. 51. MUCH ADO ABOUT NOTHING.

"—" like the fhaven Hercules, in the fmirch worm-
" eaten tapeftry;] By the *fhaven Hercules*, is meant
" *Samfon*; the ufual fubject of old tapeftry. In
" this ridicule of the fafhion, the poet has not unart-
" fully given a ftroke at the barbarous workman-
" fhip of the common tapeftry hangings then in
" ufe. What authorifed the poet to give this name
" to *Samfon*, was the folly of certain chriftian my-
" thologifts; who pretend, that the grecian *Her-*
" *cules*, was the jewifh *Samfon*. The retenue of our
" Author is to be commended: The fober audi-
" ence of that time would have been offended with
" the mention of a venerable name on fuch a light
" occafion." WARB.

However *barbarous* the workmen of the common Tapeftry may have been, I fancy, they were
hardly fo bad *chriftian mythologifts*, as to draw
Samfon (not with the jaw-bone of an afs, but) with
a *maffy club*; as he is here defcribed. But perhaps
They too, as well as our Poet, had their *commenda-*
ble retenue; and fo only *meant* Samfon, but really
drew Hercules.

If Shakefpear under this *retenue* did mean *Samfon*,
I wonder whether he intended that his *fober audience*
fhould *underftand* his meaning! if he did, he muft
either be a ftrange fellow himfelf, or think his audience were ftrange fellows; who would have been offended with the mention of a venerable name, and
yet would bear with patience the downright Burlefque of the very perfon, to whom that venerable
name belonged.

Ex.

EXAMP. XVIII. Vol. 2. P. 405. THE TAMING
OF THE SHREW.

" If love hath *touch'd* you, nought remains but fo ;
" Redime te captum quam queas minimo.]
" This line from Terence fhows, that we fhould
" read,

" If love hath *toyl'd* you—i. e. taken you in his
" *toyls*, his nets.   Alluding to the *captus eft, babet,*
" of the fame author." WARB.

That is.   The line from *Terence* fhows, that we
fhould read—*toyl'd*— ; becaufe the allufion is (not
to this but) to another line in *Terence,* where the
word *captus* does not fignify *toyl'd,* any more than
it does in the line here quoted : and the metaphor
in *redime te* plainly fhows, that *captum* does not
mean, taken, as a wild beaft, in *toyls* ; but, taken,
as a prifoner, in *battle.*

EXAMP. XIX. Vol. 5. P. 350. HEN. VIII.

——" his mind and place
" Infecting one another—] This is very fatirical.
" His mind he reprefents as highly corrupt ; and
" yet he SUPPOSES the CONTAGION of the place
" of firft minifter, AS ADDING an INFECTION to
" it." WARB.

The Satire is Mr. W's : for the paffage fuppofes
his place to be juft as much infected by his mind,
as his mind was by his place.

Suppofes as adding, for, fuppofes to add ; Excellent Grammar ! and —*Contagion adds Infection* ; Excellent Senfe ! Both in the compafs of two Lines.

Ex-

EXAMP. XX. Vol. 7. P. 69. JUL. CÆSAR.

" Remember March, &c.
" What villain touch'd his body, that did ftab,
" And not for juftice ?—] The thought here is
" infinitely noble ; yet, by reafon of the Laconic
" brevity here reprefented, it is obfcure.   We muft
" imagine *Brutus* fpeaking to this effect.   Re-
" member the Ides of March ; when we had a caufe
" in hand fo great and fanctified, that the moft cor-
" rupt men, intent only on the public, caft afide all
" private regards ; engaged in the caufe of liberty,
" and ftabb'd for juftice.   Remember too, that
" this is but the fame caufe continued ; all corrupt
" and private motives fhould therefore be neglect-
" ed and defpifed.   This is the fenfe ; in which
" the dignity of the fentiment, and the propriety
" of it to the cafe in hand, are altogether worthy of
" the character of the fpeaker. WARB.

What obfcurity Mr W. can find in this paffage,
is hard to conceive : but, as near as I can guefs, it
muft be in this Line ;

  "What *villain touch'd his body*——."

from which words, as I fufpect, Mr W. thinks that
it muft be inferred ; that fome of thofe, who *touch'd
his body*, were *villains* ; and this, I fuppofe, is the
intent and meaning of thofe words in his expofition
—" the moft corrupt men—&c." But a reader of
common fenfe and common attention need not be
told, that this Queftion—*What villain* &c— ? is fo
far from inferring This ; that on the contrary it is
a ftrong way of denying that there were any fuch a-
mong them, as were villains enough to ftab for
any caufe except that of juftice.

                                        C A N O N

CANON X.

He should not allow any poetical licences,
which He does not understand.

EXAMP. I. Vol. 6. P. 470.   CORIOLANUS.

" our veil'd dames
" Commit the *war* of white and damask in
" Their nicely gauded cheeks to th' wanton spoil
" Of Phœbus' burning kisses."

" This commixture of white and red could not,
" *by any figure of speech,* be called a *war* ; because it
" is the *agreement* and union of the colours, that
" make the beauty.   We should read,

— " the *ware* of white and damask—

" i. e. the *commodity,* the *merchandise.*" WARB.

Perhaps some other profess'd critic, disliking Mr.
Warburton's *commodity* ; and being offended with
the idea of venality, which the word *merchandise*
gives in this place ; may tell us, we should read,
Commit the *Wear*—i. e. hazard the wearing out—
commit from *commettre,* an *old* French *word* ; which
is no small recommendation to it.   But a poor
poetical reader would let this figure pass ; and not
be alarm'd (except for his own heart) on account of
this innocent *war* between the roses and lilies in a
lady's cheek ; remembering that beautiful, though
simple description of it, in the old ballad of *Fair*
Rosamond.

" The blood within her crystal cheeks
" Did such a color drive ;
" As though the *lily* and the *rose*
" For *mastership* did *strive.*"

If

If Mr. Warburton should object to the authority of this unknown poet, I hope he will allow that of Shakespear himself; who in his TARQUIN and LUCRECE has these lines,

" This silent WAR of lilies and of roses,
" Which Tarquin view'd in her fair face's field."

p. 103. Sewel's ed.

So also, in the Taming of the Shrew.

Theob. Vol. 2. p. 342.

" Such *war* of white and red within her cheeks."

Theob. edit.

There is also a like passage, in Venus and Ad. St. 58.

" To note the fighting *conflict* of her hue,
" How white and red each other did destroy."

EXAMP. II. Vol. 4. P. 380.   K. HENRY V.

" Fills the wide vessel of the *universe.*] *Universe*
" for *horizon*; for we are not to think Shakespear
" so ignorant, as to imagine it was night over the
" whole globe at once—Besides, the image he em-
" ploys, shews, he meant but half the globe; the
" *horizon* round, which has the shape of a vessel, or
" goblet."   WARB.

Here Mr. Warburton unnecessarily interferes with his minute philosophy : As if the whole might not be poetically used for a part. Virgil, when he said,

——" silet omnis ager,"

never was thought to mean precisely every field in the habitable world. The only reason our critic could have for writing this curious note, was to make ostentation of his knowlege in philosophy; and this he does very unhappily : for it appears, that

he

he does not know the difference between the *hori-zon* and *hemisphere.* Besides, he ought to have re-membered; that if this goblet, he is so fond of, re-presents the hemisphere, which was then dark; it must mean that part which was over our heads, and consequently it is a goblet turned upside down; the most improper situation for being fill'd in, that even Mr. Warburton could imagine.

EXAMP. III. Vol. 7. P. 10.   JULIUS CÆSAR.

" His *coward* lips did from their *colour* fly.] A'
" plain man would have said, the *colour* fled from
" his lips; not his *lips* from their colour. But the
" false expression was from as false a piece of Wit:
" a poor quibble, alluding to a *coward* flying from
" his *colours.*" WARB.

Shakespear had no such miserable stuff in his head. The expression is classical; and the figure of speech as common, as any poetical ornament whatever.

" In nova fert animus mutatas dicere formas
Corpora;"——Ovid.   and—Nullum
" Sæva caput Proserpina fugit." Hor.
are amongst a thousand instances of it. Where the sense is—Corpora mutata in novas formas—and—nullum caput fugit Proserpinam.

C A N O N   XI.

He may make foolish amendments or explana-tions, and refute them; only to enhance the va-lue of his critical skill.

EXAMP.

EXAMPLE I. Vol. 6. P. 370. MACBETH.

" Thou feest the heavens, as troubled with man's
 " act,
" Threaten this bloody *stage*"——

 " One might be tempted to think, the poet wrote
" *strage*, flaughter. But I, *who know him better*, am
" perfuaded, he ufed *stage* for *act*. And, becaufe *stage*
" may be figuratively ufed for *act*, a dramatic re-
" prefentation; therefore he ufes it for *act*, a deed
" done. Threatens a *tragedy.*" WARB.

None but an erring (or * errant) pedant could be
tempted to think, that Shakefpear wrote *strage* in
this place; which is a barbarous word, without any
authority produced for it. As for the intimate acquaintance Mr. Warburton boafts with Shakefpear,
one might be tempted to doubt of that; he is fo
feldom let into the poet's meaning: particularly, in
the prefent inftance, the obvious fenfe, which any
body but a profefs'd critic might have feen, is; "that
" Heaven, troubled with man's act [the murder of
" Duncan] threatens the bloody ftage, where the
" murder was committed; i. e. the world in gene-
" ral, or at left Scotland, which on this occafion
" was covered with darknefs; as appears by the
" following line,

" That darknefs does the face of th' earth entomb."

There was therefore no occafion for inventing that
forites of nonfenfical figures; of *stage* for *act*, a dramatic reprefentation; therefore, as he *doth* add, for
act, a deed *done*; and therefore, as he *should have*
added, for a deed *to be done*; for a threaten'd tra-

* See Mr. W.'s *Note* on "erring Barbarian," OTHELLO, VOL. 8.
P. 302.

gedy is not paſt, but future. But ' thus it will be,' (as Mr. Warburton obſerves) ' when the author is ' thinking of *one* thing, and his critic of *another* *.'

EXAMP. II. Vol. 3. P. 99. ALL'S WELL THAT ENDS WELL.

" We loſt a jewel of her; our *eſteem*
" Was made much poorer by it———"

" What is the meaning of the king's *eſteem* be-
" ing made poorer by the loſs of Helen? I think,
" it can only be underſtood in one ſenſe; and that
" ſenſe wo'n't carry water: i. e. we ſuffered in our
" eſtimation by her loſs.——We muſt certainly read
" therefore,
———" our *eſtate*
" Was made much poorer by it——
" that is the certain conſequence of loſing a
jewel." WARB.

This very ſage obſervation our critic gave us in Mr. Theobald's edition; Vol. 2. P. 443. However, he has ſince ſtopped the leaks; and *eſteem* in his own edition carries water very well, with only this cover-ing; *eſteem* for *eſtimation,* in the ſenſe of *worth,* " *eſtate.*" WARB.

EXAMP. III. Vol. 6. P. 387. MACBETH.

" Augurs, that underſtood relations, have
" By magpyes and by choughs and rooks brought
" forth
" The ſecret'ſt man of blood.——] By *relations* is
" meant, the *relation* one thing is ſuppoſed to bear
" to another. The ancient Soothſayers, of all
" denominations, practiſed their art upon the prin-
" ciple of *Analogy.* Which Analogies were found-

* Vol. 1. P. 445.

" ed

" ed in a superstitious Philosophy, arising out of
" the nature, of ancient Idolatry; which would
" require a Volume to explain. If Shakespear
" meant, what I suppose he did, by *relations*; this
" shews a very profound knowledge of Antiqui-
" ty. But, after all, in his licentious way, by
" *relations* he might only mean *languages*; i. e. the
" languages of *Birds*." WARB.

Shakespear, without all this *very profound* knowledge of nobody knows what analogies, founded
on superstitious philosophy, arising out of ancient
idolatry; which 'tis well if it would not require
above one volume to explain; might yet have e-
nough, fully to answer his present purpose: and,
I think, had a great deal too much; to mean, first,
by *relations — languages*; and then, by *languages*
simply, to mean the languages of *Birds*.

The only part of this learned note, which the
Critic himself seems certain of, is the assertion
in the first sentence of it. And That, for the un-
deniable truth of it, is worthy of honest *Bardolph*
himself; " * who, when he should define, puts us
" off, for want of a *synonimous* term, even with
" the same term differently accommodated."

The *relations* Shakespear means are only those,
which the cries and flights of sundry birds are su-
perstitiously supposed to bear, to the actions of men;
and the events or accidents of human life: of
which kind of superstition many a *prophecying* old
Aunt at this day will supply Mr. W. with any
quantity he has occasion for, as good cheap as
can be had of e'er an ancient Soothsayer of 'em
all.

* Vol. 4. P. 257. 2 HEN. IV. Note 9.

CANON XII.

He may find out an immodest or immoral mean-ing in his author ; where there does not appear to be any hint that way.

EXAMPLE I. Vol. 7. P. 266.   CYMBELINE.

" If she be up, I'll speak with her; if not,
" Let her lie still and dream."——

" *If she be up,* &c.] It is observable ; that Shake-
" spear makes his fools deal much in that kind of
" wit, called the *double entendre,* with only a *single*
" *meaning* ; since his time transferred to the fine
" gentleman of the drama."   WARB.

True is that old proverb,
  As the fool thinketh,
  The bell clinketh.

For the *meaning* here is so *single* ; that nobody, but a man of Mr. Warburton's penetration, could find out a *double entendre.*

EXAMP. II. The same penetration discovered in that line in KING LEAR, Vol. 6. P. 6.

" Which the most precious *square of sense* possesses."

That, " by the *square of sense,* we are to under-
" stand the *four* nobler senses ; *viz.* the sight, hear-
" ing, taste, and smell.   For a young lady could
" not with decency insinuate, that she knew of any
" pleasures, which the *fifth* afforded. This is ima-
" gined with great propriety and delicacy."

I believe, that Shakespear uses *square* for the full complement of all the senses : and that this ima-gined propriety and delicacy Mr. Warburton ought
to

to have the praise of; who feems to have been thinking of the *fixth* fenfe, inftead of the fifth; when he
wrote that note.

EXAMP. III. Vol. I. P. 398.   MEASURE FOR
MEASURE.

Duke. " ———— Thou art not noble;
" For all th' accommodations, that thou bear'ft,
" Are nurs'd by bafenefs :"——

" *Are nurs'd by bafenefs :*] This enigmatical fen-
" tence, fo much in the manner of our author, is
" a fine proof of his knowledge of human nature.
" The meaning of it being this, Thy moft *virtuous*
" actions have a *felfifh* motive; and even thofe of
" them, which appear moft *generous*, are but the more
" ARTFUL DISGUISES OF SELF-LOVE." WARB.

It is as plain, as words can make it; that Shakefpear is not here confidering man as a *moral* agent:
but is fpeaking of *animal* life; the *accommodations*
[conveniencies] of which, he fays, are *nurs'd* [fup-
plied and fupported] by *bafenefs*; [thofe that are
efteemed the lower and meaner parts of the creation;
fuch as wool, filk, the excrements of beafts and in-
fects; &c. or by the labor and fervice of the meaneft
people.] K. LEAR fell into the fame reflection,
on feeing the naked beggar : " Confider him well.
" Thou oweft the worm no filk, the beaft no hide,
" the fheep no wool, the cat no perfume. Ha !
" here's three of us are fophifticated. Thou art the
" thing itfelf; *unaccommodated*, man is no more,
" but fuch a poor bare forked animal as thou art."
Vol. 6. P. 82.

This is plainly the fame thought. And our poet
was too good a writer, as well as too honeft a man,

L 3

to think of this fine enigma; which is impertinent
to the subject he is upon, and contains a doctrine
most execrable, and destructive of all virtue; the
original inventer of which must either have had a
very bad heart, if he found it true *at home*; or
must have kept very bad *company*, and from such
uncharitably judge the hearts of all the rest of
mankind.

This reflexion, I have heard, has been reckoned
too *severe*; I cannot but think, the case *required* se-
verity; and I have the good fortune to be supported
in my censure, by an authority; which, how much
soever others may think slightly of it, Mr. Warburton will allow to be the *best* : I mean that of the ingenious gentleman, who wrote *A critical and philosophical enquiry into the causes of* Prodigies *and* Miracles; printed in 1727. " But there is (says he, p. 26.)
" a sect of antimoralists, who have our Hobbes and
" the French Duke de la Rochefoucault for their
" leaders; that, give it but encouragement, would
" soon rid our hands of this inconvenience; [an en-
" thusiastic love of one's Country;] and most effec-
" tually prevent all return from that quarter : For,
" whereas it was the business of ancient philosophy,
" to give us a due veneration for the dignity of hu-
" man nature; they described it, as really it was, be-
" neficent, brave, and a lover of its *species*; a prin-
" ciple become sacred, since our divine Master made
" it the foundation of his religion : These men, for
" what ends we shall see presently, endeavouring to
" create a contempt and horror for it; have painted
" it base, cowardly, envious, and a lover of it's
" *self.* A view so senseless, and shocking to the
" common notices of humanity; that I *affirm him
" no honest man, and uncapable of discharging the of-
" fices of a son, a subject, or a father; that in the
" sudden,*

" *sudden, and even involuntary workings of the affec-*
" *tions, does not perceive the fucus.*"

And a little lower, P. 28.

" But when once we can be brought to persuade
" ourselves, that this love of the species is chimeri-
" cal; that the notion was invented by crafty *knaves,*
" to make *dupes* of the young, the vain, and the
" ambitious; that nature has confined us to the
" narrow sphere of *self-love*; and that our *most pom-*
" *pous boasts* of a generous disinterestedness, are
" but the ARTFUL DISGUISES OF THAT PASSION ;
" we become, like Ixion, ashamed of our fondness
" for a mistaken Juno ;" &c.

Mr. Warburton should have remember'd too, an
observation of his, on a passage in CORIOLANUS ;
Vol. 6. P. 528. " Shakespear, when he chooses to
" give us some weighty observation upon human
" nature, *not much to the credit of it* ; generally
" (as the intelligent reader may observe) puts it
" into the mouth of some *low buffoon* character." ·

CANON XIII.

He needs not attend-to the low accuracy of or-
thography or pointing ; but may ridicule such
trivial criticisms in others.

EXAMPLE. I. Vol. 7. P. 64. JULIUS CÆSAR.
" And things *unluckey* charge my fantasy."
So spelt, for unlucky, *five* times, in the text and note.

EXAMP. II. *Attellanes,* for Atellanes, Vol. 5. P.
339.

EXAMP. III. *Bain'd,* for Baned, Vol. 1. P. 452.

EXAMP.

EXAMP. IV. *Boney*, for Bony, Vol. 2. P. 319.

EXAMP. V. *Consture*, for Construe, Vol. 4. P. 399.

EXAMP. VI. *Furtber*, for Farther, — *paffim*.

EXAMP. VII. *Gal'd*, for Gall'd, Vol. 4. P. 110.

EXAMP. VIII. *Grotb*, for Growth, Vol. 8. P. 70.

EXAMP. IX. *Jolitry*, for Jollity, Vol. 2. P. 346.

EXAMP. X. *Lain* open, for Laid open, Vol. 3. P. 237.

EXAMP. XI. *Levar*, for Liever, Vol. 5. P. 4.

EXAMP. XII. The *L'ouvre*, for the Louvre, Vol. 1. P. 114. Fr.

EXAMP. XIII. *Nautioufly*, for Naufeoufly, Vol. 1. P. 100.

EXAMP. XIV. *Pennants*, for Pendents, Vol. 1. P. 304.

EXAMP. XV. *Spleenatic*, for Splenetic, Vol. 1. P. 99.

EXAMP. XVI. *Syncerus*, for Sincerus, Vol. 5. P. 350. Lat.

EXAMP. XVII. *Synonimous*, for Synonymous, Pref. xij, xvj. Vol. 4. P. 257.

EXAMP. XVIII. *Utopean*, for Utopian, Vol. 1. P. 34.

EXAMP. XIX. *Warey*, for Wary, Vol. 7. P. 323.

EXAMP. XX. *Eifel*, vinegar, fpelt right by Mr. Theobald, Vol. 8. P. 250.

EXAMP. XXI. *Oar*, fpelt right by Mr. Theobald, Vol. 3. P. 69.

EXAMP. XXII. *Ofprey*, fpelt right by Mr. Theobald, Vol. 6. P. 536.

EXAMP. XXIII. Vol. 7. P. 189.

" Commend unto his lips thy *•favoring* hand."

• " Here Mr. Theobald reftores an *f*, depofed by " the printer; to make room for an *f*," WARB.

EXAMP

EXAMP. XXIV. *Ibid.* P. 214. " and lighted up
" the little ᵇ O o'th' earth."

ᵇ "A round O restored by Mr. Theobald." WARB.

EXAMP. XXV. Vol. 3. P. 235.

" Shall love in ᵃ *building* grow so ruinate ?"

ᵃ " *buildings.*] Mr. Theobald has here removed
" a superfluous letter." WARB.

EXAMP. XXVI. Vol. 6. P. 436.

" The one side must have ᶜ *bale.*"

ᶜ This word spelt right by Mr. Theobald.

EXAMP. XXVII. *Ibid.* P. 464.—" What harm
" can your ᵉ *bisson* conspectuitys glean out of his
" character"—

ᵉ *bisson* (blind) spelt right by Mr. Theobald.

EXAMP. XXVIII. Vol. 3. P. 43.

Note 1. Commas and points here set exactly right
by Mr. Theobald.   So Vol. 2. P. 148.

EXAMP. XXIX. *Ibid.* P. 459.

Note 7. A point set right by Mr. Theobald.

EXAMP. XXX. Vol. 1. P. 217.

With my *master's ship.*] This pun restored by
Mr. Theobald.

EXAMP.

EXAMP. XXXI. Vol. 1. P. 259.

" I hope upon familiarity will grow more *con-*
tempt."
A conundrum reſtored by Mr. Theobald.

EXAMP. XXXII. Vol 2. P. 197. — *but ſo ſo.*]
A quibble reſtored by the Oxford editor.

EXAM. XXXIII. Vol. 3. P. 404. *ſhrew*] ſpelt
right by Mr. Theobald.

EXAMP. XXXIV. Vol. 2. P. 251.

N. 3. O. U. A poor conundrum, as Mr. Theobald rightly calls it, reſtored by him to its place.

EXAMP. XXXV. Vol. 6. P. 94.

ſulled] ſpelt right by Mr. Theobald.

EXAMP. XXXVI. Vol. 7. P. 306.

deſtroying] ſpelt right by Mr. Theobald.

EXAMP. XXXVII. Vol. 4. P. 218.

Ch. Juſt. " You follow the young Prince up
" and down, like his *ill* angel."
Falſt. " No, my lord, your *ill* angel is light." &c.

" A pun in ill angel, which, Mr. Theobald tells
" us, he has reſtored and brought to light." WARB.

CANON XIV.

Yet, when he pleaſes to condeſcend to ſuch
work, he may value himſelf upon it ; and not
only

only reſtore loſt puns, but point-out ſuch quaint-
neſſes, where perhaps the author never thought of
them.

EXAMPLE I. Vol. 5. P. 257. K. RICHARD III.
   Note 2. " I have alter'd the pointing of this paſ-
" ſage; whereby a ſtrange and ridiculous anticli-
" max is prevented." WARB.

EXAMP. II. Ibid. P. 346. KING HENRY VIII.
   Note 1. ' This ill pointing makes nonſenſe of
' the thought. I have regulated it, as it now ſtands.'
WARB.

EXAMP. III. Vol. 6. P. 189. TIMON OF ATHENS.
        " it ſhould ſeem by th' ſum,
" ' Your maſter's confidence was above mine."
   " ' *Your maſter's confidence*] Play on the word
" *confidence.*" WARB.

EXAMP. IV. Ibid. P. 432. CORIOLANUS.
  — " let us revenge ourſelves with our pikes, e'er
" we become rakes."
  "—Time, *who* has done greater things, has here
" ſtifled a miſerable joke; which was then the ſame, as
" if it had been now *wrote*; Let us revenge ourſelves
" with *forks*, e'er we become *rakes*;" &c. WARB.

EXAMP. V. Vol. 1. P. 276. " This abſurd paſ-
" ſage may be pointed into ſenſe."

EXAMP. VI. Vol. 2. P. 154. " The wrong point-
" ing has made this fine ſentiment nonſenſe."

EXAMP.

EXAMP. VII. Vol. 6. P. 161. TIMON OF ATHENS.

—— "We should read and point this nonsense
"thus." WARB.

EXAMP. VIII. Vol. 6. P. 345.

——"This nonsense, made worse by ill pointing,
"should be read thus." WARB.

EXAMP. IX. Vol. 4. P. 121. 1 HENRY IV.

—— "there's ne'er a king in Christendom could be
"better *bit*, than I have been since the first cock."

"Time has here added a pleasantry to the expres-
"sion. For, I think, the word *bite* was not then
"used in the cant sense to deceive, or impose
"upon." WARB.

EXAMP. X. Vol. 1. P. 87. TEMPEST.

"O, touch me not; I am not *Stephano*, but a *cramp*."

"In reading this play, I all along *suspected*;
"that Shakespear had taken it from some Italian
"writer —— I was much confirmed in my suspicion,
"when I came to this place. It is plain, a joke
"was intended; but, where it lies, is hard to say. I
"*suspect*, there was a quibble in the original, that
"would not bear to be translated; which ran thus
"—— I am not *Stephano*, but *Staffilato : staffilato* signi-
"fying in Italian, a man well lashed or flayed;
"which was the real case of these varlets." WARB.

The plain meaning of Shakespear's words is,

"O, touch me not; for I am sore, as if I were
"cramped all over."

He must have a good nose at a conundrum, who
can hit it off upon so cold a scent as is here. But
I   "Sowter

"Sowter will cry upon it, though it be not as rank
"as a fox *." He *suspects* a jest here, which he cannot make out in English; and so, having *suspected*
before, that Shakespear had taken or translated
this play from an Italian writer; away he goes to his
Italian Dictionary, to hunt for some word; whose
like sound might be a pretense, though a poor one,
for his suspicion. The best he could find, was this
same *staffilato*; which signifies simply *lashed*; not
well lashed; much less *flayed*: but this it must signify, and this too must be *the real case of these varlets*; the one, in defiance of the Italian language, and
the other, in defiance of Shakespear; who fully explanes their punishment, and this consequence of
it, in Prospero's commission to Ariel; P. 73.

"Go charge my goblins, that they grind their joints
"With dry *convulsions*; shorten up their sinews
"With aged *cramps*; and more *pinch-spotted* make
   "them,
"Than pard or cat o'mountain."

Had not the Dictionary helped Mr. Warburton to
this foolish conundrum, I suppose this passage would
have been degraded; as a nonsensical interpolation
of the player: and I do not know, which proceding
would have been more worthy of a Professed Critic;
or have done more justice to Shakespear.

I cannot help taking notice here of the unfair
arts Mr. Warburton uses, to make his suspicion
pass on his readers for truth. He first, to the word
lashed, which *staffilato* does signify; tacks *flayed*,
which it does not signify; as if they were the same
thing: just as he did in interpreting the word *sheen*,
under Canon VII. Example 15. and then, to prove,

* TWELFTH NIGHT, Vol. 3. P. 158.

that

that this (flaying) *was the real cafe* of thefe varlets,
he mifquotes Shakefpear——

——" pricking gofs and thorns,

" Which enter'd their frail *skins*"——

infinuating, as if they were torn and raw all over :
whereas Shakefpear fays,

" Which enter'd their frail * *shins*"——

Nor let Mr. Warburton cavil, that their fhins could
not be fcratched, without the thorns entering their
fkins ; fince fcratched fhins can never put a man in
the condition, which Stephano here reprefents himfelf in ; or which *He* would have to be meant by
his *ftaffilato.*

The inftances above, of corrections in pointing,
are brought ; not to blame Mr. Warburton for
rectifying miftakes of that nature : but to fhew the
unreafonablenefs of his ridiculing that care in
others ; when the want of it may make nonfenfe
of the beft of writings : and, as he acknowledges,
has frequently done fo in Shakefpear.

EXAMP. XI. Vol. 7. P. 323. CYMBELINE.

" ———————— Young one,

" Inform us of thy fortunes ; for, it feems,

" They crave to be demanded : who is this,

" Thou make'ft thy bloody pillow ? what was he,

" That, otherwife than noble Nature *did*,

" Hath *alter'd* this good picture? what's thy intereft

" In this fad wreck ? how came it ? and who is it?"

" The Editor, Mr. Theobald, cavils at this paf-
" fage. He fays, ' It is *far from being* ftrictly
" grammatical ;' " and yet, what is ftrange, he fub-
" joins a paraphrafe of his own ; which fhows it

* P. 70.

" to

" to *be* strictly grammatical. For, says he, the con-
" struction of these words is this : who hath *altered*
" that good picture, otherwise than nature *altered*
" it ? I suppose then, this Editor's meaning was,
" that the grammatical *construction* would not
" conform to the *sense* ; (for a bad *writer*, like a bad
" *man*, generally says *one* thing, and means *ano-*
" *ther* : He subjoining, Shakespear *designed* to say,
" if the text be genuine, who hath *altered* that
" good picture, from what nature at first *made* it ?
" Here *again* he is mistaken, Shakespear *meant*,
" like a plain man, just as he *spoke* ; and as our
" Editor has paraphrased him : who hath *altered*
" that good picture, otherwise than nature *altered*
" it ? And the solution of the difficulty in this sen-
" tence, which so much perplexed *him*, is this :
" The speaker sees a young man without a head ;
" and consequently much *shortened* in stature : on
" which he breaks-out into this exclamation ; who
" hath *altered* this good form, by making it *shorter* ;
" so contrary to the practice of nature, which by
" yearly accession of growth *alters* it by making it
" *taller*." WARB.

I transcribe the former part of this note ; merely for the sake of observing, once for all ; that he,
who besides stopping-at our great critic's grosser
errors and absurdities, should stay to peck-at every
minute inaccuracy, where his meaning is obvious ;
(as he here serves poor *Theobald:*) might easily write
a Book as *big* at least, as the *Divine Legation*; however it might be for *goodness*.

As for the explanatory part of the note ; — " The
" speaker sees a young man" &c— It contains a
paltry miserable *quibble* ; never thought-of by
Shakespear, and utterly unworthy of him ; and
very

very hardly to be collected from the words of the paffage.

Shakefpear certainly *meant*, as Mr. Theobald explains him; who hath *altered* the picture from what Nature *made* it? And if Mr. W. won't allow us Mr. Theobald's conjecture of—*bid* for *did*—, we muft fuppofe *did*, not to be the fign of the paft tenfe, but to be itfelf a verb, *did* or *made*—; perhaps ufed in the technical fenfe—*did* the picture, i. e. painted it.

EXAMP. XII. Vol. 1. P. 443. MEASURE FOR MEASURE.

" *Duke.*————————This is moft likely!
" *Ifabel.* Oh! that it were as *like*, as it is true!"

She was confcious, that her accufation was *true*; and very naturally replies to the Duke's ironical words, that fhe wifhes it were equally *probable, or credible*, as it was true.

But Mr. W. won't be fatisfied; without making the fenfible and virtuous *Ifabel*, gay enough to quibble, in a cafe of the utmoft ferioufnefs; and abfurd or wicked enough to wifh, that *Angelo's* adultery and murder might appear *feemly*.

" *Like* is not ufed here for *probable*, but for
" *feemly*. She catches-at the Duke's word, and
" turns it to another fenfe; of which there are a
" great many examples in Shakefpear and the wri-
" ters of that time." WARB.

'Tis pity, when he put himfelf to the trouble *
' of fhewing the *peculiar* fenfe of this word;' that he did not alfo (according to his promife) explain
' the caufe, which led the poet to fo *perverfe* an ufe of it.'

* Pref. p. 16.

CANON

CANON XV.

He may explane a difficult passage, by words absolutely unintelligible.

EXAMPLE I. Vol. 8. P. 298. OTHELLO.

" Nor to comply with heat the young affects
" In my *defunct* and proper satisfaction.
" i. e. with that heat and new affections, which the
" indulgence of my appetite has raised and created.
" This is the meaning of *defunct* ; which has made
" all the difficulty of this passage." WARB.

  If there can any sense be made of this, there are still two small difficulties : 1. how *defunct* comes to signify *raised and created by indulgence* ; and 2. how the appetite can be said to be *defunct,* or indulged ; when *Othello* had not yet enjoyed the object of his affections.

EXAMP. II. Vol. 3. P. 237. COMEDY OF ERRORS.

" Sing, Syren, for thyself, and I will dote ;
" Spread o'er the silver waves thy golden hairs,
" And as a bed I'll take thee, and there lye ;
" And in that glorious *supposition* think,
" He gains by death, that hath such means to die."
  —" in that glorious *supposition*] Supposition, for the *thing lain open.*" WARB.

  I am in some doubt, whether this note should be placed under this, or the XIIth Canon ; because from Mr. Warburton's exposition of the word * *supposed,* propping or supporting, Vol. III. P. 25. I suspect,

* See the *Glossary.*

M

that *lain open* is a false print for *lain upon*; and that Mr. Warburton had his eye on a passage in Horace, Sat. 2. Lib. i. *Hæc ubi suppofuit, &c:* or else he would have told us, what this glorious thing lain open [or upon] was. What ideas can this great master of languages have; to talk of thinking *in* a thing *lain open* or *upon*!

Not to take notice, that to *lay* is *ponere*, and *cubare* is to *lie*, which would form *lien*, or *lyen upon*; *suppofition* here is used, in its ordinary sense, for *imagination, fancy*. I suspect, there is a slight mistake of one letter in the third line; we should probably read *them* for *thee*.

" Spread o'er the silver waves thy golden hairs:
  " And as a bed I'll take *them*, and there lie;
" And in that glorious suppofition think,
  " He gains by death, that hath such means to die."

Examp. III. Vol. 7. P. 223. Antony and Cleopatra.

———" Come, mortal wretch;
" With thy sharp teeth this knot Intrinsecate
" Of life at once untie:"

———" *this knot intrinsecate*] The expression is
" fine; it signifies a hidden, secret [*intrinfecus*]
" knot, as that which ties soul and body together."
Warb.

How, secret *as* that which ties soul and body together? Why, it is that very knot she speaks of. But, what a lingua franca is here! a secret *intrinfecus* knot! How long has *intrinfecus* been an adjective? and, if it be not, how will he construe the sentence? Had our critic read Shakespear with any attention, he might have known; that he uses *intrinfecate* for *intricate, intangled,* or *tied in hard knots*;
" Like

" Like rats, oft bite the holy cords in twain,
" Too' *intrinsecate* to' unloose."

K. LEAR, Vol. 6. P. 50.

Had it signified *bidden*, *secret*, it could no more have
been *bitten in twain*, than *untied*, before it was *found
out*.

EXAMP. IV. Vol. 6. P. 386. MACBETH.

——————" You make me strange
" Even to the disposition that I owe ;
" When now I think you can behold such sights,
" And keep the natural ruby of your cheeks ;
" When mine is blanch'd with fear.——] Which
" in plain English is only—*You make me just mad.*
WARB.

If this *be* the meaning, Shakespear has indeed
done here, as Mr. W. describes him elsewhere to do;
viz. *' When he came to draw-out his contempla-
' tions into discourse, he took-up with the first words'
' that lay in his way.' For, except by supposing this'
sort of chance-medley, it is impossible to make
Shakespear's text tally with Mr. W's *balderdash* explanation.

The plain meaning is——Though I am *bold* enough
myself, (i. e. *owe* or *have* enough of that *disposition* ;)
yet I cannot but wonder, when I think——&c.

N. B. In some of these instances, Mr. W's words,
though not unintelligible in themselves, yet are utterly so, considered as explanatory of Shakespear's
words. If therefore these examples may be thought
not to range exactly under this canon, or perhaps
under any of the present ones ; They must then be
provided (as they deserve) with a new CANON
of their own : which Mr. W. himself will, with a

* Pref. P. 16,

M 2

very

very fmall addition, furnifh † very proper terms for.

> To common terms he may affix meanings of his own, unauthorifed by Ufe ; and not to be juftified *either* by Analogy, *or any thing elfe.*

CANON XVI.

He may contradict himfelf ; for the fake of fhewing his critical fkill on both fides of the queftion.

EXAMP. I. Vol. 6. P. 347. MACBETH.

" the golden round,
" Which fate and metaphyfical aid *doth feem*
" *To have thee* crown'd withal."

" *Doth feem to have thee* crown'd withal, is not
" fenfe. To make it fo, it fhould be fupplied thus ;
" *doth feem defirous to have.* But no poetic licence
" would excufe this," &c. WARB.

Yet, page 335. in his Note on this line,

" So fhould he look, that *feems* to fpeak things
ftrange."

he fays, " i. e. feems as if he would fpeak."
Which is much the fame thing as *defirous.*

So alfo in ALL'S WELL THAT ENDS WELL. Vol. 3. P. 13.

" our deareft friend
" Prejudicates the bufinefs, and would feem
" To have us make denial.

Exactly in the fenfe here required ; and not re-marked-on by Mr. W.

† Pref. P. 15.

Ex-

EXAMP. II. Vol. 2. P. 197. LOVE'S LABOUR
LOST,

—" taken *with* the manner."

" We should read, taken *in* the manner; and this
" was the phrase used to signify, taken in the fact."
WARB. And he quotes Dr. Donne's authority for it.

But in Vol. 4. P. 142. 1 HENRY IV. he says,
—" taken *in* the manner."

" The Quarto and Folio read, *with the manner*;
" which is right. *Taken with the manner* is a law
" phrase, and then in common use; to signify *taken*
" *in the fact.*" WARB.

Great wits have short memories.

But such things will happen, when a critic must
furnish such a quota of Notes; whether he have any
thing worth publishing or no.

EXAMP. III. Ibid. P. 249.

" Sown cockle reap'd no corn."

" i. e. If we do not take proper measures for
" winning these ladies, we shall never atchieve them."
WARB. in Theobald's ed. Vol. 2. P. 146.

In his own, the explication is this;

" Sown cockle," &c.

" This proverbial expression intimates; that, be-
" ginning with perjury, they can expect to reap
" nothing but falshood." WARB.

This seems to be the true explication; but he
ought to have confessed, as he does sometimes in a
sort of triumph, that he had led Mr. Theobald into a foolish mistake. If it should be thought hard

M 3

to quote upon a man a note, which he may seem to have recanted; it cannot be reckoned so toward Mr. Warburton: who in Page 293. of this Volume, published at length a mistaken Note of Mr. Theobald, as he expresly says, in order to *perpetuate* it; when his *modesty* suffered him to withdraw it from his second edition.

Hither also may be referred the last example under Canon I.

Examp. IV. Vol. 6. P. 367. Macbeth.

" *Ban.* Our royal master's murder'd. *Lad.* Woe,
 " alas;
" What in our house! ——

" This is *very fine.* Had she been innocent, no-
" thing but the murder itself, and not any of its ag-
" gravating circumstances, would naturally have
" affected her. As it was, her business was to appear
" highly disordered at the news. Therefore, like
" one who has her thoughts about her, she seeks for
" an aggravating circumstance; that might be sup-
" posed most to affect her *personally:* not considering,
" that, by placing it there, she discovered rather a
" concern for *herself,* than for the *King.* On the
" contrary, her husband, who had repented the
" act, and was now labouring under the horrors of a
" recent murder; gives all the marks of sorrow for
" the fact itself." Warb.

I transcribe the whole Note; to shew, how strong-ly Mr. W. seems to *feel* the difference between the Lady's affected and *Macbeth*'s real sorrow. And yet, in the very next page, he has utterly forgotten all this; and *Macbeth* is represented to be just as great a hypocrite, as his Wife is here.

" His *silver* skin lace'd with his *golden* blood.]
 " The

" The allufion is fo ridiculous, on fuch an occafi-
" on ; that it difcovers the *declaimer* not to be af-
" fected in the manner he would reprefent himfelf.
" The whole fpeech is an unnatural mixture of far-
" fetched and common-place thoughts ; that fhews
" him to be acting a part." WARB.

CANON XVII.

It will be neceffary for the profefs'd critic
to have by him a good number of pedantic and
abufive expreffions ; to throw-about upon proper
oecafions.

EXAMPLE I.—" To this the Oxford editor gives
" his *Fiat*." Vol. 4. P. 101.

EXAMP. II. — " To which the Oxford editor
" fays, *Recte*." Vol. 6. P. 227.

EXAMP. III. " Was there ever fuch an *afs* ; I
" mean, as the tranfcriber?" Ib. P. 226.

EXAMP. IV. " This is an *idle blunder* of the
" editors." Vol. 1. P. 110.

EXAMP. V. "—The word *well*—is an intrufion,
" and fhould be thruft-out again ; as it burdens
" the diction, and obftructs the eafy turn of the
" thought." Vol. 1. P. 263.
An intrufion thruft out—What language is this ?
as Mr. Warburton fays on another occafion.

EXAMP. VI. Vol. 1. P. 390. " The old *blunder-*
" *ing* folio having it *invention*, this was enough for
" Mr. Theobald to prefer *authority* to *fenfe*."

M 4   EXAMP.

EXAMP. VII. P. 403.—"Bite the law by th'nose," "This is a kind of *bear-garden* phrase; taken from "the custom of * driving cattle," &c. WARB.

EXAMP. VIII. Vol. 3. P. 93. "This is *into*- "*lerable nonsense.* The *stupid* editors," &c.

EXAMP. IX. "This is *nonsense.* We should "read, *frontlet.*" Vol. 4. P. 109. 1 HENRY IV.

EXAMP. X. "This *stupidity* between the hooks "is the players." Vol. 4. P. 110.

EXAMP. XI. "This *foolish* line is indeed in the "folio of 1623: but it is evidently the players' "*nonsense.*" Vol. 4. P. 189.

EXAMP. XII. "A *paltry* clipt *jargon* of a mo- "dern *fop.*" Vol. 6. P. 469.

EXAMP. XIII. "This *nonsense* should be read "thus." Vol. 2. P. 410.

EXAMP. XIV. "This *unmeaning* epithet, *em*- "*braced.*" Vol. 1. P. 133.

EXAMP. XV. "The *stupid* editors, mistaking "*guards* for satellites." Vol. 1. P. 402.

EXAMP. XVI. "The words have been *ridicu*- "*lously* and *stupidly* transposed and corrupted." Vol. 2. P. 229.

* Because drovers have a connection with butchers; and but-chers with the bear-garden.

CANON

CANON XVIII.

He may explane his Author, or any former Editor of him ; by supplying such words, or pieces of words, or marks, as he thinks fit for that purpose.

EXAMPLE I. Vol. 1. P. 355. MEASURE FOR
MEASURE.

In a note on the title of this play, Mr. Pope had told us ; that the story of it was taken from Cinthio's Novels, Dec. 8. Nov. 5 : by which a plain man would imagine he meant, that it was taken from the fifth Novel of the eighth Decade, as indeed it happens to be, in Cinthio : but Mr. Warburton puts it in words at length, *December 8. November 5.* though, whether he thought the story was so long, that it held for two days ; and, not being finished the first, was resumed again at almost a twelve-month's distance ; or, whether he designed to hint, that Cinthio wrote his Tale on the *eighth of December,* and Shakespear his Play on the *fifth of November ;* we can only conjecture.

This is the *only* passage, in all this book ; which has been honour'd with Mr. Warburton's particular notice. In a note on v. 175 of Mr. Pope's imitation of Horace, book ii. epist. 2. the ridiculous blunder here laugh'd-at is charged on the Printer ; and the author of the Canons abused grossly, for imputing it to the Editor. Both parts of this answer should be replied-to. ' The Printer, it seems, ' *lengthened* Dec. and Nov. into December and No- ' vember.' If Mr. W. can give a single instance of any such *lengthening,* or any thing like it, in Printers ; except this and two or three more which
might

might be mention'd, as having happen'd to *Himself*; (one is to be found under Canon VIII. Ex. 28.) and one *famous* one, which is said to have happen'd to a Writer, lately the subject of much controversy; the benefit of it shall be allow'd him very readily.   As to the *Duncery*, or *Knavery*, of imputing to Mr. W. himself this pretended blunder of his Printer; we would observe, in the first place, that the very great number of cancell'd leaves in his edition of Shakespear led us to think; that it was revised with extraordinary care and exactness: and consequently, that the many blunders in spelling, pointing, and the like, were as certainly *His*; as those in reasoning and emending: in the second place, He must knowingly and wilfully mistake our design; if he supposes it was *anywhere* intended to charge such gross ignorance upon him; or any thing more *here*, than to expose his heedless haste and very slovenly inattention; in a work, which came abroad with such vast expectation.

EXAMP. II. Vol. 7. P. 241.   CYMBELINE.
——————" or e'er I could
" Give him that parting kiss, which I had set
" Betwixt two charming words"——

Mr. Warburton, in his note on this passage, has had the felicity to discover; *what* were the two charming words, between which Imogen would have set her parting kiss: which Shakespear probably never thought-of. He says; " without que-
" stion, by these two charming words she would be
" understood to mean,
" ADIEV, POSTHVMVS.
" The one *religion* made so; and the other *love*."

Imogen

Imogen muſt have underſtood the etymology of our language very exactly; to find out ſo much *religion* in the word *adieu:* which we uſe commonly, without fixing any ſuch idea to it; as when we ſay, that ſuch a man has *bidden adieu* to all religion. And, on the other ſide, ſhe muſt have underſtood the language of *love* very little; if ſhe could find no tenderer expreſſion of it, than the name, by which every body elſe called her huſband.

EXAMP. III. Vol. 2. P. 229. LOVE'S LABOR LOST.
—" and ſuch barren plants are ſet before us, that
" we thankful ſhould be; which we taſte and *feel-*
" *ing are*, for thoſe parts that do fructify in us more
" than he."

The words have been, as Mr. Warburton ſays, tranſpoſed and corrupted; and he " hopes, he has " reſtored the author," by reading thus;

—" and ſuch barren plants are ſet before us,
" that we thankful ſhould be for thoſe parts (which
" we taſte and feel *ingradare*) that do fructify in us
" more than he." WARB.

Our Critic's deſire to ſhew his ſkill in the Italian, would not let him ſee; that Sir Thomas Hanmer reſtored this paſſage to ſenſe, without the help of his *ingradare*; which does not mend the matter much, and which he has not the leſt pretenſe of authority for palming upon us as Shakeſpear's; and this is done in the Oxford edition, by *thruſting-out the intruſion,* as Mr. Warburton * ſays; and printing the paſſage, as the rhyme directs;

" And theſe barren plants are ſet before us, that we
" thankful ſhould be
" For thoſe parts, which we taſte and feel do fruc-
" tify in us more than he."

* Vol. 1. P. 263.

which

which is a couplet of the fame fort of long verfes, as
thofe which follow. This unreafonable and unbridled affectation in Mr. Warburton, of dragging
into the text of Shakefpear, as well as into his notes
on him, all, and more-than he underftands, of the
modern languages; cannot but put one in mind of
a moft unlucky note of his a little lower, p. 233.
note 3.

——" thofe, who know the world, know the *pedant*
" to be the *greateft affecter of politenefs.*" WARB.

When the critic *does* not underftand a paffage,
 he may explane it by putting a proper quantity of afterifks, where he fuppofes fome words
 are wanting.

EXAMP. IV. Vol. 3. P. 46. ALL'S WELL
   THAT ENDS WELL.

——" for doing I am paft; as I will by thee in
" what motion age will give me leave."

 " Here is a line loft after *paft*; fo that it fhould be
" diftinguifhed by a break with afterifks. The very
" words of the loft line, it is impoffible to retrieve;
" but the fenfe is obvious enough. *For doing I am*
" *paft*; age has deprived me of much of my force
" and vigour; yet I have ftill enough to fhew the
" world I can do myfelf right, *as I will by thee in*
" *what motion* [or in the beft manner] age will give
" me leave." WARB.

By this fagacious difcovery *Lafeu,* an old lord of a
high fpirit, (who is treating with the moft contemp-
tuous ridicule *Parolles,* an infamous coward; who
receives all that can be laid on him with the moft
abject patience) is made fo far to forget his character
and dignity; as to give a challenge to this pitiful
fcoundrel. Is this like Shakefpear? The fenfe, fuch
as it is, feems to be plainly this;

        " I can-

" I cannot do much, ſays *Lafeu* ; doing I am *paſt:*
" as *I will by thee* in what motion age will give me
" leave. i. e. as I will *paſs* by thee as faſt as I am
" able ;" and he immediately goes out : it is a play
on the word *paſt* ; the conceit indeed is poor ; but
Shakeſpear plainly meant it, and nothing more ; and
conſequently nothing is left-out. In the very next
ſpeech *Parolles* conſiders it not as a challenge, but
as an excuſe on account of his age ; and threatens
to fight his ſon for it :

" Well, thou haſt a ſon ſhall take this diſgrace
" off me ;" &c.

Examp. V. Vol. 3. P. 38. All's well that
ends well.

" *Parolles.*—he's of a moſt facinerious ſpirit,
" that will not acknowledge it to be the——
" *Lafeu.* Very hand of heaven.
" *Par.* Ay, ſo I ſay.
" *Laf.* In a moſt weak——
" *Par.* And debile miniſter, great power, great
" tranſcendence ; which ſhould indeed give us, a
" farther uſe to be made, than alone the recovery
" of the King ; as to be——
" *Laf.* Generally thankful.——

" Between the words *us* and *a farther,* there ſeem
" to have been two or three words dropt ; which
" appear to have been to this purpoſe.—*ſhould in-*
" *deed give us* [notice, that there is of this] *a far-*
" *ther uſe to be made.* — So that the paſſage ſhould
" be read with Aſteriſks for the future." WARB.

. He is in the right to put the Aſteriſks, not the
Words into the text ; becauſe They do indeed give
us [notice, that there is in Them] as much additional meaning, as there would be in thoſe words
which they ſo properly repreſent.

Ex-

EXAMP. VI. Vol. 6. P. 232. TIMON OF
ATHENS.

" *Tim.* You that way, and You this ; — *But two*
" *in company.* —
" Each man apart, all single and alone,
" Yet an arch villain keeps him company.
" If, where *Thou* art, two villains shall not be ;
" Come not near *Him.* — If *Thou* would'st not reside,
" But where one villain is ; then *Him* abandon."

" This is an imperfect sentence ; and is to be
" supplied thus. But two in company spoils
" all." WARB.

The sentence is certainly complete ; and has reference to the words preceding it. The whole speech
turns upon the same quibbling conceit ; *viz.* That
each of them, though alone, has a villain in his
company : i. e. is *himself* a villain.

CANON XIX.

*He may use the very same reasons for confirm-
ing his own observations ; which He has disallowed
in his adversary.*

EXAMPLE I. Vol. 8. P. 350. OTHELLO.
" Let him command ;
" Nor to obey shall be in me *remorse* :
" What bloody business ever."

" The old copies read, *And* to obey — but evident-
" ly wrong : some editions read, *Not* to obey ; on
" which the editor, Mr. Theobald, takes occasion
" to alter it to *Nor* to obey ; and thought, he had
3 " much

" much mended matters. But he miſtook the ſound
" end of the line for the corrupt ; and ſo, by his
" emendation, the deep deſigning Iago is fooliſhly
" made to throw-off his maſk, when he has moſt
" occaſion. for it ; and, without any provocation,
" ſtand before his captain a villain confeſs'd ; at a
" time when, for the carrying on his plot he ſhould
" make the leaſt ſhew of it :" &c. WARB.

To avoid this flagrant inconſiſtency of character,
Mr. Warburton aſſures us ; that Shakeſpear wrote,
and pointed the paſſage thus ;
             " Let him command,
" And to obey ſhall be in me. *Remord*
" What bloody buſineſs ever.

For the word *remord*, he quotes the authority of
Skelton. The force and beauty of that phraſe—
to obey ſhall be in me, to expreſs *I will obey*, is ſo
ſelf-evident ; that it needs no authority.

But now, in the very next note on thoſe words of
Iago, ſix lines lower,
             ——" My friend is dead ;"

Mr. Warburton, having forgotten all the fine reaſoning, on which this criticiſm is founded ; ſays,
in flat contradiction to it ; " I cannot but think,
" this is a very artful imitation of nature. Iago,
" while he would magnify his ſervices, betrays his
" villainy. For was it poſſible he could be honeſt,
" who would aſſaſſinate his friend ? And not to
" *take* at this, ſhew'd the utmoſt blindneſs of jea-
" louſy." P. 341, 352.

EXAMP. II. Vol. 5. P. 120. 3 HENRY VI.

" Will *coſt* my crown] Read COAST, i. e. hover
" over it." WARB.

How often has Mr. Warburton taken offenſe at
                                        Mr.

Mr. Theobald and the Oxford editor, for violating the integrity of metaphors? Yet here he brings-in, unneceſſarily, *coaſt*, a term belonging to *ſailing*; to tally with a deſcription, wherein the images are taken from *flying* — wing'd with deſire — like an eagle. —

CANON XX.

As the deſign of writing notes is not ſo much to explane the Author's meaning, as to diſplay the Critic's knowlege; it may be proper, to ſhew his univerſal learning, that He minutely point out, from whence every metaphor and alluſion is taken.

EXAMPLE I. *Paſtry.*

Vol. 1. P. 387. MEASURE FOR MEASURE.

— " prayers from *preſerved* ſouls,
" From faſting maids " —

" The metaphor is taken from fruits, *preſerved* in " ſugar." WARB.

In order to continue the metaphor, we ſhould alter *faſting* maids to *pickled* maids.

EXAMP. II. *Chandlery.*

Vol. 1. P. 396. Ibid.

" you ſhall *ſtifle* in your own report,
" And *ſmell* of calumny."

" Metaphor taken from a *lamp* or *candle* going " out." WARB.

EXAMP. III. *Embroidery.*

Ibid. P. 422. " Doth *flouriſh* the deceit" —
" A metaphor taken from *embroidery.*" WARB.

Ex-

EXAMP. IV. *Chess.*

—P. 429.—" lay myself in *bafard.*"

" A metaphor taken from Chess-play." WARB.
Rather, from Tennis.

EXAMP. V. *Bird-catching.*
Vol. 8. P. 328. OTHELLO.

" That shall *enmesh* them all."

" A metaphor from taking birds in meshes." P.
Note, this will serve also for fishing.

EXAMP. VI. *Music.*
Vol. 6. P. 531. CORIOLANUS.

" He and Aufidius can no more *atone,*
" Than violenteft contrarietys."

" *can no more atone*] This is a very fine expression,
" and taken from *unison-strings* giving the same tone
" or found." WARB.

Attone, or rather *attune,* has that signification,
but *atone* is *unite, make one.*

Thus Mr. W. himself explains *atone* in ROMEO
AND JULIET. Vol. 8. P. 74.

The Deputy *set at one* certain of the West Lords,
that were at variance. K. Edw. VI's Journal P. 15.
in Burnet's Hist. of the Ref.

So also in Othello. Vol. 7. P. 461.

" I would do much to *atone* them."

EXAMP. VII. *Traffic.*
Vol. 7. P. 302. CYMBELINE.

" Thou *bidd'st* me to my loss."

N

" A phrase

" A phrafe taken from *traffic*," &c. WARB.

EXAMP. VIII. *Baking.*
Vol. 6. P. 50. KING LEAR.

    " *Unbolted* villain"

" Metaphor from the *bakehoufe*." WARB.

EXAMP. IX. *Bowling.*
Ibid. P. 53.

  " Will not be *rubb'd* or ftopp'd."
" Metaphor from *bowling*." WARB.

EXAMP. X. *Man's or Woman's Taylor;*
Vol. 7. P. 23. JULIUS CÆSAR.

    " And fince the quarrel
" Will bear no *colour* for the thing he is,
" *Fafhion* it thus"

" The metaphor from the wardrobe; when the ex-
" cellence of the fashion makes out for the defect of
" the colour." WARB.

EXAMP. XI. *Pocket-book.*
Vol. 4. P. 273. 2 HENRY IV.

" wipe his TABLES clean] Alluding to a *table-
book* of flate, ivory," &c. WARB.

EXAMP. XII. *Arithmetic.*
Vol. 6. P. 180. TIMON OF ATHENS.

—" and thefe hard *fractions*] An equivocal allu-
" fion to *fractions* in decimal *Arithmetic.*" WARB.

 But why in *decimal arithmetic?* I doubt, Mr.
Warburton does not underftand, that *decimal fractions*
           are

are much eafier than *vulgar fractions.* What Shakefpear calls *fractions* here, were the breaks in the anfwer of the fenate ;

—————" are forry—you are honourable—
" But yet they could have wifh'd—they know not—
" Something hath been amifs—a noble nature
" May catch a wrench—would all were well—'tis
    " pity," &c.

So again in ANT. AND CLEOP. Vol. 7. P. 141.

" I know not what *counts* hard fortune cafts up-
" on my face] Metaphor from making marks or
" lines in cafting accounts in Arithmetic." WARB.
And again in the Two GENT. OF VERONA P.
229.

" He lov'd her out of all *nick*] A phrafe taken
" from Accounts ; when Calculations were made
" by picking of numbers upon a ftick. WARB.

EXAMP. XIII. *Aldermen and men of worfhip.*
Vol. 7. P. 189. ANTONY AND CLEOPATRA.

" *Chain* my arm'd neck] Alluding to the Go-
" thic cuftom of men of worfhip, wearing gold
" chains about the neck." WARB.

Your humble fervant, Mr. Alderman Antony—
Your *worfhip* is fo fine to day ; that I vow I fcarce
know you. But you will hardly thank Mr. Warburton, for the honor he does you.

Chain my arm'd neck, means, entwine me, armed
as I am, in thy embraces. A chain, which a gallant man would prefer before any gold one.

EXAMP. XIV. *Navigation.*
Vol. 7. P. 189. ANTONY AND CLEOPATRA.
—————" Leap thou, attire and all,

         " Through

" Through proof of harnefs, to my heart; and there
" Ride on the pants triumphing.

" *Ride on the pants triumphing*] Alluding to an
" Admiral fhip on the billows after a ftorm. The
" metaphor is extremely fine." WARB.

There are fome points, which our Profeffed Critic
fhould never touch; for, whenever he does, he only
fhews his ignorance about them. He quite miftakes
the nature of the *pants* here, as well as the *chain*
above.

But why *triumphing* like an admiral fhip on the
billows after a ftorm? I thought victories gained,
not ftorms efcaped, had been the matter of triumphs;
and I fuppofe, other fhips dance on the billows, juft
after the fame manner as the Admiral's does.

Vol. 3. P. 426, KING JOHN.

—" untrimmed bride]—The term is taken from
" Navigation: we fay too, in a fimilar way of
" fpeaking, *not well manned*." WARB.

EXAMP. XV. *Mathematics.*

Vol. 6. P. 36. K. LEAR.

" Which like an *engine* wrench'd my frame of
" nature] Alluding to the famous boaft of Archi-
" medes." WARB.

Perhaps rather alluding to the rack.

EXAMP. XVI. *Monkery or Confectioner*.

Vol. 4. P. 446. 1 HENRY VI.

" Field Prieft—] Alluding to his *fhaven crown*;
" a metaphor taken from a *peel'd orange*." Mr.
POPE.

The

The true word is *pilled*; which Mr. Warburton, if he looks for Pilled Garlick in Skinner, will find to import a feverer farcafm, than any thing which alludes to his fhaven crown.

Examp. XVII. *Physic and Surgery.*

Vol. 3. P. 108. ALL'S WELL THAT ENDS WELL.

—" *diet* me]—A phrafe taken from the fevere " methods taken in curing the venereal difeafe." Warb.

Again, Vol. 6. P. 209. On the word *Tubfaft*, he gives you the whole procefs of the cure.

Examp. XVIII. *Conftables and Officers of juftice.*

Vol. 6. P. 349. MACBETH.

—"nor keep peace between] Keep peace, for go " between, *fimply*. The allufion to officers of ju- " ftice; who keep peace between rioters, by going " *between them*." Warb.

A conftable, who fhould think to keep the peace between rioters, in the manner Mr. Warburton de- fcribes, would go between them *fimply* indeed.

Examp. XIX. *Pigeons.*

Vol. 6. P. 169. TIMON OF ATHENS.

" *Serring of becks*] A metaphor, taken from the " billing of pigeons." Warb.

Examp. XX. *Gaming.*

Vol. 6. P. 197. TIMON OF ATHENS.

—" and *lay* for *hearts*] A metaphor, taken from " card p'aying. So in CORIOLANUS—*lurch'd all* " *fwords*." Warb.

N 3　　　　　　　　EXAMP.

EXAMP. XXI. *Aſtrology or conjuring.*
Vol. 6. P. 344. MACBETH.

" To find the mind's *conſtruction* in the face]
" This metaphor is taken from the conſtruction of a
" ſcheme, ih any of the arts of prediction." WARB.

EXAMP. XXII. *Hyperaſpiſts.*
Ibid. P. 402.

" *Beſtride* our down-fallen birth-doom]—The
" alluſion is to the *Hyperaſpiſts* of the antients ; who
" *beſtrode* their fellows fallen in battle, and covered
" them with their ſhields." WARB.

I wonder this learned note did not come-in before, in 1 HENRY IV. Vol. 4. P. 187. where Fal-
ſtaff ſays to the Prince, " Hal, if thou ſee me down
" in the battle, and *beſtride* me, ſo ; 'tis a point of
" friendſhip." But need Shakeſpear go ſo far as
the Hyperaſpiſts of the antients for this inſtance of
friendſhip ? or is not this rather brought-in to ſhew
the critic's learning ?

EXAMP. XXIII. *Bear-garden.*
Vol. 6. P. 490. CORIOLANUS.

—" why *rule* you not their *teeth*] The metaphor
" is from mens ſetting a bull-dog or maſtiff at any
" one." WARB.

EXAMP. XXIV. *Goldſmiths or refiners.*
Vol. 6. P. 515. CORIOLANUS.

" My friends of noble *touch*] Metaphor taken
" from *trying gold on the touch-ſtone.*" WARB.

EXAMP.

EXAMP. XXV. *Hawking.*

Vol. 7. P. 29. JULIUS CÆSAR.

—" *high-sighted* tyranny]. The epithet alludes to
" a *hawk soaring on high,* and intent upon its prey."
WARB.

EXAMP. XXVI. *Archery.*

Vol. 1. P. 358. MEASURE FOR MEASURE.

" We have with a prepar'd and leaven'd choice
" Proceeded to you"]

" Leaven'd has no sense in this place: we should
" read *level'd choice.* The allusion is to archery,
" when a man has *fixed upon* the object, after taking
" good aim." WARB.

I thought, people generally *fixed upon* the object
they would shoot at, before they *took aim.*

EXAMP. XXVII. *Law-proceedings.*

Vol. 7. P. 198. ANTONY AND CLEOPATRA.

—" *seal* then, and all is done] Metaphor, taken
" from civil contracts; where, when all is agreed
" on, sealing completes the contract." WARB.

EXAMP. XXVIII. *Bawdyhouse.*

Vol. 8. P. 253. HAMLET.

" As peace should still her wheaten garland wear,
" And stand a comma 'tween their amities"]

" The poet without doubt wrote,
" And stand a *commere,* &c. The term is taken
" from a trafficker in love, who brings people to-
" gether; a procuress." WARB.

Mr. Warburton, who brought-in this *middling*

gossip,

goffip, as he afterwards calls her, ought beft to know from whence fhe came.

EXAMP. XXIX. *Undertakers.*

VOL. 7. P. 147. ANTONY AND CLEOPATRA.

" For this
" I'll never follow thy *pall'd* fortunes more."

Pall'd feems to mean *decayed.* But Mr. Warburton fays,

" *Pall'd,* i. e. *dead.* Metaphor taken from *funeral*
" *folemnities.*"

And this leads us to

EXAMP. XXX. *Doctors Commons.*
Ibid. P. 216.

" I cannot *procter* my own caufe fo well]—The
" technical term, to plead by an advocate." WARB.
And this is note-writing!

CANON XXI.

*It will be proper, in order to fhew his wit,
efpecially if the critic be a married man, to take
every opportunity of fneering at the fair fex.*

EXAMPLE I. Vol. 6. P. 468. CORIOLANUS.

" My gracious *filence,* hail."

" The expreffion is extremely fublime ; and the
" fenfe of it conveys the fineft praife, that can be
" given to a good woman." WARB.

I always thought fpeaking well and to the purpofe deferved a greater commendation ; or, in Mr.
War-

burton's phrafe, a *finer praife*, than holding
tongue.

P. II. Vol. 3. P. 287. THE WINTER'S TALE.

owerful think it"] "After this there are
lines of infamous fenfelefs ribaldry, ftuck in
oy fome profligate player, which I have cafhier'd;
" and hope no—*fine Lady* will efteem this a *caftra-*
" *ted* edition; for our having now and then, on the
" fame neceffity, and after having given fair notice,
" taken the fame liberty." WARB.

EXAMP. III. *Ibid.* P. 480.

——" the fourth [*part of thy wit*] would return
" for confcience fake, to help thee to get a wife."

" A fly fatirical infinuation, how fmall a capacity
" of wit is neceffary for that purpofe. But every
" day's experience of the fex's prudent difpofal of
" themfelves, may be fufficient to inform us how
" unjuft it is."

EXAMP. IV. Vol. 1. P. 260. MERRY WIVES OE WINDSOR.

" I keep but three men and a boy yet," &c.

" As great a fool as the poet has made Slender;
" it appears by his boafting of his wealth, his breed-
" ing, and his courage, that he *knew how to win a*
" *woman.* This is a fine inftance of Shakefpear's
" knowledge of nature." WARB.

I know not, what Mr. Warburton's experience
may have taught him; but the fuccefs of Mr. Slender's addrefs could give no hint for this good-na-
tured reflexion; for however Mrs. Anne's father
might

might favor him, it is plain, that *her* heart was set upon a more worthy man; and the poet has very properly made Mr. Fenton marry her.

EXAMP. V. Vol. 2. P. 264. LOVE'S LABOR LOST.
" Fair Ladies mask'd are roses in the bud,
" Or angels veil'd in clouds"——

After quarrelling with Mr. Theobald for not using his whole emendation, Mr. Warburton adds;

" It was Shakespear's *purpose* to compare a fine
" lady to an angel; it was Mr. Theobald's *chance*,
" to compare her to a cloud: and perhaps the ill-
" bred reader will say, a lucky one." WARB.

None but an *ill-bred* reader would say so; and probably no body at all would have had such a thought on this occasion, if an *ill-bred* critic had not suggested the complement.

EXAMP. VI. Vol. 2. P. 457. THE TAMING
OF THE SHREW.

Cath. " Why, Sir, I trust I may have leave to
" speak," &c.

" Shakespear here has copied nature with great
" skill. Petruchio, by frightening, starving, and
" over-watching his wife, had tamed her into
" gentleness and submission. And the audience
" expects to hear no more of the *Shrew*: when, on
" her being crossed in the article of fashion and
" finery, *the most inveterate folly of the sex*, she flies
" out again, though for the last time, into all the
" intemperate rage of her nature." WARB.

Our critic is a great admirer of Shakespear's knowledge of nature; whenever he can pay a complement to it, at the expense of the fair sex. Here,

in

in order to set, what he calls *their most inveterate folly,* in the strongest light, he misrepresents Shake-spear in every circumstance.

1. It does not appear, that Petruchio had as yet *tamed her into gentleness and submission*; for almost the last words she spoke before this sentence are a general curse upon his family.

2. She does not on this occasion fly-out into *all the intemperate rage of her nature.* She insists indeed, with more heat and obstinacy than one would wish in a wife, upon having the gown and cap in question; but does not, as on some former occasions, support her resolution either with ill language, or blows.

3. And lastly, It is not the last time that her temper appears. For twice afterwards she is debating with her husband; once about the hour of the day, and once about the sun and moon; nor is it till the XIIIth Scene, that she appears to be perfectly *tamed into gentleness and submission.*

EXAMP. VII. Vol. 7. P. 273. CYMBELINE.

" And Cydnus swell'd above its bank, *or for*
" *The press of boats, or pride*] This is an agreeable
" ridicule on poetical exaggeration, which gives
" human passions to inanimate things;"&c. WARB.

This reflexion seems to be made merely to bring
in what he says a little after—" The very same kind
" of Satire we have again, on much the same occa-
" sion, in THE TWO GENTLEMEN OF VERONA;
" Vol. 1. P. 215. where the false *Protheus* says to
" his friend, of his friend's mistress,

——" *and she hath offer'd to the doom,*
" *Which unrevers'd stands in effectual force,*
" A sea of melting pearl, which some call tears.
" A cer-

" A certain gaiety of heart, which the speaker strives
" to conceal, breaking-out under a Satire; by which
" he would insinuate to his friend, *the trifling worth*
" *of a woman's tears.*" WARB.

This polite complement did not occur to our critic, when he was at work on the play he quotes;
but as he was unwilling to lose the reputation of it
among the ladies, he has forced it in here without
fear or wit; I say, forced; because there is no
ground, but in his imagination, for thinking that
Shakespear meant any such thing.

EXAMP. VIII. Vol. 7. P. 291.

———" so thou, Posthumus,
" Wilt lay the leven to all proper men;
" Goodly and gallant shall be false and perjur'd
" From thy great fall."
" When Posthumus thought his wife false, he
" unjustly scandalized the whole sex. His wife here,
" under the same impressions of his infidelity, at-
" tended with more provoking circumstances, ac-
" quits his sex; and lays the fault where it was due.
" The poet paints from nature. This is life and
" manners. The man thinks it a dishonor to the
" superiority of his understanding, to be jilted; and
" therefore flatters his vanity into a conceit, that
" the disgrace was inevitable from the general infi-
" delity of the sex. The woman, on the contrary,
" not imagining her credit to be at all affected in
" the matter, never seeks for so extravagant a con-
" solation; but at once eases her *malice*, and her
" grief, by laying the crime and damage at the
" door of some obnoxious coquette." WARB.

I have nothing to object to what is said in this
learned note of the effects of Jealousy upon men;
except

except that the whole might properly be referred to
Canon XXIII. But, for what he says of the women,
there seems to me no foundation here. Imogen
surely does imagine her credit to be affected, when
she says just before,

" Poor I am stale, a garment out of fashion."

Nor does she shew any *malice* here, but a proper
resentment of a crime, which could not be committed without the assistance of some *obnoxious* female, either *prude* or *coquette.*

CANON XXII.

*He may misquote himself, or any body else, in
order to make an occasion of writing notes; when
He cannot otherwise find one.*

EXAMPLE I. Vol. 2. P. 24.   MUCH ADO ABOUT
NOTHING.

" She would infect the north star] i. e. there
" is nothing of so pure and keen a brightness, that
" her calumnious tongue will not sully." WARB.

Mr. Warburton's text, as well as all others, read,

" she would infect *to* the north-star:"

and it is the diffusedness, or extent of her infection
which is here described. But Mr. Warburton will
contradict his author, and himself too, rather than
lose what he thinks a brilliancy.

EXAMP. II. Vol. 2. P. 185.   MERCHANT OF
VENICE.

" Fair ladies, you drop *manna* in the way
" Of starved people."]   " Shakespear is not more
" exact

" exact in any thing, than in adapting his images
" with propriety to his speakers ; of which he has
" here given an instance, in making the *young*
" *Jewess* call good fortune, *manna.*"   WARB.

But in Mr. Warburton's own text, as well as in
other editions, the speech is not given to the *young*
Jewess, but to *Lorenzo*, and is in answer to two,
addressed by Portia and Nerissa to him.   If there
were a necessity of making a reflexion here, it might
have been—How easily do we learn to talk the language of those we love? And this would have been,
as Mr. Warburton says, *to the purpose* ;   but it
would have been out of his element.

EXAMP. III. Vol. 2. P. 437.   TAMING OF THE
SHREW.

In note 2, where he is abusing old ballads, he
says,
" Shakespear frequently ridicules both them and
" their makers with exquisite humor.   IN MUCH
" ADO ABOUT NOTHING, he makes Benedict say,
" *Prove that ever I lose more blood with love, than I*
" *get again with drinking,* prick out *my eyes with a*
" *ballad-maker's pen.*   As the bluntness of it would
" make the execution extremely painful." WARB.

Where, for the sake of this refined explanation,
he quotes the passage, *prick* out *my eyes*, whereas his
own, as well as the other editions, have it, *pick out*
(Vol. 2. P. 11.) and the humor lies, not in the pain-
fulness of the execution, but the ignominy of the instrument, and the use he was to be made of after the
operation ; " *and hang me up at the door of a brothel-*
" *house, for the sign of a blind Cupid.*"

EXAMP.

EXAMP. IV. Vol. 1. P. 87. TEMPEST.

——" which enter'd their frail *shins.*"]

Mr. Warburton in his note quotes it, *their frail skins*; because it suited his purpose better. See Canon XIV. Example 7. But in the text, P. 70, he gives it right, *shins.*

EXAMP. V. Vol. 6. P. 224. TIMON OF ATHENS.

" The Sea's a thief, whose liquid surge resolves
" The *moon* into salt tears"——]

" The Sea melting the *moon* into tears, is, I
" believe, a secret in philosophy; which nobody
" but Shakespear's deep Editors ever dreamed of."
WARB.

As it is evident from the latter end of Mr. W.'s note, that his alteration of the text here, is upon his *own* authority, not that of any copies which he had seen; it seems a little hard in him to lay the old reading to the charge of the Editors; which ought certainly to be given to Shakespear himself. They, poor Ignorants! went to work without their tools, and never dreamed of these true Warburtonian Canons of Criticism; and of the high privileges therein annexed to the character of the Critic by profession: by the 2d and 6th of which he is empowered to alter any thing, which he does not understand; or, any word that will do; provided he can think of any thing, which he imagines will do better.

Armed with this Authority, Mr. W. boldly pronounces; that " 'tis more reasonable to believe,
" that Shakespear may allude to this opinion; viz.
" that the saltness of the Sea is caused by several
" ranges,

3

" ranges, or *Mounds* of rock-falt under water; with
" which *refolving* liquid the Sea was impregnated.
" This I think a *fufficient* Authority for chang-
" ing—*moon*—into—*mounds.*" WARB.

And was this Term—the *Mounds* —fo familiarly
known in Shakefpear's time, as the Name of thefe
Ranges of rock-falt; that they would convey the
Idea of thefe Ranges without any addition or explanation? No Mortal, but one, can believe it.
And, after all, Mr. W.'s criticifm gives us Salt
inftead of Water.

As for his philofophy, it is like *Gonzalo's* commonwealth in the *Tempeft* ;— ' the latter end of it
' forgets the beginning ' — for no farther back than
P. 48. of this Vol. he tells us ; that— ' the natural
' philofophy of that time was, that the rays of
' the moon were *cold* and *moift* ' —and fays ; that
Shakefpear himfelf alludes to this latter property in
two paffages.

—" the moonfhine's *watry* beam." ROM. & JUL. and
" Quench'd in the *chaft* beams of the *watry* moon."
                    MIDSUMMER NIGHT'S DREAM.

fufficient authorities, both thefe, for us to conclude
that Shakefpear in this paffage too, wrote— *Moon*.
And, indeed the tenor of the paffage demands it.
All things fteal from each other. The Sun robs
the Sea ; the *Moon* robs the *Sun* ; and the Sea again
robs the *Moon*.

The old *notion* of the Moon's influence upon the
Weather, and the known *fall* of its influence on the
Tides, are very ample grounds for any poet to fay,
that the Moon fupplies the Sea with Water.

' I cannot take leave of this Note, without juft
pointing out the fingular perfpicuity of the follow-
                                                    ing

ing fentence : " The Sea is impregnated with
" mounds of rock-falt refolving liquid." •

EXAMP. VI. Vol. 7. P. 21. JUL. CÆSAR.

———— " the complexion of the *Element*

" Is fev'rous"——] " We find from the preceding
" relation, (P. 17) that it was not *one* Element only,
" which was difturbed, but *all :* being told, that
" all the fway of *Earth* fhook like a thing infirm ;
" that the *Winds* rived the knotty oaks ; that the
" *Ocean* raged and foamed ; and that there was a
" tempeft, dropping *Fire.* So that all the *four*
" Elements appeared to be difordered. We fhould
" read therefore——

" ———— the complexion of the *Elements*————
" which is confirmed by the following line

" Moft *bloody*, *fiery*, and moft *terrible.*
" *Bloody* referring to the *Water* ; *Fiery* to the *Air*
" and *Fire :* and *Terrible* to the *Earthquakes.*"

WARB.

Thus Mr. W. For what reafon, except to force
the word *complexion* from its common meaning of
colour to the lefs ufual fenfe of *conftitution*, I own
I cannot conceive. There is not the left reafon to
think, that any thing is here alluded to ; but fome
extraordinary meteors in the Air. But Mr. W.
having laid hands on a fpeech of *Cafca* (P. 17)
where the words Earth, Winds, Ocean, and Fire
happen all to occur, he immediately falls to his
work ; and ftirring them together with his *uncre-
ative* paw, he brews us up this horrid Chaos of the
Elements. And from the midft of all this turmoil
of his own raifing, comes ftaring out and tells us,
that " Bloody refers to the Water, Fiery to the

O   " Air

" Air and Fire, and Terrible to the Earthquakes."
as well as I can conjecture, for thefe reafons. Bloody
to the Water, becaufe No mention is made of Water in the paffage : Fiery to the Air and Fire, becaufe, The Air was on Fire, and 'tis hard if a thing
may not refer to its felf : and laftly, as for *Ter-*
rible to the Earthquakes ; when Mr. W. gives us,
any reafon, why *Terrible* muft refer to Earthquakes,
rather than to any other objects of terror ; except,
becaufe *Terra* is Latin for the Earth ; I promife to
take this off his hands again.

The paffage Mr. W. refers to (P. 17) has nothing in it that can lead us to imagine any thing
is there meant, except diforders and commotions
in the Air.—Shakes the *earth*—evidently relates
not to an Earthquake, but to the *Thunder*.—A
tempeft dropping Fire, is a proof, that the Air is
in diforder ; but the Element of Fire is no more difturbed in This, than in any other of its common
operations. As for the riving Winds and the foam-
ing Ocean, they are not fpoken of by *Cafca*, as
circumftances then prefent, but as things which he
had formerly feen.

It may be thought perhaps, that the difference
between the two readings is not of confequence e-
nough to fpend fo much time about : but however
trifling may be that difference, Mr. W.'s reafoning
about it is abfurd and ridiculous ; and

——————we muft not give advantage
To ftubborn Critics ; apt, without a theme,
For depravation.——
TROILUS AND CRESSIDA. Vol. 7. P. 472.

CANON

C A N O N XXIII.

The Profess'd Critic, in order to furnish his quota to the bookseller, may write NOTES OF NOTHING ; *that is, Notes, which either explane things which do not want explanation ; or such as do not explane matters at all, but merely fill-up so much paper.*

EXMAPLE I. Vol. 6. P. 143. K. LEAR.

" Friends of my soul] A Spanish phrase. Amigo " de mi Alma." WARB.

Just with the same acuteness a Spanish critic meeting with the expression, Amigo de mi alma, might say,
An English phrase. " Friends of my soul."

EXAMP. II. Vol. 1. P. 61. TEMPEST,
" If thou dost break her virgin knot," &c.
" *Virgin knot*] Alluding to the Latin phrase of " Zonam solvere." WARB.

EXAMP. III. Vol. 2. P. 99. MERCHANT OF
VENICE.
—" *peep through their eyes*] This gives us a very " picturesque image of the countenance in laugh-" ing, when the eyes appear half shut." WARB.

EXAMP. IV. *Ibidem.*
—" shew their teeth in way of smile] Because " such are apt enough to shew their teeth in anger." WARB.

EXAMP.

EXAMP. V. Vol. 6. P. 552. CORIOLANUS.

—" he no more remembers his mother now,
" than an eight year old horse] Subintelligitur, re-
" members his dam." WARB.

EXAMP. VI. Vol. 8. P. 349. OTHELLO.
—" swell, bosom, with thy fraught;
" For 'tis of aspics tongues.
" i. e. swell, *because* the fraught is poison." WARB.

Such recondite observations as these, shew the
great judgment of the critic; and are much to the
edification of the gentle reader.

EXAMP. VII. Vol. 3. P. 94. ALL'S WELL THAT
ENDS WELL.

" It rejoices me that I hope, I shall see him e'er I
" die"]

" It is not hope that rejoices any one; but that
" that hope is well grounded. We should read
" therefore,

" It rejoices me, that hope, that I shall see him e'er
" I die." WARB.

Do people hope, when they think their hope not
well grounded? This surely is criticising for criticising sake.

EXAMP. VIII. Vol. 1. P. 29. TEMPEST.

" My spirits, as in a dream, are all bound up]
" Alluding to a common sensation in dreams,
" when we struggle, but with a total *impuissance*
" in our endeavours, to run, strike," &c. WARB.

This

This is only saying in prose, what Shakespear had said in verse; but it serves to introduce that fine word *impuissance,* instead of the obsolete English *impotence.*

EXAMP. IX. Vol. 1. P. 95. MIDSUMMER NIGHT'S DREAM.

" As she is mine, I may dispose of her:
" Which shall be either to this gentleman,
" Or to her death, according to our law."

" By a law of Solon's, Parents had the absolute
" power of life and death over their children. So
" it suited the poet's purpose well enough, to sup-
" pose the Athenians had it before. Or perhaps he
" *neither thought nor knew any thing of the matter.*"
WARB.

Very possible. And therefore, it might have been as well, if Mr. Warburton had not *said any thing of the matter.*

EXAMP. X. Vol. 2. P. 123. MERCHANT OF VENICE.

" 'Tis vile, unless it may be quaintly ordered."

This is spoken of their going a masking. Upon which Mr. Warburton quotes,

" Ut gratas inter mensas symphonia discors,
" Et crassum unguentum, et Sardo cum melle pa-
"   paver
" Offendunt, poterat duci quia coena sine istis." HOR.

Which puts one in mind of those lines in PRIOR's Alma,

" Here, Dick, I could display much learning,
" At least to men of small discerning."

EXAMP.

Examp, XI. Vol. 1. P. 113. Midsummer
night's Dream.

Note 2.——" She (Mary queen of Scots) is called
" a *Mermaid*, to denote——her beauty and *intem-*
" *perate luft.*

——" Ut *turpiter* atrum
" Definat in piscem mulier formosa superne."

Which those who do not underftand Latin, will
perhaps think, is a proof of what our critic afferts;
or at left fomething to his purpose.

Examp. XII. *Ibid*. P. 114.

" The emperor Julian tells us, Epift. xii. that
" the Sirens—contended for precedency with the
" Mufes, who overcoming them, took away their
" *wings*. The quarrels between Mary and Elizabeth
" had *the fame cause*, and *the fame issue*." Warb.

Not to take notice of the famenefs of the *cause*;
if what Mr. Warburton fays of the *issue* be true,
then *heads* and *wings* are the *fame*; for Queen Mary
loft her *head*.

Examp. XIII. Vol. 8. P. 230. Hamlet.

" O how the *wheel* becomes it!] We fhould read
" *weal*. She is now rambling on the ballad of the
" fteward and his lord's daughter; and in thefe
" words fpeaks of the ftate he aflumed." Warb.

But how can " the *weal* becomes *it*" fignify " the
" *ftate he* aflumed?" I fuppofe, becaufe the *common-
weal* fignifies the *ftate* or government, therefore
weal muft fignify *ftate* or *dignity*. Our critic feems
here to ramble as much as poor Ophelia, and this
is

is called explaning; he had better have owned, that he did not underftand the paffage.

———" Edmund the bafe

" Shall *be* the legitimate] Here the Oxford editor
" would fhew us, that he is as good at coining
" phrafes as his author; and fo alters the text thus,

" Shall toe the legitimate] i. e. fays he, ftand on
" even ground with him; *as he would with his au-*
" *thor.*" WARB.

Poor Sir Thomas! Woe be to you, if you invade Mr. Warburton's prerogative; of *coining* words
for Shakefpear! One may fairly fay here, that " the
" toe of the *peafant* comes fo near the heel of our
" *courtier*; that it galls his kibe *." But Mr. Warburton ought to have taken notice, that the old reading is *fhall* to *tb' legitimate*; which though it mifled
Sir Thomas, may perhaps direct to the right word;
———" Edmund the bafe
" Shall *top* the legitimate :"

which he would do, if he got the inheritance from
him; though that could not make him *be* the legitimate.

———" matter deep and dangerous,
" As full of peril and adventurous fpirit
" As to o'erwalk a current roaring loud
" On the unfteadfaft footing of a fpear."
" i. e. of a fpear laid acrofs." WARB.

* HAMLET, Vol. 8. P. 246.

I, fuppofe

I fuppofe it would not be fo dangerous to walk *over* a current, on a fpear laid *along* it; but it would be more difficult: as the man obferved, about peoples getting at bridges, if they were built in that manner.

EXAMP. XVI. *Ibid.* P. 135.

" Here's lime in this fack too; there is nothing " but roguery to be found in villainous man."

Here, when he has properly quoted Sir Richard Hawkins, to prove the cuftom of putting lime into fack; he runs-out into a differtation, about lime's being the caufe of the ftone; which he contradicts by Mrs Stephens's fuccefs with her medicine, and upon this occafion fpins out a tedious note, which is nothing to the purpofe, fince there is no mention of the ftone here; and if lime be good againft that, it may be unwholfome in other refpects, efpecially if the wine be over-dofed with it; as Sir John's feems to have been, when he could diftinguifh it at firft tafte.

EXAMP. XVII. Vol. 2. P. 99. MERCHANT OF VENICE.

—" Now by two-headed *Janus*] Here Shake- " fpear fhews his knowledge in the antique," fays Mr. Warburton; I fuppofe, to fhew *his own* knowledge; for the fingle epithet of *Jane Bifrons* would ferve Shakefpear's turn as well as all the collections of antiques, and the books of Montfaucon, Spanheim, &c. which he makes fuch a parade with.

EXAMP. XVIII. Vol. 8. P. 284. OTHELLO.

" By *Janus*, I think no] There is great propriety " in making the double Iago fwear by *Janus*, who " had

" had two faces. The addrefs of it is likewife re-
" markable; for as the people, coming up, appear-
" ed at different diftances to have different fhapes;
" he might fwear by *Janus,* without fufpicion of
" any other emblematic meaning." WARB.

· There are a great many of this fort of notes, too
many to tranfcribe; which, with a fhew of refinement, may throw a duft in the reader's eyes; but,
when one comes to reflect on them, contain nothing at all; or, what is worfe than nothing, nonfenfe. All this dream of an *emblematic meaning* has
no more foundation, than his conceit of people's
having different *fhapes* at different diftances; different appearing *magnitudes* they may have, but not
different *fhapes*; nor, if they had, would that help
him; unlefs at fome diftance or other they had
two faces.

EXAMP. XIX. Vol. 7. P. 231. CYMBELINE.

" You fpeak him far."] " i. e. largely in his
" praife. Shakefpear with his common licence
" only ufes the *Length* for the *Breadth.*" WARB.

It may perhaps be improper to range this example under Notes of *Nothing*; fince the acute reader will difcover in it no lefs than *three* Things,
viz. Not only the *Length* and *Breadth,* but the
Thicknefs alfo of our notable critic's Head-piece.
Why he explains *far* by *largely,* except for the
fake of his doughty remark on Shakefpear's licence;
is hard to conceive. If Shakefpear had been abfurd enough to *mean—breadth,*— I truft, he would
alfo have been nonfenfical enough to *fay —* You
fpeak him *wide* (far, length; wide, breadth.) But
the beft of it is, this fpeaking him *far,* or extending his praife, in the very next note fignifies both
length

length and *breadth*; and with a witnefs too: for it
fignifies drawing out (or extending) it, *beyond its
lifts and compafs.* i. e. beyond its extent. Mr. W.
fneers at poor *Theobald* for explaining the words,
— I do extend him within himfelf — by thefe — I
extend him within the lifts and compafs of his merit — ; which, fays our merry Critic, is juft as proper
as to fay, *I go out within doors.* Now we have exactly the fame reafon to fay, that Mr. W.'s explanation of the word *extend,* is juft as proper as
to fay, *I ftay at home without doors.*

EXAMP. XX. Vol. 5. P. 278. RICHARD III.

" I think there's ne'er a man in Chriftendom,

" Can leffer hide his love or hate than he."] " This
" character is what *Ennius* gives of himfelf, and
" in the fame words. Ego eo ingenio nàtus fum,
" amicitiam atque inimicitiam in frontem promp-
" tam gero. Ap. Non. in Inimic. But this is no
" imitation: For the thought, which is a common
" one, could hardly be expreffed otherwife."
WARB.

What a flippery ground is critical confidence!
Vol. 6. P. 284.

No two fentences, expreffing the fame fentiment,
can well be more different in the *form* of them than
thefe two.

Ennius fpeaks *directly* of him-felf, by a fimple
affirmation;

promptam gero. I fhow it openly.

Haftings fpeaks of *Richard obliquely,* by a com-
parifon of him to other men; and his expreffion is
negative: defcribing him as — *not hiding* his love
and hatred.

CANON

CANON XXIV.

He may dispense with truth; in order to give the world a higher idea of his parts, or of the value of his work.

For instance,

1. He may assert, that what he gives the public, was the work of his younger years; when there are strong evidences of the contrary. This Mr. Warburton has done, in so many words, in his Preface; P. 19.

" These (observations on Shakespear) such as
" they are, were among my younger amusements;
" when, many years ago, I used to turn over these
" sort of writers, to unbend myself from more se-
" rious applications," &c.

From a very great number of these notes, one would think this to be true; though it is but a bad complement to the public, *at this time of day, to trouble* them with such trash; but when one reflects on the passages in almost every page, where Sir Thomas Hanmer's edition is corrected; and on the vast numbers of cancelled sheets, which give pretty strong evidence, that the book was in a manner written while it was printing off; beside several other evident marks of haste, these circumstances render this assertion impossible to be true; without construing away the obvious meaning of his words.

2. He may assert, that he has collated the text of his author with *all* the former editions; when at the same time it appears undeniably in his work, that he has not done it.

In the title page of his edition, Mr. Warburton says, that the text is collated with *all* the former

editions;

editions; how truly this is said, will appear by the following inftances.

EXAMPLE. I. Vol. 2. P. 72. MUCH ADO ABOUT NOTHING.

" Let them be in the hands of Coxcomb]—But
" the editor (Mr. Theobald) adds, *the old Quarto*
" *gave me the firft umbrage for placing it* [*this fpeech*]
" *to Conrade.* What thefe words mean, I do not
" know; but I *fufpect*, the old Quarto divides the
" paffage as I have done." WARB.

I SUSPECT! Is this the language of a man, who had actually collated the books? I am afraid from thefe words, the world will more than *fufpect*, that he knew nothing of the matter; and that where he quotes the old editions, it is only at fecond hand.

EXAMP. II. Vol. 1. P. 67. TEMPEST.

" And like the bafelefs fabric of *their* vifion."]

" Not to mention the aukward expreffion of
" *their* vifion; which Mr. Theobald, *upon what*
" *authority* I *know not*, changed into *this* vifion."
WARB.

It is ftrange, that Mr. Warburton fhould not know; that it was upon the authority of the firft Folio, which has this reading.

EXAMP. III. Vol. 3. P. 149. TWELFTH NIGHT.

" Unftaid and fkittifh in all *motions* elfe] The
" Folio reads, *notions*." WARB.
Both the Folio's read, *motions*.

EXAMP.

EXAMP. IV. Vol. 6. P. 5. K. LEAR.

—" and 'tis our faſt intent] This is an interpola-
" tion of Mr. Lewis Theobald," &c. WARB.

Hardily faid—but not very honeſtly; for FAST
is the reading of both the Folio editions.

CANON XXV.

*He may alter any paſſage of his author, with-
out reaſon and againſt the Copies; and then quote
the paſſage ſo altered, as an authority for altering
any other.*

EXAMPLE. I. Vol. 6. P. 348. MACBETH.

——" the raven himſelf *is* hoarſe,
" That croaks the fatal enterance of *Duncan*
" Under my battlements"—] " I ſuppoſe the text
" to be corrupt; and that we ſhould read——

" The raven himſelf's *not* hoarſe——;

" The meſſenger tells her of one, who has juſt
" brought the agreeable news of *Duncan*'s coming.
" Give him tending, anſwers ſhe; he brings great
" news: i. e. treat him as the bringer of good news
" deſerves. This is ſo very acceptable; that it would
" render the moſt ſhocking voice harmonious, the
" moſt frightful bearer agreeable. A thought ex-
" preſſed in the moſt ſublime imagery conceivable,
" and beſt adapted to the confidence of her views.
" For as the raven was thought a bird of omen, it
" was the propereſt to inſtance in; both as that
" imagination made its hoarſe voice ſtill naturally
" more odious; and as that was a notice of the
" deſigns of fate, which ſhe could confide in. But
" this effect of the diſpoſition of the mind upon
" the

" the organs of sense, our poet delighted to de-
" scribe. Thus in a contrary case, where the
" chaunting of the Lark in *Romeo and Juliet*
" brings ill news, he makes the person concerned
" in it to say,

 " 'Tis said, the Lark and loathed Toad chang'd
  eyes:
 " Oh now, I wot, they have chang'd voices too."
            WARB.

This couplet had passed Mr. W.'s forge, before
it could be made fit for the purpose 'tis here used
for. As Shakespear wrote it, it has no relation to
any *effect of the disposition of the mind upon the
organs of sense*; but is a simple Wish. Thus it
stands in the Original;

Oh now I *would* they had changed voices too!
and how happily Mr. W. has changed I *would* for
I *wot*, may be seen in CANON VIII. Ex. 52. P.
68.

This Reflexion, as is observed above, in
CANON IX. Ex. 2, is undoubtedly raised in
her mind by what is there said about the Messen-
ger's being almost dead for breath. The old reading,

 The raven himself is hoarse——
is right; and the sentiment seems to be this:

 The raven himself, whose ominous croaking is
always hoarse; (a voice of ill omen, and therefore
finely insinuated to be disagreeable to the Ear) is
more particularly so, when he croaks the fatal entrance of *Duncan*, &c. because *Duncan*'s death is
fixed and determined on with a resolution more than
commonly steady and immoveable. *A thought,
indeed expressed in the most sublime imagery conceivable;
and best adapted to the confidence of her views.*

I   EXAMP.

EXAMP. II. Vol 6. P. 351. MACBETH.

Unto our *gentle senses.*—Mr. W. reads, *general
sense ;*—and supports himself by reasons, which are
endeavoured to be confuted in CANON VIII.
Ex. 43. But he has one hold still left him. i. e.
Authority ; which (as the good SCRIBLERUS
says in the first note on the Dunciad) is—at all
times with Critics *equal,* if not *superior,* to *Reason*
—especially, if it be their *own* Authority ; which
is the case here with Mr. W.

" *General* has been corrupted to *gentle* once a-
" gain in this very Play." See Note, Act 3.
Scene 5. WARB.

It is at P. 385. Where Mr. W. instead of
gentle weal—without any reasonable cause, and *con-
fessedly* against the concurrent testimony of all the
Editions, thrusts into the Text by his own Authority—*general* weal.

He quotes indeed a passage in *Timon of Athens,*
in support of his alteration ; where the commonwealth is called the *general* weal.

————take the bridge quite away
Of him, who his Particular to foresee
Smells from the general weal.————

But here the word *general* is necessary ; because the
public good is spoken of, in opposition to the *private* advantage of a *particular.*

So that in *both* places the *gentle* or *general* readers (i. e. the readers in general) will be apt to believe, that *gentle* has been corrupted into *general ;*
and not, as Mr. W. would have it, *vice versâ.*

ESSAY

ESSAY

TOWARDS A

GLOSSARY.

ABSENT, " unprepared." Vol. 4. P. 42.
See Can. P. 70.

AFFAIRS, " proffeffions." Vol. 5. P. 394.
"——their *affairs* are righteous."

APPEAL'D, " brought to remembrance." Vol. 6.
P. 518.
" Your favor is well *appeal'd* by your tongue."
This word Mr. WARB. brought-in upon conjecture.

ARGUMENTS, " natures." Vol. 6. P. 179.
" and try the *arguments* of hearts by borrowing."
Perhaps rather, contents.

ARISE, a word ufed to ufher in a matter of
" importance." Vol. 1. P. 13.
" Now I *arife*."

AUNTS, " old women," Vol. 6. P. 366.
" *Aunts* prophefying," &c.
The text was, *And* prophefying. But Mr.
Warburton brought-in his *Aunts*, on purpofe to
make old women of them; in order to which he
wrongly

wrongly interprets " *accents terrible of dire combus-*
" *tion*" to mean articulate sounds or words, P. 365.

BELIEVE a thing, " act conformably to it."
Vol. 8. P. 135.
" —so far to *believe* it."

BELIGHTED (introduced to Shakespear's acquaintance by Mr. Warburton.) Vol. 8. P. 299.
" If Virtue no *belighted* beauty lack"] white,
fair, W.
It should rather signify lighted-up, as a room is
with candles. See Can. P. 9.

BROOCH, " a chain of gold." Vol. 4. P. 240.
" Your *brooches*, chains, and owches.
Rather, a bodkin or some such ornament, from
broche, Fr.

CAP, " property," bubble." Vol. 6. P. 221.
" Thou art the *cap* of all the fools alive.
Rather the top, chief.

CARBONADO'D, *rectius* CARBINADO'D,
" mark'd with wounds made by a *carabine*."
POPE confirmed by WARB. Vol. 3. P. 95.
So when Kent in King *Lear* says, *I'll carbonado
your shanks for you*; he means, *I'll shoot you in the legs
with a carabine*, which will carry the antiquity of
that weapon much higher than Henry IV. of
France.
But *carbonaded* means *scotched*, or cut as they do
steaks before they make *carbonadoes* of them.

CEMENT, " cincture or inclosure, because both
" have the idea of holding together."
" Your temples burn'd in their *cement*." Vol. 6.
P. 532.

COMES-OFF, " goes-off." Vol. 6. P. 149.
" —this *comes-off* mighty well."

P   CON-

CONSEAL'D, a word of Mr. Warburton's own
  invention ; and which is, as he says, "—a very
  "proper designment of one just *affianced* to her
  " Lover." Vol. 8. P. 69.

CRESTLESS, "one who has no right to Arms."
  i. e. Coat of Arms. Vol. 4. P. 467.
  just as headless would signify one who has no
  legs.

CURIOSITY, " scrutiny." Vol. 6. P. 3. See
  Can. II. Ex. 12.

DANGER, " wickedness." Vol. 6. P. 19.
  "—on no other pretence of *danger*."

DEAR, " dire." Vol. 6. P. 288.
  " —with this *dear* sight."

DECK'D, " honor'd." Vol. 1. P. 12.
  " When I have *deck'd* the sea with drops full
  " salt."
  To *deck* signifies to adorn.

DEROGATE, " unnatural." Vol. 6. P. 37.
  —from her *derogate* body never spring
  A Babe, to honour her !—
  I imagine, Shakespear meant degenerate.

DESPITED, " vexatious." Vol. 8. P. 282.

DISTEMPER, " sudden passions." Vol. 4.
  P. 344.
  " If little faults proceding on *distemper*
  " Shall not be wink'd at."
  But the distemper here alluded-to was drunken-
  ness.
  " —we consider,
  " It was *excess of wine* that set him on."

EFFECT, " executioners." Vol. 5. P. 222.
  " Thou wert the cause and most accurst *effect*."
But

But Richard replies,
" Your beauty was the caufe of that *effect*."
Does *effect* mean executioner here too ? Perhaps
the firft line fhould be read,
" Thou wert the caufe of that moft curs'd ef-
" fect ;"
i. e. the timelefs deaths of Henry and Edward.
ENDEAVOURS, " for deferts." Vol. 5. P. 406.
" —I confefs your royal graces,
" Shower'd on me daily, have been more than
" could
" My ftudied purpofes requite ; which went
" Beyond all man's *endeavours :* my *endea-*
" *vours.*
" Have ever come too fhort of my defires."
Rather, for endeavours.
ENRACED, " rooted." Vol. 2. P. 133, a word
of his own bringing-in. See Can. P. 53.
ENVY, " for evil." Vol. 5. P. 397.
" You turn the good we offer into *envy*."
Rather, you put an invidious conftruction on
what we mean well.
EQUIPAGE, " ftolen goods." Vol. 1. P. 280.
" I will retort the fum in *equipage*."
ERRANT, " one who has no houfe nor coun-
try." Vol. 8. P. 302.
A man that has no *houfe*, one has a tolerable
notion of ; but to fay a man has no *country*, is
a piece of nonfenfe, not to be fuffered in any,
except one, Country.
To EXTEND a thing, " to draw it out beyond
its lifts or compafs. Vol. 7. P. 231.
FANTASTICAL, " fupernatural, fpiritual."
Vol. 6. P. 339.

P 2　　　　　　　　　rather,

rather, creatures of the brain, merely ideal, or as Shakefpear fays in another place—unreal mockeries.

So in, 1 Hen. IV. Vol. 4. P. 198.

—————————art thou alive?

Or is it Fancy plays upon our eyefight?

FEARLESS, carelefs. Vol. 2. P. 113.

" See to my houfe, left in the *fearlefs* guard

" Of an unthrifty knave."

FISSURE (another word introduced by Mr. Warburton) " Socket, the place where the eye is."
Warb. Vol. 3. P. 382. See Can. II. Ex. 6.

But Fiffure would fignifie, flit, or the parting of the eyelids; not the focket of the eye.

To FLOUT, " to dafh any thing in another's " face." Vol. 6. P. 335."

" Where the Norweyan banners *flout* the fky."

FORMAL, " common."

—to any *formal* capacity. Vol. 3. P. 158. it means,—whofe capacity, i. e. faculty of reafoning is in any form, or method, and thus Mr. W. himfelf explains the word in Measure for Measure.

" *Formal,* a thing put into form or method."
Vol. 1. P. 447.

So in Antony and Cleopatra. Vol. 7. P. 135.

Thou fhould'ft come like a fury crown'd with fnakes,

Not like a *formal* man.——

i. e. a man in his fenfes.

tho' Mr. W. here too choofes to fay—

Formal, ordinary.

FOULED (a word of Mr. Warburton's) " trampled under foot." Vol. 6. P. 537.

FRAINE

FRAINE (another word of Mr. Warburton's making) for "refraine, keeping back farther favors." Vol. 2. P. 62. See Can. 7. Ex. 5. So one may upon occasion use 'fractory for refractory, 'bellion for rebellion, &c.

FREE, "grateful." Vol. 6. P. 390.
"Do faithful homage, and receive *free* honors." *i. e.* Our allegiance on one side and our honors and privileges on the other shall be put on a certain and known footing. The sentiment is the same as Shakefpear has, P. 420.
———"The time approaches,
"That will with due decision make us know,
"What we shall say we *have* and what we *owe*.

To FROWN, "to project or execute laws." Vol. 6. P. 493.
"Than ever *frown'd* in Greece."
By the same rule of construction, it may signifie to write angry notes, and call names.

FULL, "beneficial." Vol. 1. P. 439.
so interpreted in order to confute a reading of Mr. Theobald.

To GAUDE, "rejoice." from the Fr. Gaudir. Vol. 3. P. 272. a word of Mr. W's coining.

To GEAP, "jeer, ridicule." Vol. 2. P. 239. This word was made by him to fit the place, instead of *leap*.
"How will he triumph, *leap*, and laugh at it?" But, if he must be altering, he should have taken the true word *jape*, which is used by the old Authors in the sense he would have; though there is no need of it.

GEER,

GEER, " eatables." Vol. 6. P. 84.
" But rats and mice, and such small *Geer*,
" Have been Tom's *food* for seven long year."

GENERAL, " speedy." Vol. 6. P. 179.
" I knew it the most *general* way."

GENTLEMAN-HEIR, " a Lady's eldest son."
Vol. 3. P. 132.
This is a phrase fresh from the mint. But Mr.
Warburton may take it back, and lay it by for his
own use : Shakespear has no need of it ; as any
body will own, who considers that Sir Toby was
drunk, and interrupted in his speech by his
pickled herrings.
" 'Tis a Gentleman here—a plague of these
　" pickle herrings ! "

GRAVE, " Epitaph." Vol. 3. P. 369.
" ————————so must thy *grave*
" Give way to what's seen now." See Can.
P. 87.

GROTH, " Shape." Vol. 8. P. 70.
" Thy tears are womanish, thy wild acts denote
" The unreasonable fury of a beast,
" Unseemly woman in a seeming man,
" And ill beseeming beast in seeming * *both*,"
　　　　　　　　　　　　　　　　* *Groth.* W A R B.

This passage Mr. Pope threw-out as *strange non-*
sense ; and Mr. Warburton restores it into absolute nonsense, by a word of his own making, and
wrong interpreting the word joined with it ; for
there is no such word as *groth* ; and if he means
Growth, that signifies *increase*, not *shape* ; then,
what is *seeming shape?* for I deny that *seeming* is
used for *seemly*, as he says. Nor is there any reason for all this pother and amendment ; but that
Mr. Warburton cannot understand Shakespear,
　　　　　　　　　　　　　　　　　　　　　　　till

till he has brought him down to his level, by making nonsense of his words.

The meaning of the sentence, which is full of gingle and antithesis, is; " You discover a strange
" mixture of womanish qualities, under the ap-
" pearance of a man; and the unseemly outrage-
" ous fury of a beast, under that compound of
" Man and Woman." This should properly have come under Canon VIII.

GUST, " aggravation." Vol. 6. P. 194.
" To kill I grant is sin's extremest *gust.*"
Mr. Warburton writes with great *gust,* when he makes notes on the Dunciad.

HAIR, men of, " nimble, that leap as if they re-
" bounded." not, *hairy* men. Vol. 3. P. 347.
See Can. IX. Ex. 2.
" —they have made themselves all men of hair,
&c.

HARD HANDS, " signifie both great labor and
" pains in acquiring, and great unwillingness to
" quit one's hold." Vol. 7. P. 72.
" —wring from the *hard hands* of peasants."

To HEDGE, " obstruct." Vol. 5. P. 401.
Shakespear uses it for pursuing ones end's ob-
liquely, cunningly. So Falstaff in the MERRY
WIVES OF WINDSOR says——Vol. 1. P. 281.

I, I, I myself sometimes, leaving the fear of
heaven on the left hand, and hiding mine honour in my necessity, am fain to shuffle, to
hedge and lurch.

but here Mr. W. had nothing to say to the word. Indeed it was not so proper a passage, wherein to introduce, or convey his interpretation.

P 4 HER.

HERMITS, " Beadfmen." Vol. 6. P. 352.
　　ignotum per ignotius is one of the Canons of
　　Lexicography.

HINT, " prognoftic." Vol. 1. P. 30.
　　Shakefpear means the fame as in three lines
　　lower is expreffed by—our theam of woe.

HYM, "a particular fort of Dog. POPE. Vol. 6.
　　P. 89.
　　" Hound or fpaniel, brache or *hym*."
　　Unlefs Mr. Warburton finds it out in Horace's
　　Epode to Caffius Severus, there is no fuch dog
　　as *Hym*.
　　Sir T. Hanmer reads it rightly *Lym*. See Caius
　　de Canib. Brit. and Skinner under *Limmer*.

IGNORANT, " bafe, poor, ignoble." Vol. 6.
　　P. 349.
　　" Thy letters have tranfported me beyond
　　" This *ignorant* prefent time."
　　Rather, time *of ignorance*; as in Othello, Vol. 8.
　　P. 375. *ignorant* Sin for Sin *of Ignorance*.
　　" Alas! what ignorant Sin have I committed?"
　　In the two firft fenfes properly applicable to many
　　of Mr. Warburton's notes.

IMPAGE, " grafting." Vol. 3. P. 34.
　　from impe, a graff, or flip, or fucker. WARB.
　　fo we may fay Pimpage, procuring, pimping,
　　from Pimp, procurer.

IMPART, " profefs." Vol. 8. P. 128.
　　evidently in the latin fenfe of impertio, give,
　　beftow.

INCHASE Subft. " the temperature, in which
　　" the feafons of the year are fet". Vol. 1. P. 111.

INCISION to make, " a proverbial expreſſion for
" to make to underſtand." Vol. 2. P. 334.
" God help thee, ſhallow man. God *make inci-*
" *ſion* in thee."
By this place we muſt explane that of Piſtol.
Vol. 4. P. 245.
" What, ſhall we have *Inciſion?*" *i. e.* under-
ſtanding.

INCORRECT, " untutor'd." Vol. 8. P. 127.
" A will moſt *incorrect*"———
This explanation, I hope, is not ſuggeſted to Mr.
Warburton by a view of Shakeſpear's text, as it
ſtands in his edition ; for, though he has *tutored*
him with a vengeance, in the moſt pedantic ſenſe
of that word, he has left him ſtill—moſt *incorrect.*

INSTANCE, " for ſenſe." Vol. 3. P. 191.
" So far exceed all *inſtance,* all diſcourſe ; "
Rather, example.

INTRAITMENTS, " coyneſs." Vol. 8. P. 139.
A word (he ſays) uſed among the *old* Engliſh
writers. I doubt, no *older* than the Hypercritic of the Dunciad. But he knows not what
to make of *intreatments,* the true reading.
" Set your *intreatments* at a higher rate."
Why may it not ſignifie *entertaintments,* i. e. the
opportunities you give him of converſing with
you ?

LAY-BY, " ſtand-ſtill." Vol. 4. P. 102.

LEARNING, " being taught." Vol. 7. P. 267.
See Can. P. 49.

To 'LEVE, " to add to the beauty of a thing."
Vol. 1. P. 95. See Can. P. 51.

LIMITS, " eſtimates." Vol. 4. P. 99. rather,
orders, limitations.

LORD

LORD of the Presence, *i. e.* Prince of the blood.
Vol. 3. P. 393.
" *Lord of the presence*, and no land beside." (*Thy*
Presence is the old reading.)
So afterwards, when K. John, speaking of him-
self, says, he is " Lord of our presence ;" P. 411.
he means, that he is *a Prince of his own blood.*
" *Lord of our presence*, Angiers, and of you.

MEAL'D, " mingled." Vol. 1. P. 427.
" ———were he *meal'd*
" With that which he corrects"———
If *mingled* were the meaning, it should be *mell'd*.
It seems to mean *dawb'd* with the same spots
that he finds fault with in others.

MEAN, " mediocre condition." Vol. 6. P. 97.
" Our *mean* secures us"———
Extremely edifying to his English reader ; he
should have added the Latin and Greek too.

To MEMORIZE, " to make." Vol. 6. P. 335.
" Or *memorize* another Golgotha."
Perhaps rather, render famous in History.

MERSOPS' SON, " Bastard, base-born." Vol. 1.
P. 213.
" Why, Phaeton, for thou art *Merop's son*
" Wilt thou aspire to guide the heavenly car ?" *&c.*
The Duke is here reproving Valentine for his am-
bition, in attempting his daughter ; and calls him
Merops' son, as a synonymous term with *Phaeton*.
He is too well bred to call a Gentleman son of a
whore for no reason at all, this is language fit
only for profess'd Critics and Car men ; but since
Clymene was *Phaeton*'s mother, and *Merops*, *Cly-
mene*'s husband ; how comes calling him *Merops'
son* to signifie calling him *bastard* ? for, though
Mr.

Mr. Warburton is acquainted with Clymene's amours, the Duke is not talking of them here.

MING (another word of Mr Warburton's, made out of a *wing turned the wrong way*) mixture. Vol. 3. P. 11.

" ———a virtue of a good *ming*." (or *wing*.)

MOTIVE, " affiftant." Vol. 3. P. 89. " inftrument." Vol. 4. P. 9. " pledge." Vol. 6. P. 403.

MUCH, " marry come up." Vol. 4. P. 243.

MUCH-BEDIGHT, " much bedeck'd and a-" dorned, as the meadows are in fpring time." Vol. 2. P. 286. See Can. P. 17.

Which being his *own word*, he pays it this complement; " *the* epithet *is proper, and the* com-" pound *not inelegant*."

MUSTER TRUE GATE, i. e. " affemble to-" gether in the high road of the fafhion." Vol. 3. P. 29.

I wifh, Mr. Warburton had given us fome authority for this, out of Skelton at left, if not from Shakefpear; for it is too much to take upon his bare word.

NATIVE, " civil." Vol. 4. P. 387.

" ———and out-run *native* punifhment."——

The fenfe of the paffage is, that war overtakes and punifhes *abroad* fuch men as have fled from the juftice of the law, and efcaped punifhment at *home*, which Shakefpear calls *native* punifhment.

NATURE, " human." Vol. 6. P. 349.

NICE, " delicate, courtly, flowing in peace." Vol. 7. P. 178.

" ———when my hours
" Were *nice* and lucky———

NOBILITY, " magnitude." Vol. 8. P. 127.
" And from no less *nobility* of love."

OATS, ' a distemper in horses.' Vol. 2. P. 442.
" ——the *oats* have eat the horses."
I hope, Mr. Warburton takes care to keep his horses from this dangerous distemper.

PEACE to keep, " to go between simply." Vol.
6. P. 349. See Can. XX. Ex. 18. P. 124.

PIKED or PICKED, " formally bearded." POPE.
Vol. 3. P. 396.

'PLOY'D, " for imploy'd." Vol. 7. P. 328.
" —have both their eyes
" And ears so *'ploy'd* importantly as now."
This is Mr. Warburton's word (*'ploy'd* for *imploy'd*, he should have said *employ'd*) instead of *cloyed*, But Shakespear never thought of circumcising his words at this rate, as our Critic does to fit them for any place which he wants them to fill. By the same rule we may say, 'PTY and 'PIRE are English words, signifying *empty* and *empire*.

POSSESSION, " satisfaction." Pope, Vol. 4.
P. 328.
" King Lewis's *possession*."——
A man must be very unreasonable, who will not be *satisfied* with *possession*.

POWER, " execution of a sentence." Vol. 6. P.
10.
" To come betwixt our sentence and our *power*."
Rather, power to execute the sentence.

PREGNANT, " ready." Vol. 3. P. 164.
—" most *pregnant* and vouchsafed ear."
Ready, for what ?

PRE-

PRESUPPOSED. " impofed." Vol. 3. P. 204.
" ——forms which there were *prefuppofed*
" Upon thee in the letter."
i. e. forms beforehand defcribed in the letter, fuch
as yellow ftockings, crofs-garters—&c.

'PRIS'D, " taught." Vol. 2. P. 155.
"— and am well *'pris'd*
" To wifh it back again"——— See Can. P. 38.
This is a word which Mr. Warburton has fub-
ftituted inftead of *pleas'd*, which is Shakefpear's.
I fuppofe, by the apoftrophe, he ufes it for *appri-
fed*; and fo, for the eafe of all future Poets and
Critics, they may ufe *'ply*, *'pear*, *'proach*, for *apply, appear, approach*, &c.

QUESTION, " force, virtue." Vol. 7. P. 440.
" During all *queftion* of the gentle truce."

RACK, " the veftige of an embodied cloud."
Vol. 1. P. 68.
" Leave not a *rack* behind." See Can. XV and
XVII.

RASH, " dry." Vol. 4. P. 284.
" As ftrong as—*rafh* gunpowder."
The true fenfe here is fudden, eafily inflammable.

RATED, " foughtfor, bought with fupplication."
Vol. 4. 299.

TO RECONCILE, "to bear with temper." Vol.
6. P. 407.

REFLECTION, " influence." Vol. 7. P. 238.

RESOLUTION, " confidence in another's words."
Vol. 6. P. 422.

RESPECT, " requital." Vol. 5. P. 320.
" Is the determin'd *refpect* of my wrongs."
Mr. Warburton put-in this word; and therefore,

perhaps, he may interpret it as he pleases.
—also, " One in honorable employment."
Vol. 6. P. 56.
" To do upon *respect* such violent outrage."
Rather, the reverence due to one in honorable
employment.

To RETORT, " to pay again." Vol. 1. P. 280.
Hence, no doubt, comes a RETORT, a vessel
used by the Chemist ; because it *repays* the Ope-
rator whatever he puts into it with Interest ; Che-
mistry being well known to be a very gainful employment.

To RETURN, " to reply aversely." Vol. 7. P.
384.
By *replying aversely to adverse fortune*, Mr. Warburton, I suppose, means ; to reply with his
back turned upon her. But the word here seems
only to mean *Echos.*
" And, with an accent tun'd in self-same key,
" *Returns* to adverse fortune"——

To REVYE a man, " to look him in the face."
Item, " to call upon him to hasten." Vol. 3.
P. 90.
" —And time *revyes* us." A word of Mr. War-
burton's bringing into the text.

RIVALS, " partners." Vol. 8. P. 116.
" The rivals of our watch"——
But *rivals* generally would have *all.*

SEASON, " infuse." Vol. 8. P. 137.

SELF-CHARITY, " charity inherent in the per-
" son's nature." Vol. 8. P. 323.
" Unless *self-charity* be sometimes a vice ;
" And to defend ourselves it be a sin."
So *self-defense* and *self-murder*, I suppose, are *de-
fense* and *murder* inherent in a person's nature.

SEEM-

SEEMING, " seemly, Vol. 8. P. 70. See GROTH.

SERRING (a word of Mr. Warburton's) " join-
" ing close together." Vol. 6. P. 169.
" *Serring* of becks."

SHAPELESS, " uncouth or diffused." Vol. 2.
P. 265.
" Disguis'd like Muscovites in *shapeless* geer."
i. e. of a strange shape, or a large shape.

SHINE, " prosper." Vol. 6. P. 372.
" —If there come truth from them,
" As upon thee, Macbeth, their speeches *shine*."
Rather, promise good fortune to.

SHOTTEN, " any thing that *is* projected; as a
" shotten herring is one that *hath* cast its spawn."
Vol. 4. P. 367.
" In that *nook-shotten* isle of Albion."

SICK, " prejudiced." Vol. 5. P. 356.
" By *sick* interpreters."——
Whether prejudiced signifies *hurt*, or *partial*,
and if partial, whether *for* or *against*, Mr. Warburton does not say.

SILENCED, " recalled." Vol. 5. P. 347.
" Is it therefore
" Th' embassador is *silenced* ?"
There is no mention of any recalling; the mean-
ing is, that the French Embassador was refused
audience by our King.

SINCERE, " legitimate." Vol. 5. P. 350.
" From *sincere* motions."

SOLLICITED, " brought-on the event." Vol.
8. P. 265.
" —the

" —the occurrents more or less.
" Which have *follicited*—the rest is filence."

SOLLICITING, " information." Vol. 6. P. 342.
" This fupernatural *folliciting*
" Cannot be ill."——
So a *Solliciter* is an *Informer.*

SNIPE, " a diminutive woodcock." Vol. 8. P.
303.
Juft as a partridge is a diminutive pheafant.

SOME, " that part which." Vol. 7. P. 333.
" ——that *fome,* turn'd coward."

'SPERSE, for difperfe. Vol. 8. P. 345. See Introd.
P. 20.
This is a word of Mr. Warburton's making; and
fo he may write '*fturb* and '*finttion.* But *fperfe*
fhould rather mean fprinkle.

SPURS, " an old word, for the fibres of a tree."
Pope, Vol. 7. P. 311.
" ——mingle their *fpurs* together".
It is a common word; and fignifies the larger
roots, in contra-diftinction to the fibres or fmaller
roots; fo the fpur of a poft is ufed in allufion to
the large root of a tree.

STRANGE, " dangerous." Vol. 6. P. 350.
" Your face, my Thane, is as a book, where
" men
' May read *ftrange* matters."

STRATAGEM, " vigorous action." Vol. 4. P.
206.

STRIFE, " action, motion." Vol. 6. P. 140.

SUBSCRIBED, " foften'd." Vol. 6. P. 94.
" All cruels elfe *fubfcribed.*"
                                                    —*Item,*

——*Item*, aliened, transferred. Vol. 6. P. 17.
" The King is gone from hence *fubfcrib'd* his
" power."

SUBSCRIPTION, " obedience." Vol. 6. P. 73.
" You owe me no *fubfcription.*"

SUDDEN, " capricious." Vol. 6. P. 404.
" ——I grant him bloody,
* * * * * * * * * * *
" *Sudden*, malicious, *&c.*"
It feems to mean paffionate, wrathful.

SUPPOSED, ' undermined." Vol. 4. P. 293.
" Wounding *fuppofed* peace."
——*item*, " propping, fupporting." Vol. 3. P. 25.
" If you fhould tender your *fuppofed* aid.',
i. e. the help you fuppofe you can give the King.

SUPPOSITION, " the thing laid open *(or per-
haps upon).*" Vol. 3. P. 237.
" And in that glorious fuppofition think."
See Can. P. 109.

SURMISE, " contemplation." Vol. 6. P. 343.
" My thought, whofe murder yet is but fan-
" taftical,
" Shakes fo my fingle ftate of man ; that Fun-
" ction
" Is fmother'd in *furmife.*"
I cannot but obferve, that Mr. Warburton is very
fudden (capricious) in his *contemplations* about the
meaning of words.

TO THEM, " Have at *you.*" Vol. 5. P. 446.
See Can. P. 8.

TRICK, " fafhion." Vol. 1. P. 455.
" I fpoke but according to the *trick.*"
" So to trick-up fignifies to drefs according to
" the mode."

Q   The

The trick signifies *habit, custom*; as, he has gotten a *trick* of doing so or so : † but to *trick-up* signifies to dress up, to adorn, in general; without necessarily implying the mode or fashion. Skinner derives it from *intricare,* innectere et implicare capillos.

To VICE a man, " to draw, persuade him." Vol. 3. P. 294.
As he had seen't, or been an instrument to *vice* you to't.

UNBOOKISH, " ignorant." Vol. 8. P. 365.
" ——his *unbookish* jealousy."——
It may be so here; but there are instances of *bookish* men, who are very *ignorant* nevertheless.

UNIMPROVED, " unrefined." Vol. 8. P. 120.
" Of *unimproved* mettle hot and full."
Shakespear seems to use it for *unproved.* However that be, Mr. Warburton has fully convinced the world; that *refinement* and *improvement* are two very different things.

UNIVERSE, " horizon." Vol. 4. P. 380.
" Fills the wide vessel of the *universe*"——
See Can. P. 95.

UNKNOWN, " supernatural." Vol. 3. P. 37.

UNTRIMMED bride, " unsteady." A term taken from Navigation: we say too, in a similar way of speaking, *not well manned.* Vol. 3. P. 426. See Can. P. 85.
" In likeness of a new *untrimmed* bride."

To WOOE, " to ogle." Vol. 5. P. 240.
" ——reflecting gems
" That *wooed* the slimy bottom of the deep."

† So Mr. W. himself explanes it, in Cymbeline. Vol. 7. P. 288. Note. 1.

The

The figure of *wooing the deep* is as far fetched, as
the extremity of metaphorical writing will admit; but Mr. Warburton thinks, there can never
be too much of a good thing; and so by his explanation, *wooed* for *ogled*, makes downright
burlefque of it.

YAWN, " gape." Vol. 8. P. 394.
  " ——and that th' affrighted earth
  " Should *yawn* at alteration."

As this Note is juft at the conclufion of his work,
I am afraid his readers have yawn'd often before
they came to it; and it is a proper complement
to take leave of ———————— him with.

The following REMARKS *are copied from* Mr. Roderick's *papers, and inserted here; as containing acute yet sober criticisms on* Shakespear's *words, and judicious yet easy explanations of his sense: a circumstance, which recommends also many of the foregoing examples, both to the Canons and Glossary; far more than their polemic merit: of which however the candid and intelligent reader will by no means esteem them void.*

I. Vol. 3. P. 313. THE WINTER'S TALE.

" ————— Sir, be prosperous
" In more than this deed does require; and
    " Blessing,
" Against this Cruelty, fight on thy Side!
" Poor thing condemned to loss."———

Antigonus takes his leave with two wishes. The 1st, " That the King may enjoy *more prosperity* " than such a deed as this of exposing the child, " could with any right *demand*, or in reason *expect*." (for this must be the meaning of those words—*be prosperous in more than this deed does require*—) The 2d wish is, " That the *Blessing* of " heaven may protect the poor child, *condemned to* " *be exposed*, against the intended effects of its father's *Cruelty*." The whole passage should be read and pointed, as follows.

" ————— Sir, be prosperous,
" In more than this deed does require! And
        " Blessing

                                " Against

" Against *his* Cruelty (*addressing himself to the*
  " *Child*) fight on *thy* Side,
" Poor Thing, condemn'd to loss !"

  N. B. The word *require* has afterwards in this
play the same sense which I have supposed it to
have here—

  " — I love'd him, as in honour he *required.*"
i. e. " with such a pure love, as the honour and
" dignity of his royal character demanded on my
" part."

II. Ibid. P. 316.

" Even to the guilt—&c."

This line should be written as follows,

" Even to the guilt, or the purgation."

in order to throw the greater stress on the word—
Even—which is here to be understood, not as an
adverb — *etiam* — but as an adjective — *æqualis* —
" Justice shall have its due course ; *equal* to the
" guilt, or the innocence, which shall appear in
" the Queen upon the trial." Shakespear often
uses the word—*Even*—in this sense.

III. Ibid. P. 318.

" ——— The Gods themselves
" (Wotting no more than I) are ignorant."

  The Parenthesis confounds the sense : which is,
—" The Gods, *if they know no more of it than I do,*
" know nothing at all of it."

IV. Ibid. P. 404. K. JOHN.

" Liker in feature to his father Geoffrey,
" Than thou and John———"

It does not appear, that Elinor and John were

Q 3

alike

alike in *feature* ; though they were Mother and
Son : and what follows,

" —— in *manners* being as like
" As rain to water, or devil to his dam—"

comes in but aukwardly. But the tranfpofition of
one comma makes all eafy and natural.

John had before been pretty rough with K. Philip ; and Elinor, in the fpeech to which this is an
anfwer, calls Conftance's fon, Arthur, a Baftard :
To which fhe, taunting Elinor's grofs expreffion,
fays in reply ; that her fon Arthur is—

" Liker in *Feature* to his father Geoffrey,
" Than Thou and John in *Manners* ;"

i. e.—as like him as poffible ; for (fays fhe) you
two are equally unmannerly—and in that as like one
another, as Rain and Water, or Devil and Dam.

V.   Ibid. P. 405.

" That he's not only plagued, &c."

A poor paffage this, at beft ! But yet, tho' low
and paltry, is not (when properly pointed, and only a fingle letter inferted) utterly unintelligible ;
which, as it ftands now, it is.

It is not worth many words. The matter in
fhort is this — She had before faid, that Elinor's
fins were vifited upon her Grandfon, Arthur : in
this fpeech fhe adds farther—That He was not only punifhed for Her fins, but that God had been
pleafed to make ufe of Her as the Means, the Inftrument, whereby that punifhment was inflicted
on him.——This is all the fentiment of the fpeech ;
which (for the fake of a miferable gingling between
Plague and *Sin*) is thrice repeted, with varied expreffions. Read and point thus.

" Tha

" That He's not only plagued for Her fin,
" But God hath made Her fin and Her the
    " Plague
" On this removed Iffue ; plague'd for Her,
" And with Her plague'd ; Her fin, His Injury,
" Her injury the Beadle to Her Sin."

The laft line and half may want fome little explanation.

" Her fin, his *injury*"—i. e. his lofs, his damage, his punifhment.

" Her *injury* the Beadle to her Sin"——

Her injury—her injuftice—her violence in taking part with K. John in his endeavours to rob him of his right to the crown. (And by the way—This ufing the fame word—*Injury*—in the fame fentence, in two different fenfes, is not at all difagreeable to Shakefpear's ufual manner : numberlefs inftances of which might eafily be collected, if it were worth while, from the worft parts of his works.) But to procede—

" Her injury the *Beadle* to her Sin"——

The Beadle in a Corporation is the officer, whofe bufinefs it is to execute the fentences pafs'd upon any offenders ; fuch as, Whipping—&c. to which Shakefpear alludes ; and becaufe her injuftice was the inftrument, by which the punifhment of her fins was inflicted upon Arthur ; he therefore calls it—the *Beadle* to her fins.——

This may, perhaps, be thought at firft fight to be a hard and unnatural explanation : but the more we are acquainted with Shakefpear's licentious manner, the more, I doubt, we fhall have occafion to think ; that this was the meaning defigned by this

expreffion.

expreſſion.   He has the ſame alluſion again in
Henry V.

" Now if theſe men have defeated the law, and
" outrun native puniſhment ; though they can out-
" ſtrip Men, they have no wings to fly from God.
" War is his *Beadle,* War is his vengeance ; ſo
" that here men are puniſhed for before-breach
" of the King's Laws, in the King's quarrel now."

VI.   Ibid. P. 444.

" Well, ſee *to* live."—Read—

" Well ; See, *and* Live."———For though there
is nothing ſaid as yet in this ſcene, about killing
him ; yet it is plain, from Hubert's next ſpeech,
that the King intended his death ſhould follow his
blindneſs.

" *Hub.* Your Unkle muſt not know, but you
" are dead.

VII.   Ibid. P. 449.

" From *France* to *England* never ſuch a power, &c."

Read—thus—

" From *France* to *England*.   Never—&c.—"

The meaning is, that—" There never was ſuch
" a power levied by *France,* for any foreign pre-
" paration ; as this, wherewith they are at preſent
" ready to invade us."
But the conſtruction, as it ſtands, will ſcarcely
bear this.   With the alteration of the pointing all
procedes eaſily.

" ——— How *goes* all in *France* ?" (ſays the
King.)
" From *France* to *England*." (anſwers the Meſ-
ſenger.)

                                              j. e,

i. e. All *in* France goes *from* France *to* England—
and then goes-on defcribing the formidable power
defigned for the invafion : as if every man in *France*
were engaged in it.

This may perhaps be called a poor conceit ; but,
I doubt, it is but too likely that Shakefpear intended it.

VIII. Ibid. P. 477.

" —— Such offers of *our* peace,
" As we with honour and refpect may take."

The word *our* has little meaning here : and, as
the preceding word ends in *f*, I conceive it might
come originally from the Poet,—*fair* Peace.

IX. Vol. 4. P. 19. KING RICHARD II.

" —— Now no way can I ftray,
" Save back to England : All the world's my
" way."

The fenfe is, " I am now in no danger of lofing
" my way ; fince, except one way, i. e. back to
" England, the whole world is open to me—all
" the world is my way." The paffage therefore
muft be pointed thus.

" —— Now no way can I ftray ;
" Save back to England, all the—&c."

X. Ibid. P. 52.

" —— throw-away Refpect,
" *Tradition*, Form, and ceremonious Duty."

I have fometimes thought, that it might be better to read—*Addition*. Titles of honour were called in Shakefpear's time, very commonly, *Additions* :
and he ufes the word in this fenfe himfelf, in many
paffages. ——

" They

" They clepe us drunkards ; and with fwinifh
    " phrafe
" Soil our *Addition*."————HAMLET.
" The name and all th' *Addition* to a King."
                          LEAR.

XI. Ibid. P. 342. KING HENRY V.

" But till the King come forth, and not till then,
" Unto Southampton do we fhift our fcene."

This ftrange blunder in expreffion, " till the
" King come forth, and not till he come forth,"
feems very unaccountably not to have ftop'd or re-
volted any of the editors ; though the paffage has
been gravely produced by one, as an argument for
changing the place of the Chorus' coming-in.
When the King does come forth, he comes forth
at Southampton ; merely to reproche the Confpi-
rators, and go directly aboard for France.   All
that was done at Southampton is pafs'd over, and
own'd to be omitted, in this Chorus ; as all that
was done in England is, in that between the fourth
and fifth Acts.

It is plain therefore, that we muft read here,

" But, till the King come forth, and *but* till then,"

that is, till the King appears next, you are to fuppofe the fcene fhifted to Southampton ; and no
longer : for, as foon as he comes forth, it will
fhift to France.

It is well known, how often *not* and *but* are confounded.

XII. Ibid. P. 353.

" But though we think it fo, it is no matter."

The Conftable has been extolling the character
of Henry V. which the Dauphin difbelieves.——
                                  " Well

" Well (fays he) it is *Not* fo—but that's no mat-
" ter—for though we don't think it is fo, yet pru-
" dence, in cafes of defence, fhould always incline
" us to think better of our adverfary, than he feems
" or perhaps truly is; for by the contrary beha-
" viour, i. e. by undervaluing our adverfary, we
" often hazard our fecurity; making too flight
" and weak a preparation for our defence."

  Read therefore——

" But though we think't *not* fo—&c."

<h3 style="text-align:center">XIII. Ibid. P. 420.</h3>

" And all our vineyards, fallows, meads, and
 " hedges,
" Defective in their nurtures, grow to wildnefs.
" Even fo our houfes—&c."——

The many diforders arifing from want of agri-
culture, are very fully and very beautifully defcribed in thirteen lines immediately preceding thefe;
and the inftances there given are exactly the fame
with thefe here: fo that this couplet is not only
flat and infipid, after what goes before; but alfo moft fhamefully tautological. Take the whole
paffage, as I think it fhould be read and pointed:

" —— Lofing both beauty and utility.
" And *as* our vineyards, fallows, meads, and
 " hedges,
" Defective in their nurtures, grow to wildnefs;
" Even fo our houfes, and our felves and children,
" Have loft, or do not learn, for want of time,
" The fciences, that fhould become our country.

and the recapitulation thus thrown to the following lines, at left is no blemifh; indeed, in my opinion, is a Beauty.

XIV.

XIV.　Ibid. P. 433.　1 KING HENRY VI.

" Brandifh your *cryftal* treffes in the fky."

I have fometimes thought, we fhould read—*triftful*—perhaps Shakefpear wrote—

"　——　your treffes in the cryftal fky."

Certainly cryftal treffes is very aukward, not to fay worfe of it : though it is to be remember'd, they are not common treffes ; but the bright and fhining ones of Comets.

XV.　Ibid. P. 438.

" He being in the *vaward*—&c."—

The words immediately following make it neceffary to read—*rereward*—or fome word of like import.

XVI.　Ibid. P. 446.

" I'll canvafs thee in thy broad Cardinal's Hat."

Gloucefter ufes many low and vulgar expreffions in this Dialogue.　Particularly, he feems fond of fhowing his contempt of Winchefter's Ecclefiaftical Character ; by threatening to put the parts of his Cardinal's Habit to ridiculous ufes.　Thus afterwards he fays, he will ufe his fcarlet robe to carry him off in, like a child's mantle—that he'll trample on his Hat—and here, having threatened to fift and examine into all the bad parts of his character, he carries on the allufion too far ; and fays, (as if the thing was really to be done with a material *Sieve)* that he would ufe his broad Cardinal's Hat inftead of fuch an utenfil.

Canvaffing comes to have this fenfe of examining from the Canvafs ufed in the bottom of a Sieve.

XVII.

XVII. Ibid. P. 449.

For—*Went*—Read—*View*—

XVIII. Ibid. P. 495.

" 'Tis much when fcepters are in childrens hands,
" But more, when envy breeds unkind divifion ;
" There comes the ruin, there begins confufion."

Point and read thus—

" 'Tis much, when fcepters are in childrens hands,
" But envy breeds unkind divifion :
" There comes the ruin—&c."——i. e.

" When Children are Kings, 'tis *odds* but that
" the envy and emulation of thofe about them,
" breed divifions ; and this is the Ruin and Con-
" fufion, which we now are threatened with."

'Tis *much* but This produces That—is a common form of fpeech. But—'tis much there comes
—inftead of—'tis much *but* there comes—is not
Englifh. And—'tis *more* there comes—ufed in the
comparative degree, taken from—'tis much but
there comes—is ftill farther from being Englifh.
Befides, if the expreffion were allowed, the fenfe
would be very paltry and trivial: it would then
be—

Often, when children reign, and efpecially, if
envy breeds divifion, at fuch a time there comes
ruin and confufion——*Often?*—Why 'tis *always*
fo—Divifion in its nature tends to ruin and confufion.

XIX. Vol. 5. P. 60. 2 K. HENRY VI.

" —— a timely-parted *ghoft*"—

The *fenfe* here is plain enough ; and the *expref-*
fion, in a very loofe fenfe of it, may perhaps be juf-
I   tified.

tified. Methinks however, it were better to read—
"   ——— timely parted *coarse.*

XX.   Ibid. P. 101.

Perhaps, for — fell-*lurking* — it were better to
read—fell-*barking*—for they were not oppofing by
ftealth, and privately, but openly withftanding with
threats and menacing language.

XXI.   Ibid. P. 102.

" Wilt thou go dig a grave to find out war?"

The fenfe is—" Wilt thou, in thy old age, go
" to war, and feek death in the field of battle?"
Read therefore—

" Wilt thou go find-out war, to dig a grave?"

Conformable to which fentiment is the lamen-
tation of young Clifford for the death of his father
in the next fcene.

"   ——— Waft thou ordained, O dear Father,
" To lofe thy Youth in peace, and to atchieve
" The filver livery of advifed age;
" And in thy reverence, and thy chair-days thus
" To die in ruffian battle?"———

XXII.   Ibid. P. 103.

" And dying *mens* cries do fill the empty air."

This word—*mens*—comes in here fo as to lame
the meafure; and, in my opinion, to lower the
expreffion alfo. Would it not be more poetical to
fay—dying cries—?

XXIII.   Ibid. P. 142.   3 K. HENRY VI.

" (As if a channel fhould be call'd the fea.)"
Expunge the Parenthefis———

A *Chan-*

A *Channel* here means not—an Arm of the Sea—but—what we write now—*Kennell*—which fenfe, though it adds to the groffnefs, yet improves (indeed is neceffary to) the propriety of the fimilitude.

XXIV. Ibid. P. 312. K. RICHARD III.

" But how long fhall that *title*, ever, laft?"

I have fometimes fufpected, Shakefpear wrote,

" But how long fhall that *little* Ever laft?"

At left it muft be owned, that calling—Ever—a *Title*—inftead of—a *Word*—is fomewhat aukward: unlefs it may be underftood in a forenfic fenfe.

XXV. Ibid. P. 313.

" Which now, *two* tender bed-fellows for duft,
" Thy broken faith hath made a prey to worms."

The word—*two*—here is without any force; and—bed-fellows for duft made a prey to worms—is a poor repetition of the fame thing over again. It were better to read—

" Which now, *too* tender bed-fellows for Duft!
" Thy broken faith hath made a prey to worms."

Too tender for duft—i. e. Too young for the grave in the courfe of nature.

XXVI. Ibid. P. 344. KING HENRY VIII.

" ———— Each following day
" Became the *next*-day's mafter, till the *laft*
" Made former wonders *its*."

If this be the true reading, then by the word—*next*-day—we muft underftand, by an uncommon application of the phrafe—the *preceding* day—the day *next before* it—unlefs we imagine, that the defign

fign is to fay—" That each day became the *maf-*
" *ter* (i. e. the inftructor, the pattern) of that which
" was to fuccede it ; which is both hard, and un-
" natural ; and alfo lowers the fanfe of the paf-
" fage."

The intended meaning certainly is—" That each
" fucceding day became the mafter to the preceding
" one (i. e. overcame it—was fuperior to it) in the
" pomp and magnificence of its pageantry ; till
" the laft of all engrofs'd to itfelf all the admira-
" tion which was before given to the former days ;
" —made former wonders, *its.*—(i. e. *its own.*)

The Paffage, I apprehend, fhould be read thus ;
with the tranfpofition of only two words :

"   ———— Each following day
"   Became the *laft* day's mafter, till the *next*
"   Made former wonders, *its.*"

XXVII.   Ibid. p. 345.

" Order gave each thing view : The office did
" Diftinctly his full function."————

—i. e. Every part of the fhow was clearly feen and
perfectly comprehended by the fpectators ; both becaufe they were placed in due order, and alfo were
fully and completely executed.   The fenfe would,
I think, be more fully feen, if inftead of — *The*
office—we fhould read—*Each* office.—

XXVIII.   Ibid. p. 384.

"   ————————— *forty pence,* no :"

Read—" *for two-pence,* no :"   This completes
the fentence ; and two-pence is altogether as worthy a bett for the old Lady to lay, as forty pence.

XXIX.

XXIX. Ibid. P. 407.

" ———— Every function of your power
" Should, notwithstanding that your bond of
" duty,
" As 'twere in love's particular, be more
" To me your friend than any."

i. e. " You should use all your endeavours to do me service, upon the account of love towards me: (*in love's particular*) setting aside, not considering (*notwithstanding*) the obligation arising from the duty towards me as king.

An extraordinary and peculiar use this of—*notwithstanding!*

XXX. Ibid. P. 453.

It is very observable, that the measure throughout this whole Play has something in it peculiar; which will very soon appear to any one, who reads aloud; though perhaps he will not at first discover wherein it consists. Whether this particularity has been taken notice of by any of the numerous commentators on Shakespear, I know not: though I think it can scarcely escape the notice of any attentive pronouncer. If those, who have published this Author, have taken no notice of it to their readers, the reason may be; that they have chosen to pass-by in silence a matter, which they have not been able to account for. I think however, 'tis worth a few words.

1. There are in this Play many more verses, than in any other, which end with a redundant syllable—such as these:

" Healthful| and e|ver fince| a fresh| admi|rer.
" Of what| I saw| there an| untime|ly a|gue.

R   " I was

" I was| then pre|sent saw 'em| salute| on horse|-
    " back.
" In their| embrace|ment as| they grew | toge|-
    " ther—&c."—

The measure here ends in the syllables—mi—a
—horse—ge—and a good reader will, by a gentle
lowering of the voice, and quickening of the pronunciation, so contract the pairs of syllables—mirer
—ague—horseback—gether—as to make them
have only the force of one syllable each to a judicious hearer.

This Fact (whatever Shakespear's design was in
it) is undoubtedly true ; and may be demonstrated
to Reason, and proved to Sense : the first, by com-
paring any Number of Lines in this Play, with an
equal number in any other Play ; by which it will
appear, that this Play has very near *two* redundant verses, to *one* in any other Play. And, to
prove it to Sense ; Let any one only read aloud an
hundred lines in any other Play, and an hundred in
This ; and, if he perceives not the tone and cadence
of his own voice to be involuntarily altered in the
latter case from what it was in the former ; I would
never advise him to give much credit to the information of his ears.

Only take Cranmer's last prophetic speech about
Queen *Elizabeth* ; and you will find, that in the
49 lines which it consists of, 32 are redundant,
and only 17 regular. It would, I believe, be difficult to find any 50 lines together (out of this Play)
where there are even so many as 17 redundant.

2. Nor is this the only peculiarity of measure in
this play. The *Cæsuræ*, or Pauses of the verse, are
full as remarkable. The common Pauses in English verses are upon the 5th or the 6th syllable (the

                                                            6th

6th I think moſt frequently.) In this Play a great number of verſes have the Pauſe on the 7th ſyllable : ſuch as (in the aforeſaid ſpeech of *Cranmer*) are theſe :

" Which time ſhall bring to ripeneſs—ſhe ſhall
   " be.
" A pattern to all princes—living with| her.
" More covetous of wiſdom—and fair vir|tue.
" Shall ſtill be doubled on her—truth ſhall
   " nurſe| her.
" And hang their heads with ſorrow—good goes
   " with| her.
" And claim by thoſe their greatneſs—not by
   " blood.
" Nor ſhall this peace ſleep with her—but as
   " when.
" As great in admiration—as herſelf.
" Who from the ſacred aſhes—of her ho|nour.
" Shall be and make new nations—he ſhall
   " flou|riſh.
" To all the plains about him—childrens chil|-
   " dren.

3. Laſtly, it is very obſervable in the meaſure of this Play ; that the emphaſis, ariſing from the ſenſe of the verſe, very often claſhes with the cadence that would naturally reſult from the metre. i. e. ſyllables that have an emphaſis in the ſentence upon the account of the *ſenſe* or *meaning* of it, are put in the uneven places of the verſe ; and are in the ſcanſion made the firſt ſyllables of the foot, and conſequently ſhort : for the Engliſh foot is Iambic.

Take a few inſtances from the aforeſaid ſpeech.

" And all that ſhall ſuccede. Shĕbā was ne|ver.
R 2   " Than

" Than this bleſt ſoul ſhall be. all princely
  " gra|ces.
" Her foes ſhake, like a field of beaten corn.
" And hang their heads with ſorrow ; good
  " grows with| her.
" In her days, every man ſhall eat in ſafe|ty,
" Under his own vine what he plants, and ſing.
" Nor ſhall this peace ſleep with her ; but as
  " when.
" Wherever the bright ſun of heav'n ſhall ſhine.
" Shall be, and make new nations. He ſhall
  " flou|riſh.
" Shall ſee this, and bleſs heav'n."———

What Shakeſpear intended by all this, I fairly
own myſelf ignorant ; but that all theſe peculiarities were done by him advertently, and not by
chance ; is, I think, as plain to all ſenſe ; as that
Virgil intended to write Metre, and not Proſe, in
his Æneid.

If then Shakeſpear appears to have been careful
about meaſure ; what becomes of that heap of e-
mendations founded upon the preſumption of his
being either unknowing or unſollicitous about it ?
Alterations of this ſort ought ſurely to be made
more ſparingly, than has been done ; and never
without great harſhneſs indeed ſeems to require it,
or great improvement in the ſentiment is obtained
by it.

XXXI. Vol. 6. P. 35. KING LEAR.

" Does any here know me ? This is not Lear.
" Does Lear walk thus ? ſpeak thus ? where
  " are his eyes ?
" Either his notion weakens, his diſcernings
" Are lethargied—Ha ! waking !—'tis not ſo ;
" Who is it that can tell me who I am ?
                                        Lear's

"" Lear's fhadow ? I would learn ; for by the
    " marks
  " Of foveraignty, of knowledge, and of reafon,
"" I fhould be falfe perfuaded I had daughters.
  " Your name ? fair gentlewoman."——

  The whole force of thefe words is not perceived,
without fome attention ; and befides, I think, they
have been flightly corrupted. The import of them
I take to be—thus.

By Goneril's telling him in the preceding fpeech,
that through his choleric difpofition he is tranfported beyond himfelf ; he naturally falls into a taunting and ironical affent to that opinion, and confe-
quent affertion, That he is indeed not Lear.

  " Does any one know me—&c."—

  " Either my fenfes are weakened, and my dif-
" cernment ftupified ; or, if I am really *awake*,
" and have the due ufe of my faculties, 'tis as
" you fay, I am not Lear—*'tis not fo*."—
Here therefore, I would read—

  " Are lethargied ; *or*, waking, 'tis not fo."

  The Players, in all probability, loving an exclamation, which gives the Actor opportunity of
mouthing, and tearing things to tatters, made this
alteration, for that reafon ; in prejudice to the
fenfe. But, to procede.

The King, having faid he is not Lear, goes on—

  " Who is it that can tell me who I am ?"

Where I would rather it were—

  " Who is it then, can tell me who I am ?

At this point the Irony ceafes ; and the fpeech
takes a different caft, of ferious refentment. A
good Actor therefore would, by changing his man-

R 3   ner

ner and tone of voice, pronounce the remaining part of the fpeech, with a refolute firmnefs of tone and gefture, juft within the bounds of paffion ; and by that means give his audience a clear conception of the different genius of the two parts of this fpeech,

" Who then can tell me who I am ? What ? am
" I no more than Lear's *fhadow* ? (i. e. am I fo
" ufed by you, as if you thought me no more
" than fo) *I would learn* — I would fain be an-
" fwered as to this point ; for, if I were to be
" perfuaded by the marks of (i. e. the diftinction
" and refpect due to) my *fovereignty* (as king) my
" *knowlege* (as an old man, one of long experience)
" or my *reafon* (as a man, one of the fuperior fex ;)
" if from any of thefe confiderations I fhould ima-
" gine that *I had daughters* (and that you were
" one of them) it would appear that I was *falfly*
" *fo perfuaded* ; in as much as you give me not
" that reverence, which is due to me in any of
" thofe characters, of Kingfhip, Age, or Man-
" hood. Therefore furely you are not my daugh-
" ter, but a ftranger ; and as fuch I accordingly
" treat you, and demand — *Your name, fair gen-*
" *tlewoman ?*

All this fentiment, which cannot be explaned in words, without much circumlocution ; would be perceived intuitively by one gefture, one fignificant look of a judicious Actor.

XXXII. Ibid. P. 37.

" —— her mother's pains and benefits."

(i. e.) the pains of child-birth, and benefits both of nurfing and inftruction. The fmall difficulty here arifes from the word —*Pains*— being applica-ble to one perfon, and —*Benefits*— to another—The *Mother's* pain—The *Child's* benefit.

A moft

A most exquisite stroke of Nature here is in danger of being lost, only by being couched under one little syllable—HER——.

Lear is wishing to her child (if she is to have one) the severest curses, that can happen; to defeat and then destroy the natural pleasure which parents take in their children : that is, a froward and curst disposition both of mind and body : (for the words —*thwart, disnatured*—are so happily chosen, as to be applicable to both :) and suddenly, without giving the hearer any previous notice, he talks of the supposed child as a *Daughter*, not a *Son*. For so, I think, the passage ought to be understood; in order to give it it's full force. Not *only* ' Turn her ' mother's pains and benefits to laughter and con- ' tempt' (i. e.) make them ridiculous and contemptible to others *passively*, by the form and temper both of her body and mind; but also *actively*, by tauntingly and contemptuously undervaluing and setting them at naught. Nor do I think, that this is too much refining on this passage : for tho' the general character of Shakespear be justly that of an impetuous and incorrect writer; yet He will do him great injury, who shall apply this to all parts of his works indiscriminately : and particularly, the passion of Lear in this scene seems to me to be as much laboured, and as highly finished, as any passage in any writer. Any one, that reads it over attentively, will, I think, perceive; that the Sentiment is nicely and accurately studied, the language full, compleat and nervous, nothing in it superfluous, nothing lax or weak, every word is striking, and as exactly placed as it is judiciously chosen. In short, this passage seems to me, for true sublimity of spirit, and exact fulness and mag-

nificence

nificence of ftile, to be worthy of the higheft and
correcteft Genius of Antiquity.

XXXIII. Ibid. P. 39.

" You are much more *at tafk* for want of wif-
" dom,
" Than praife'd for harmful mildnefs."——

This has much the air of that of Cicero—*Salu-
taris rigor vincit inanem fpeciem clementiæ*—

At tafk—i. e.—blamed—cenfured—the word is
ftill ufed in this fenfe—to take one *to tafk*—i. e. to
reprehend—to animadvert on one with feverity.

—*harmful mildnefs*—ftronger than—*inanem fpeciem clementiæ.*

XXXIV. Ibid. P. 60.

" ———— O Regan, fhe hath tied
" Sharp-toothe'd unkindnefs, like a vulture,
" here."   (Points to his heart.)

There is fomething very hard and unnatural in
this expreffion, of tying unkindnefs to his heart ;
I fufpect, it fhould be read and pointed thus—

" ———— O Regan, fhe hath *tired*,
" (Sharp-tooth'd unkindnefs !) like a vulture—
" here."

i. e. She hath preyed on my heart——

' An hawke tyryth upon rumpes,
' She fedyth on all manere of flefhe.'

                    Jul. Barns de Re accipitrariâ.
The word occurs in our author 3 HENRY VI.
Vol. 5. p. 120. " Like an empty eagle *Tire* on
" the flefh of me and of my fon."

Unkindnefs, I conceive, here to have the force
of—*unnaturalnefs*—Kind and Nature—in the old
writers are fynonymous.

XXXV.

XXXV. Ibid. P. 82.

" —— the web and the pin"—Diforders of the Eye. Skinner explains them, as both names of the fame diforder.

A *Pin* or *Web* in the Eye. Male Higgin. *Suf-fufio.* Potius *Pterygium* feu *Unguis.* Credo ab Anglo-Sax. Pynban, Includere. Sic dictum quia totum oculum Claudit et Circumveftit. See Pin.

Gouldman explains Pterygium —— Vitium unguium vel oculi, cum ab eis caro recedit, et ad inftar alarum (πἰερυγίων) panditur excrefcendo. Eft et Pinna. A fkin growing from the corner of the Eye, and in continuance covering the fight.

Unguis (fays the fame Gouldman) is a difeafe in the Eye called a Haw ; and in his Englifh Dictionary for a Haw in a horfe's eye he gives us the Latin word Pterygium,

Skinner explains a Haw in the Eye a fimilitudine quadam fructûs vulgo dicti a Haw.

Sir T. H. to remark once for all on the Authority of his Gloffary, explains *Pin* in the very words of Nat. Bailey, Φιλολογ☉ : A horny induration of the membranes of the eye. In the other word *Web* indeed he ventures to deviate from his great mafter ; for whereas the aforefaid Philologift faith, it is a Spot or Pearl in the Eye ; his Pupil omitteth the words—*or Pearl*—and in the ftead thereof giveth us a Glofs of his own, defcriptive of the property of a fpot. *Web,* A fpot in the Eye, injurious to the fight.

XXXVI. Ibid. P. 132.

" —— *My* great employment
" Will not bear queftion."——

Thus reads Mr. Theobald, againft the concurrent

rent authority (as he confeſſes) of all the copies; which have—*thy* great employment (as he thinks) erroneouſly. I confeſs, I ſee no difficulty in the paſſage; but what is occaſioned by the comment.

In the firſt place—*thy* great employment will exactly as well admit of Theobald's own explication, as—*my* great employment: but—

In the ſecond place, this explication of his does not, I think, give us the true meaning of the words.

Edmund having whiſpered his deſign to the Captain (which was to kill Cordelia and Lear, as appears in a following ſpeech of his, " —— My Writ is on the life of Lear and of Cordelia") gives him the Note, which was to be his Warrant; and promiſes him promotion upon his execution of his inſtructions. The Captain however ſhows ſome diſmay and irreſolution; and therefore Edmund goes on to encourage him, by telling him—" that " men ſhould accommodate themſelves to the cir- " cumſtances of the times; and that tender-heart- " edneſs or compaſſion is not in character in a " ſoldier.

" —— know thou this, that men
" Are as the time is; to be tender-minded
" Does not become a ſword."——

But, ſeeing him ſtill wavering, he bids him either peremptorily promiſe to do it; or not engage at all in it: for that in ſuch kind of buſineſs as this a man ſhould be clear and determined.

" —— $\frac{my}{thy}$ great employment
" Will not bear *queſtion* (i. e. doubtfulneſs) ei-
   " ther ſay, thou'lt do't;
" Or thrive by other means."——

I

If

If there be any difficulty in this (as I confess I fee none) in the Closet, upon the Stage there would be none : for the Looks of the Actor would convey the fentiment more effectually, than any explanation can do.

XXXVII. Ibid. P. 144.

There is a vaft ftretch of invention, and confummate art, in this character of Lear ; and a particular and fine knowledge of nature is fhown in his laft appearance, and death in this fcene. He is reprefented as a man of the niceft fenfibility of mind ; and our compaffion for him is raifed to its highth, as well by the tender expreffions of his great love to his children, which are interfperfed in his fpeeches ; as by the reprefentation of his lamentable diftreffes. Indeed, the very outrageous expreffions of his refentment carry with them by implication the tendernefs of his affection ; in the feeling fenfe he fhows of his difappointment, that it was not returned towards him by his daughters.

We have feen him in the courfe of the play expreffing the moft furious tranfports of defperate rage ; pouring forth the bittereft curfes and imprecations, that I think human imagination is capable of conceiving ; and at length tranfported beyond the bearing of man's faculties ; and raifed from choler to downright madnefs. And, even in this fhattering of his fenfe and reafon, ftill giving the moft exquifite and piercing ftrokes of his quick and lively feeling of filial ingratitude.

Here, one would imagine, were *a Period :* and, far fhort of this, would have been one in any other

writer

writer but Shakespear. But he has still a reserve; another change in Lear, to a yet higher and more deplorable degree of distress, than he has yet suffered. The very fulness and perfection of misery, which (to use his own phrase) *tops Extremity*, is reserved for the last scene of his appearance.

Till the last and finishing stroke of Cordelia's death, Lear had kept-up the spirit and strength of his resentment; but here he is touched in such a point, as utterly afflicts and dismays him. From the highest struggles of fury and passion, he is here at once dejected and cast down to the lowest and most dispirited pitch of grief and desperation. Nothing now remains of his vigorous passion. All his expressions dwindle now into faintness and languor. His towering rage lowers and sinks into feeble despair; and his impetuous madness flags into sullen and unnerved stupefaction. The faculties of the mind, like the sinews of the body, become, by overstraining, weak, relaxed, and motionless.

XXXVIII.   Ibid. P. 380.   MACBETH.

" —— Light Thickens, and the Crow
" Makes way to th' *rooky* wood."——

This description of the close of day, by the circumstance of the *Crow's* flying toward the *Wood*, is very natural; and therefore beautiful. But the Crow flying to the *rooky* wood, is tautological: for Crow here must in a loose acceptation be taken for Rook.

I should rather imagine, Shakespear intended to give us the idea of the gloominess of the woods, at the close of the evening; and wrote—" Makes way
" to

" to th' *murky* (or *dusky*) wood :" words used by him on other like occasions, and not very remote from the traces of that in the text. This gives a Solemnity to the passage, of a piece with the other sentiments of this beautiful speech ; and proper to the occasion of it.

XXXIX. Ibid. P. 442. CORIOLANUS.

" Opinion, that so sticks on Martius, shall
" Of his demerits rob Cominius."

This passage, as it stands here, presents us with a strange kind of mock-reasoning.

Brutus and Sicinius are reasoning together about Martius's contenting himself with the *second* place in the army, leaving the *first* to Cominius. " Here-
" in (says Brutus) he acts prudently : for, Fame
" being his motive, and he having already an esta-
" blished Character, he by this means less risques
" the losing of it. For, in case of any miscar-
" riage, the fault will be thrown on Cominius,
" the General ; and giddy censurers will be apt
" enough to cry—It would have been otherwise ;
" if Martius had had the management !" To this observation Sicinius might very pertinently add the following : " That, moreover, if things should
" go well, the opinion of the people was so firmly
" fixed to Martius ; that he would certainly car-
" ry-off some part of the praise due to Cominius."
And this sense will be obtained by reading——

" ————— Besides, if things go well,
" Opinion, that so sticks on Martius,
" Shall of his Merits rob Cominius."——

Thus the passage goes-on very sensibly. Brutus remarks

remarks — " That by his *inferiority of place,* he
" would quit himself of all the *disgrace* of any *mif-*
" *carriage.*"—and Sicinius adds—" That by his
" *fuperiority in character,* he would poffefs himfelf
" of more than his true fhare of *merit* in any
" *fuccefs.*"

Or, probably, *Merit* and *Demerit* did in Shakefpear's time mean the fame thing; as they certainly did originally : the fuppofed oppofition in the
fenfe of thefe words being comparatively modern,
and as I apprehend altogether fantaftical.

INDEX

APPENDIX.

AS I have proved by a great number of examples, that these Canons are really drawn from Mr. Warburton's Edition of Shakespear; it may not be amifs to add a few inftances, to fhew; that, as much as he difowns them, he has actually proceeded by the fame rules; in his notes on other Authors, and in his other works.

I. In the tenth Book of Milton's Paradife loft, at line 23, he has given us a note; which may be referred to Canon IV. or VIII : for he quarrels with Milton for his fentiment; and gives no other reafon for his alteration, befides an affertion which is not true.

> ———— dim fadnefs did not fpare
> That time celeftial vifages; yet mix'd
> With pity violated not their blifs.

" Here pity is made to prevent their fadnefs
" from violating their blifs; but the latter paffion
" is fo far from alleviating the former, that it adds
" weight to it. If you read (mix'd with pity) in
" a parenthefis, this *crofs-reafoning* will be avoid-
" ed." WARB.

There is no need of this bungling parenthefis to avoid a crofs-reafoning, which is entirely Mr. Warburton's; who is fo unlucky, whenever he attempts to treat of the humane focial affections, that he feems an utter ftranger to them. How much more juft is Mr. Thyer's obfervation on this paffage; which fhews the difference of *feeling* between the

two

two Critic's ? " What a juft and noble idea (fays
" he) does our Author here give us of the bleffed-
" nefs of a benevolent temper; and how proper at
" the fame time to obviate the objection, that
" might be made of fadnefs dwelling in heavenly
" fpirits."

I think, I need not afk; which of thefe two Gentlemen beft underftood Milton, and the fubject he
was treating of.

Here too his friend Dr. Newton contradicts
him; and he muft be contradicted by every heart,
that feels what the meltings of a benevolent compaffion are.

II. We have a like inftance in his note on Book
VI. line 251.

—with huge two-handed fway, &c.

" It fhews, how entirely the ideas of chivalry and
" romance had poffeffed him; to make Michael
" fight with a two-handed fword. The fame idea
" occafioned his expreffing himfelf very obfcurely
" in the following lines of his Lycidas:

But that two-handed engin at the door
Stands ready to fmite once, and fmite no more.

" Thefe are the laft words of Peter, predicting
" God's vengeance on his Church by his miniftry.
" The making him the minifter, is in imitation of
" the Italian Poets; who in their fatiric pieces
" againft the Church, always make Peter the mi-
" nifter of vengeance. The *two-handed engin* is
" the two-handed Gothic fword, with which the
" Painters draw him. *Stands ready at the door*
" was *then* a common phrafe, to fignifie a thing im-
" minent. To *fmite once, and fmite no more*, figni-
" fies, *a final deftruction*; but alludes to Peter's fin-
" gle ufe of his fword, in the cafe of the High-
" Prieft's fervant." WARB.

Now

Now this tedious homily on thofe lines in Lyci-das is nothing but a heap of miftakes or mifrepre-fentations, of conceit and refinement; which caft a fhade, inftead of light, on a paffage; which was not obfcure, till Mr. Warburton made it fo.

1. Here is no prediction of Peter, of vengeance againft *God's church*; but it is againft negligent and unfaithful minifters.

2. Whatever the Italian poets do in their fatiric pieces, which have nothing to do here, Milton gives not the leaft hint, that this vengeance is to be executed by *Peter's miniftry*.

3. The two-handed Gothic fword is not gene-rally, if ever, the attribute of Peter, but of Paul; as being the inftrument of his martyrdom. Peter is ufually, and particularly in this place, reprefent-ed with his proper attribute *the Keys*.

> Laft came and laft did go
> The Pilot of the Galilean lake;
> Two maffy keys he bore of metals twain,
> The golden opes, the iron fhuts amain.

4. That *ftands ready at the door* was *then* a com-mon-phrafe to fignify a *thing imminent*, is not true; it *then* fignified, and ftill fignifies, *ready at hand for ufe*. If Mr. Warburton were going to ride-out, and fhould afk his fervant, whether his horfe were *imminent* or not; he muft be well fkill'd in this *worft fort of critical jargon*, if he underftood his mafter; and yet I believe, he would apprehend the meaning of that queftion, as foon as any groom in Milton's time.

5. If to *fmite once, and fmite no more*, fignifies a final deftruction; how can it allude to Peter's fin-gle ufe of his fword, in the cafe of the High Prieft's

fervant; where he only cut-off an ear? in defcribing which Hiftory, no tolerable Painter would
give him a two-handed Gothic fword.

After all this pother about nothing, the allufion moft probably is to the fword ufed in criminal
executions; and Milton feems to have been poffeffed
not with ideas of *chivalry* and *romance*, as Mr. Warburton fays, but fuch as are taken from Scripture;
which *he* was no ftranger to: and when one confiders the perfons whom St. Peter threatens, and the
vengeance threatened; it feems plain, that Milton
had in his eye that paffage in the XXIVth of Mat-
thew v. 50, 51.

The Lord of that fervant fhall come in a day when he
looketh not for him—and fhall cut him afunder, and
appoint him his portion with the hypocrites.

III. Again, under Canon VIII. we may rank
the following note on Milton, Book I. line 684.

—by him firft
Men alfo, and by his fuggeftion taught,
Ranfack'd the centre. —

" Dr. Bentley fays, the Poet affigns as two caufes
" *him* and *his fuggeftion*; which are one and the
" fame thing. This obfervation has the appear-
" ance of accuracy. But Milton is exact; and al-
" ludes in a beautiful manner to a fuperftitious
" opinion generally believed among the miners:
" that there are a fort of Devils, which converfe
" much in minerals; *where* they are frequently
" feen to bufy themfelves in all the operations
" of the workmen: they will dig, cleanfe, melt,
" and feparate the metals. See G. Agricola de
" Animantibus fubterraneis. So that Milton poe-
" tically

" tically fuppofes Mammon and his Clan to have
" taught the Sons of earth by example, and prac-
" tical inftruction; as well as precept, and mental
" fuggeftion." Warb.

Notwithftanding all the *appearance of accuracy*,
Dr. Bentley's obfervation is a Hypercritical miftake. *Him and his fuggeftion*, mean, indeed, *one
and the fame thing*; but are not affigned by the Poet
as *two caufes*, but as *one* only. We have the like
expreffions commonly in profe, " *It was you and
your perfuafion, that made me do fo or fo.*" It was
" *he and his example, which influenced others*; &c."
And we meet with a paffage in Book XI. line 261.
very like this:

> To *thefe* that fober race of men, whofe lives
> Religious titled them the Sons of God,
> Shall yield up all their virtue, all their fame
> Ignobly, *to the trains and to the fmiles
> Of thefe fair Atheifts.*——

As to Mr. Warburton's dream about devil-miners;
it really does not deferve a ferious notice. It is
more worthy of *his* † *prophefying Aunts*, than the
divine Milton; and ferves only to fhew, that he has
read, or feen quoted, G. Agricola: Or, what is
moft likely, has, *among his younger amufements*, when
he was writing notes and emendations on Poets,
ftudied the Frontifpiece to *Hales'* Golden Remains.
There he wou'd not only read-of, but fee thefe
Devil-miners; and fee too, what they are compared to: which is indeed worth his attending-to:
Mr. Hales tranflated the paffage from G. Agricola;
and this tranflation is copied by Mr. W, with all
it's peculiarities; efpecially that of ufing *Minerals*
for *Mines*: which nobody now does.

S 2   I.V. An

† See the Gloffary.

IV. An example to Canon IX. he gives us in *the last edition* of the Dunciad. Book IV. line 444:

> A drowzy Watchman; that juſt gives a knock,
> And *breaks our reſt*, to tell us what's a clock.

Verſe 444. And breaks, *&c.*

i. e. " When the feaſt of life is juſt over, calls
" on us to think of breaking-up; but never watches
" to prevent the diſorders that happen in the heat
" of the entertainment." WARB.

One would think our Critic was *aſleep*, when he wrote this note; how elſe, not to mention the propriety or probability of a Watchman's coming into Gentlemens houſes, *to prevent the diſorders which may happen in the heat of an entertainment*; I ſay, how elſe could he dream; that, *being impertinently waked out of a ſound ſleep*, and *being called upon to go home after ſupper is over*, were the ſame idea?

In the preceding note on theſe words, Mr. Warburton has vented his ſpleen againſt a worthy Gentleman in ſuch a manner; as to give us an example at once to the XVIIth and XXIId Canons. This was taken notice of in a Letter publiſhed in one of the Daily papers of February 1749. which the Reader will find at the end of the Appendix.

I could add ſeveral other Examples out of his Notes on Milton, not leſs worthy of our Obſervation; but theſe are ſufficient for a ſample, and I have neither leiſure nor inclination to follow as far as he will lead.

V. Examples to Canon XVII.

The licence of abuſe mentioned under this Canon being the Profeſſed Critic's undoubted privilege, he may. call any perſon whom he diſlikes,

* a Gen-

* a Gentleman of the Dunciad,
* a Muſhroom,
* a Gentleman of the laſt edition,
* a Grubſtreet critic run to ſeed.   And,
* a Libeller.

But I would adviſe him to be cautious, how he uſes the laſt appellation ; becauſe he may chance to meet with ſome people, who, not knowing, or not allowing his *privilege,* may very uncritically move for an Information againſt him in the Court of King's Bench.

And if the terms he chooſes to employ are ſo groſs, that he is aſhamed to uſe them in Engliſh ; he may call his betters *Son of a Bitch,* or any other hard name, in *Latin,* with ſome ſucceſs ; though his reputation for *wit* and *good manners* will not extend quite ſo far, as if the complement had been made in the vulgar tongue.

Thus Mr. Warburton has publiſhed the following extract from one of Horace's Epodes before two pamphlets, called *Remarks on ſeveral Occaſional Reflections,* &c. and printed, the one in 1744, and the other in 1745; applying it to the ſeveral Gentlemen, whom he there anſwers. Now, as there is luck in odd numbers, I would recommend it to his uſe a third time before his next Edition of the Dunciad ; and here ſubjoin a tranſlation of it, that he may have the reputation, and the world may ſee the whole force, of that fine complement he paid to Dr. Middleton, Dr. Pococke, Dr. Richard Grey, Dr. Akinſide, Dr. Sykes, Dr. Stebbing, and other Gentlemen, in the application of theſe lines to them :

S 3   Quid

* * * * * See the laſt Edition of the Dunciad, Book IV. p. 76.

Quid immerentes hofpites vexas, CANIS,
  Ignavus adverfum lupos ?
    *   *   *   *   *   *   *

Nam qualis aut Moloffus, aut fulvus Lacon,
  AMICA VIS PASTORIBUS,
Agam per altas aure fublatâ nives,
  Quæcunque præcedet Fera.
Tu, quum timendâ voce complefti nemus,
  Projectum odoraris CIBUM.

                      HOR. Epod. VI.

Here are the characters of two *Puppies*; one
Mr. Warburton gives to the Gentlemen mentioned
above, the other he applies to himfelf : but to divide and choofe, is not quite fair ; let the reader
judge, which fits each. I procede to the tranflation;

To kennel, *Looby!* yelping Cur,
Teafing the harmlefs paffenger ;
  While your great Mafter's fheep,
Thofe two fair flocks, unguarded ftray,
To foxes and to wolves a prey ;
  Thofe flocks, you're fed to keep.

See faithful *Trueman*, honeft hound,
Far from the Sheep-cotes all around,
  Chafe every ravenous beaft ;
You,—when the Hills and Vales have rung,
With echo of your tatling tongue,
  Turn tail and fcent the feaft.

  Note, *the two* flocks *in this allegory feem to mean*
preferments; *perhaps*, a Chapel in Town *and* a
Living in the Country; *and* the Feaft, Profit in
general.
  To conclude. I thought it a piece of Juftice
due to the memory of Shakefpear, to the reputa-
                                    tion

tion of Letters in general, and of our Englifh language in particular; to take fome public notice of a performance, which I am forry to fay has violated all thefe refpects. Had this been done by a common hand, I had held my peace; and left the work to that oblivion, which it deferves: but when it came out under the fanction of two great names, that of our moft celebrated modern Poet, and that of a Gentleman, who had by other writings, how juftly I fhall not now examine, obtained a great reputation for learning; it became an affair of fome confequence: chimerical conjectures and grofs miftakes were by thefe means propagated for truth, among the ignorant and unwary; and that was * eftablifhed for the *genuine* text, nay the *genuine* text *amended* too, which is neither Shakefpear's nor Englifh.

As fuch a proceding is of the utmoft ill confequence to Letters; I cannot but hope, that this reprehenfion of it will meet with excufe from all unprejudiced judges; and then I fhall have my end: which was to defend Shakefpear, and not to hurt his Editor more than was neceffary for that defenfe.

And now I hope, I have taken my leave of Mr. Warburton and his works; at left unlefs, to complete the maffacre of our beft Englifh Poets, he fhould take it into his head to murder Spenfer; as he has Shakefpear, and in part Milton too; for, by the fpecimen we have left, I cannot with Dr. Newton bewail the lofs of the reft of his annotations on that Poet; though perhaps I and every body elfe may † " apprehend, what is become of them." Upon the whole, I leave it to the Public to judge which has been engaged AGAINST Shakefpear,

S 4   Mr.

* See Mr. Warburton's Title-page.
† See the Preface to Dr. Newton's Milton.

Mr. Warburton, or I, who have, in part at left, vindicated that best of Poets from the worst of Critics; from one, who has been guilty of a greater violation of him, than that, on the authors of which he imprecated vengeance in his Epitaph;

And curs'd be he, that moves my bones.

A violation, which, were he not arm'd against the * superstition of believing in Portents and Prodigies, might make him dread the apparition of that much injured bard.   But

Carmine Di superi placantur, carmine Manes;

and, as much as Mr. Warburton thinks me his enemy, I will endeavour to appease the indignant Ghost by the following

S O N N E T :

"Rest, †rest, perturbed Spirit!" hence no more
  (Not unchastis'd at left, if aught I can)
   The half learn'd Pedant shall, allur'd by gain,
Retale his worthless drofs for thy pure ore;

Deferv'd contempt the vengeful Muse shall pour
   On that bold Man, who durst thy works profane;
   And thy chaste page pollute with mungrel strain,
Unlicens'd jargon, run from Gallia's shore.

---

  * See a Critical and Philosophical Enquiry into the causes of Prodigies and Miracles, printed 1727.
   † Hamlet.

Reign he fole King in Paradoxal Land,
And for Utopia plan his idle fchemes
Of vifionary Leagues, Alliance vain
Twixt * WILL. and WARBURTON; and with rafh hand
On Peers and Doctors force his ‡ thrice told dreams:
Let him do aught——but thy fair beauties ftain.

* The whole argument, by which the Alliance between Church
and State is eftablifhed, Mr. Warburton founds upon this fuppofition ; " that people, confidering themfelves in a religious ca-
" pacity, may contract with themfelves, confidered in a civil
" capacity." The conceit is ingenious ; but is not his own.
Scrub in Farquhar's *Beau's Stratagem* had found it out long ago ;
he confiders himfelf, as acting the different parts of all the fervants in the family ; and fo *Scrub* the Coachman, Ploughman,
or Juftice's Clerk, might contract with *Scrub* the Butler, for fuch
a quantity of Ale as the other affumed character demanded.

‡ The firft Edition of the Alliance came out without a dedication, but was prefented to all the Bifhops ; and, when nothing
came of that, the Second was addreffed to both the Univerfities ;
and, when nothing came of that, the Third was dedicated to a
Noble Earl ; and nothing has yet come of that.

Feb.

A LETTER

To———— ————— ————.

SIR,

MR. Warburton, in his new Edition of the Dunciad, has given the world a sample of what it is to expect from the consequences of Mr. Pope's legacy to him ; among other improvements, he has made that Poem a vehicle of his own private resentments against persons, whom Mr. Pope either knew not at all, or lived in friendship with : One of the latter he has abused in his notes, for no other crime ; than for shewing to the world his disapprobation of a book, published since Mr. Pope's death ; and which, as the Author has contrived it, reflects a disgrace on his memory ; but of this, perhaps, he may hear another time : my present complaint against him is for abusing a Gentleman of known merit, for no apparent reason in the world ; by misrepresenting a little passage in one of the handsomest complements to Mr. Warburton's best friend, that ever was made to Man ; and *that* made in better language, than Mr. Warburton ever could write.

The note I mean is on these words, Book IV. P. 50.

The common Soul, of Heav'n's more frugal make,
Serves but to keep Fools pert, and Knaves awake.
A drowzy Watchman ; that just gives a knock,
And breaks our rest, to tell us what's a Clock.

3   R E-

REMARKS.

" Verfe 443. A drowzy Watchman, &c. Thefe
" two lines ftood originally thus :

" And moft but find that Centinel of God
" A drowzy Watchman in the Land of Nod.

" But to this there were two Objections; the
" pleafantry was too low for the Poet, and a
" deal too good for the Goddefs. For though,
" as he told us before, *Gentle Dulnefs ever loves a*
" *joke*; and, as this fpecies of Mirth arifes from a
" Mal-entendu, we may well fuppofe it to be much
" to her tafte; yet this above is not genuine, but
" a mere counterfeit of wit; as we fhall fee by
" placing by the fide of it one of her own Jokes,
" which we find in the Rev. Mr. B———'s late Sa-
" tire upon Bath in the following words: Virum,
" quem non ego fane doctiffimum, at certè om-
" nium quotquot fuere ufpiam Literatiffimum ap-
" pellare aufim. And look, the more refpectable
" the Subject, the more grateful to our Goddefs
" is the Offering."

Scribler.

The Paffage ridiculed by the Scribler, as he
properly calls himfelf, is in a Letter called, *A Jour-
ney to Bath*, not *A Satire on Bath*: printed in the
year 1748: where, after a Defcription of the idle
lives, which the generality of people live there,
follows this Poftcript.

" Sed heus ευρηκα! tandem inveni Virum; in-
" ftar mille unum. Facile fcias eum mihi placuiffe,
" quem acceperam teftimonio commendatum tuo:
" Virum, inter Bathonienfes fuos faeile principem;
" quem undequaque praefentem parietes ipfi medius
" fidius

" fidius loquuntur : quem illuſtrat glorioſa nata-
" lium obſcuritas, fortunae eundem et virtutis
" filium; τον αυτοφυη, τον αυτοδιδακτον, και αυτοτελη.
" Virum, quem non ego ſane doctiſſimum, at certe
" omnium quotquot fuere uſpiam reperiuntur Li-
" teratiſſimum appellare auſim ; et ex commercio
" ſuo literario fructus pro merito uberrimos ſine
" invidia conſecutum."

Which elegant complement, for the benefit of
thoſe, who may chance to underſtand the original
as little as Mr. Warburton ſeems to reliſh it, I
ſhall endeavour to tranſlate ; though I cannot do
juſtice to it.

" P. S. But ſtay—I have at laſt found a Man;
" one worth a thouſand. You will believe, that it
" was natural for me to be pleaſed with a perſon
" whoſe character you recommended to me ; A
" man, by far the chief among all his fellow-citi-
" zens, whoſe preſence among them the very
" walls every where proclame; whom the want
" of high birth renders the more illuſtrious, and
" ſhews him to be at once the Child of Virtue, and
" the Favourite of Fortune ; ſelf-formed, ſelf-
" taught, and ſelf-complete. A Man, whom one
" may call, if not the moſt learned, yet certainly
" above compariſon with moſt a man of letters ;
" and one, who by his literary commerce has
" deſervedly acquired an ample and unenvied for-
" tune."

. Is not here a moſt juſt and amiable picture drawn
of Mr. Allen ? A Gentleman whoſe character is
too univerſally known and eſteemed ; to need any
commendations of mine : much leſs can it receive
any honor from ſuch groſs incenſe, as is awkwardly
offered him by this Note-writer. It is true, there is
a little ſort of pun in it; but a pun, which Tully
himſelf

himself need not have been afhamed of in the freedom of epiftolary writing; and fuch, as nothing but malice or dulnefs itfelf could conftrue into a defign'd affront upon Mr. Allen: efpecially, as it introduces that elegant complement in the conclufion, which Mr. Warburton by a partial quotation induftrioufly fuppreffed. If I were now to afk Mr. Warburton, why this unprovoked undeferved attack upon a Gentleman; who juft at this very juncture is exerting himfelf in the caufe of Letters and of his Country; who has fhewn more true tafte of the Ancients, and more true fpirit and elegance, than have appeared in any writings a great while; I doubt, the anfwer muft be in his words above, "Look, the more RESPECTABLE "the Subject, the more grateful to our Goddefs "is the Offering.

Lately

AN
ACCOUNT

OF THE

TRIAL

OF THE

Letter Υ, *alias* Y.

Printed in the Year M.DCC.LVIII.

PREFACE.

THE following little piece cannot require a long preface; it is publifhed
with a defign to put Gentlemen of learning
and leifure in mind, of fettling the orthography of our language. This is a matter, furely
worthy the attention of all who would write
correctly; which every man ought to do, at
leaft in his Mother-tongue; and therefore it
cannot be reckoned either trifling or pedantic
to attend to it: Yet fo it is, that our language
is perhaps paft it's higheft pitch of perfection;
before we have any certain rule or manner
of writing it.

The French have fettled their fpelling; but,
in doing it, they, by too great a regard to
their pronunciation, have, I think, disfigured
their language; and in numberlefs inftances
loft all traces of the Etymology of their words.
Sir Roger L'eftrange imitated their manner;
and, had his licentious way of fpelling been
generally followed, our Englifh had not been
now a language, but a jargon.

T

The

The two chief things hinted-at in this piece are, Uniformity in spelling, where the reasons from derivation are the same; and, Preserving, as much as possibly may be, the marks of our Etymology; both which, I apprehend, are necessary to the rendering any language fixed and easily intelligible. Modes of pronunciation may vary; but orthography, settled upon true principles, will last as long as the language continues.

A N

AN
ACCOUNT
OF THE
TRIAL, &c.

ONCE on a time the Englifh Commonwealth of Letters, generally called the Alphabet, was very much difturbed; that a certain Greek letter, whofe real name was * Υψιλον, had, contrary to the libertys and privileges of the Englifh letters, infinuated himfelf into the Englifh language; and invaded the province of an Englifh letter: utterly excluding the faid letter from feveral fyllables, wherein he ought of right to exercife his office.

The Vowel I was the letter chiefly concerned in point of intereft: he found himfelf wholly excluded from all jurifdiction in the end of words; and not only fo, but he was frequently banifhed from the middle; infomuch that in Chaucer's time this fugitive Greek had ufurped his power in *Wyfe, Lyfe, Knyght,* and innumerable other inftances; and almoft thruft him out of the Englifh language:

---

* Wherever in this Trial the Greek character Υ occurs, it fhould be read Hupfilon.

therefore,

therefore, in a convention of the letters, he declared ; that he could no longer bear this forein usurpation : and conjured them, as they valued the privileges of the Englifh Alphabet, which were fo notorioufly violated by this ϒ, under the name of Y ; (whofe example if others fhould follow, they had reafon to apprehend the moft fatal confequences from a Greek inundation :) that they would join with him in a petition and remonftrance to Apollo ; in order to regain his right, and have his jurifdiction fettled.

The majority of the Alphabet heartily clofed-in with the propofal ; fome of them indeed from private views, and in hopes to regain fome provinces, which they thought invaded by other letters : the moft public-fpirited amongft them thought, that fuch a remonftrance might be very advantageous ; as it would open the way to a general reformation : and be a means to fettle their refpective powers, and prevent private quarrels and incroachments on one another ; as well as fecure them againft a forein invafion.

H was not very much inclined to have matters examined into ; for fear leaft he fhould be degraded into a fimple afpiration : but was at laft prevailed-on to join in the petition by P and T, with whom he was collegue in the government of fome provinces ; and who told him, they were all equally in danger of being fupplanted by [a] Φ and [b] Θ ; who, as they were credibly informed, were come-over incognito for that purpofe.

The whole Alphabet having at length agreed, fome through fear, fome through private pique, and others from public views ; a petition was

[a] Phi.   [b] Theta.

drawn,

drawn, and figned by the Vowels firft, and then by the Confonants according to their feniority, reprefenting the illegal incroachments of ϒ, alias Y, upon the Englifh privileges ; and praying, that Apollo would fix a day for hearing the complaint of I againft the faid ϒ.

Apollo very readily granted the petition, affigned a day of hearing, and ordered ϒ to appear ; at the fame time declaring, that, if any other members of the Alphabet had any grievances to complain-of, he would then hear and redrefs them.

This declaration met with different reception, according to the different interefts of parties ; fome repented their figning the petition ; but it was too late to go back : and now the whole Alphabet was bufied, in preparing either to defend or inlarge their refpective provinces.

When the day of hearing was come, and the Court fate ; the Vowel I began in a pompous oration to fhew, that, notwithftanding ϒ was in reality a Greek letter, and had no right to a place in the Englifh Alphabet ; yet he had wrongfully intruded himfelf into it, and did actually take on him the place and power of I in numberlefs inftances, to the difinherifon of the faid I.

He reprefented ; " that, even in the beginning of words, where Y was frequently ufed, it was the real power and office of I ; that *year, yoke, you, Yorke,* &c. were pronounced, and ought to be written, *iear, ioke, iou, iorke,* &c.

" As to the middle of words, he infifted ; that, though fuch incroachments had indeed been more frequent in former times ; yet Y had ufurped his place, and ftill continued to act as I, in many words ; as *dying, flying, denying,* &c.

T 3   " And

" And for the ends of words, he was totally excluded from any place there, though the power was his in *Majesty*, *Liberty*; in, what he still valued more than either, *Lady*; in short, in all other instances where Y is generally used.

" That he apprehended it a notorious violation of English privilege; that a fugitive Greek, whose real power in his own country gave not even the least umbrage for such a clame; should thus insolently take upon him the power and jurisdiction of an English Vowel: and concluded; that he hoped, Apollo would grant him justice against this intruder: and, if he did not banish him from the English Alphabet, that he would confine him to the power of U; to which he had a much juster pretense."

U was so shocked at this unexpected motion; that, before he could recover himself enough to make any defense, E rose-up and seconded what had been said by I; beginning with scurrilous reflexions on the shape and figure of ϒ, which he compared to the Cross or *Furca* used in ancient executions: for which being reprimanded by the Court, he desired, that he might be appointed collegue with I to supplie the place of ϒ in the ends of words; according to several precedents which he quoted.

U now thought it high time for him to speak; and therefore rose-up, and with some precipitation represented the surprise he was under; to hear an insinuation, so destructive to English privilege, and so particularly injurious to himself, and that without the least ground, from a Vowel, who pretended to defend the Rights of the English Alphabet.

3

He

He pleaded; that "the same place and powers, which ϒ had in the Greek language, he stood fully intitled-to in the English; and that therefore of right he ought to be possessed of the place of ϒ even in all Greek words anglicised, as *System, Hypocrite, Hypothesis*, and the like."

ϒ, alias Y, modestly urged in his defense; "That they, who cast such illiberal reflexions on his figure, were ignorant of, or had forgotten, the deep mysterys which Pythagoras tells them are represented by it; that Custom, the great Arbiter of languages, had established him in those rights and privileges which he enjoyed; and tho' formerly they were much larger, yet when Custom abridged him of that extent of sway which he possessed in Chaucer's time, who was the great reformer and refiner of the English language, though then he might have pleaded possession time out of mind, yet he submitted without repining.

"That he could not but wonder at the ingratitude of the English Alphabet; in shewing so much spleen against the Greeks, from whom they derive their being; nay, without whose assistence they have not so much as a name; except one coined by old nurses, and borrowed by them from the * superstition of Popery.

"That, whatever might be determined as to his power and place in words properly English; he thought he had an indisputable right to keep his place in all Greek words anglicised; since, though it might not be agreable to the English pride, it was highly consonant to reason; that such words should bear the character of the language, from whence they are derived.

* The Christ's-cross-row.

T 4

Apollo

Apollo, after having heard all fides, gave his determination to this effect. "That the jealoufy, " which the Englifh Alphabet, and I in particu- " lar, had fhewn againft Υ, proceded indeed from " a laudable motive, a concern for their libertys ; " but feemed in reality entirely groundlefs : for " that Y, in all the Inftances given by I, had " nor ufurped his power ; but was indeed only a " deputy to, or more properly a different cha- " racter of I ; the power remaining wholly his : " that particularly in *dying, flying,* and the partici- " ples of all verbs ending in IE, Y was put there " only as a reprefentative of IE ; to prevent the " unfightly clufter of vowels, which would be " huddled together in *dieing, flieing,* &c."

Therefore, to prevent future difputes between the faid partys, he ordained ;

" That Y be never admitted into the middle of " Englifh words ; except in fuch participles as a- " forefaid, where he reprefents IE : provided ne- " verthelefs, that he always exercife his power of " Υ in Greek words made Englifh ; as *Style, Syftem,* " *Hypocrite, Hypothefis,* &c.

" That he act as a different character of I in " *Yoke, Year, Yorke,* and fuch like words.

" And that he ftand as the reprefentative of I or " IE, wherever they end a word ; except in mo- " nofyllables, where there is no other vowel ; as " *die, tie, lie,* &c."

This matter being thus adjudged and deter- mined, feveral Petitions and Remonftrances were prefented from other members of the Alphabet.

The Crofs-petitions of D, and TH ; each fide complaining, that the other had wrongfully taken his place in the word *Murder* or *Murther.*

" Referred

" Referred to a Committee of Anglo-Saxons,
" to determine the rights of each Complainant;
" and in the mean time the Poets had liberty given
" them to ufe either, as would beft fuit their
" rhime."

The Petition of UGH to be reftored to the end
of the words *Tho'* and *Thro'*.

The prayer of this petition granted; " and a
" Cenfure was paffed upon Sir Roger L'eftrange,
" who in a foolifh imitation of the French intro-
" duced their new-fangled way of leaving-out fuch
" letters as are not pronounced; whereby the lan-
" guage is maimed and disfigured, and the Ety-
" mology of words in danger of being loft."

The complaint of I againft E, for ufurping his
place in the words *entitle*, *entire*, &c.

Partly allowed to be juft; and accordingly " E
" was ordered to quit all pretenfions to the be-
" ginning of words compounded of the prepofi-
" tion IN; but, as to *Entire*, I was defired to
" take notice; that it being derived immediately
" from the French *entier*, his clame to that was
" not fo well grounded."

The Petition of S to be reftored to his place in
Defence, *Pretence*, &c. (words derived from the Su-
pines of Latin Verbs ending in DO) which the
Letter C had unreafonably taken from him.

Granted.

The complaint of O againft U for intruding
into the words *Honour*, *Labour*, *Superiour*, *Gover-
nour*, and the like.

" The Judge difcharged U with a reprimand
" from the final Syllable of all words derived
" from the Latines ending in OR; but, as for
" *Governer*; he faid, they neither of them had
" any thing to do there; it being an Englifh Sub-
" ftantive

" ftantive formed immediately from the Verb *Go-*
" *vern:*" and therefore he affigned that province
to E, and ordered him " to take poffeffion both
" in that and all fuch words."

The Complaint of E againft A, for intruding
into the Adjective *Left.*

E, to make good his fole clame to that word,
had brought into Court the opinion of the celebrated Dr. Wallis, exprefs in point ; that *Left,* being a contraction of *Leffeft,* ought to be fpelled
without an A ; and that the Conjunction might
for diftinction's fake be written with one.

Apollo, after he had read it, declared ; that
" He could not make a jufter Decree : and imme-
" diately ordered A to quit his place in the Ad-
" jective, and enter into the Conjunction."

Another Complaint of E againft A, for thrufting
himfelf into the words *Extream,* and *fupream.*

" Apollo banifhed A ; and gave E a double
" power in *Extreme, fupreme,* &c."

A Petition from the Letter N, praying that G
might be excluded from the words *Foreign* and
fovereign.

Upon hearing this Petition read, A immediately
joined in it ; and begged, that both E and I might
be banifhed from thofe words ; and himfelf admitted
in their room. For the latter word he brought the
Authority of Milton, who fpells it *fovran* ; and
infifted, that, the other being derived from the
Latin *Foraneus,* he had the fame equitable clame
to it.

G on the other fide maintained, that both words
were originally formed from *Regnum* ; *fuper regnum,* and *foris regno :* and therefore, if any of the
Letters fhould be banifhed, it ought to be I.

" Apollo

" Apollo faid, he had a very great refpect for
" the Authority of his beloved fon Milton ; and
" would take time to confider the cafe : in the
" mean while people fhould be at liberty to fpell
" thofe words which way they liked beft. But
" he was obferved to fmile rather contemtuoufly,
" at G's abfurd affertion."

When A heard the great opinion that Apollo
had of Milton, he pulled-out a Petition to be re-
lieved againft the incroachment of I ; who had
forced himfelf into *Parliament,* contrary to the Authority of Milton ; who always writes it *Parla-
ment :* But he was prevaled-upon to withdraw his
Petition, by his adverfary ; who whifpered him,
that he had better not move that matter ; for fear
leaft they fhould be both banifhed, and the province affigned to E ; who in truth had a better
right to it than either. However, before he fat
down, he put-in a complaint againft U ; for
wrongfully driving him out of the word *Farther,*
without the left pretenfe of reafon or cuftom to
fupport his clame.

U being called-upon to defend himfelf, faid ;
that it was but a very little while, that he had taken
poffeffion of that word ; that he did it, upon the
Authority of fome celebrated modern Authors ;
and he hoped, their Authority would be allowed
by the Court.

" I will never, faid Apollo with fome indigna-
" tion, allow of the Authority of men ; who
" write, before they can fpell. If you have no
" clame to the pofitive *Far,* what pretence can you
" have to the comparative *Farther ?* "

A Remonftrance from TH ; reprefenting, that
S had ufurped his place in the end of the third
perfon fingular of verbs.

Apollo

Apollo declared, " that he thought this a very
" great irregularity ; as it addeth very much to
" that hiffing, which is fo much complained-of
" in the language by foreiners ; that he wifhed,
" Cuftom would entirely abrogate it ; in the
" mean time he ordered TH to keep poffeffion in
" all Prayers and folemn acts of Worfhip, and cen-
" fured thofe young Divines, who, notwithftand-
" ing Mr. Addifon's reproof, will continue to
" read *pardons* and *abfolves* ; inftead of *pardoneth*
" and *abfolveth*."

The Petition of E ; fhewing, that I had unreafonably thruft himfelf into feveral Englifh words
derived from *Clamo*, *valeo*, &c : and praying, that
the faid I might be difcharged, and that he the
faid E might be added, at the end of fuch words ;
fo that thofe which are now abfurdly written *Claim*,
Prevail, &c. may hereafter be fpelled *Clame*, *Pre-
vale*, &c. He urged, that I was already difmif-
fed from *Proclamation*, *Prevalent*, &c ; and that
there was the fame reafon for what he defired.

Granted.

A Complaint of ED againft T, for juftling
him out of the ends of Verbs of the preterperfect Tenfe, and of Participles.

The Court had fat late, and therefore referred
this petition to another Day ; and adjourned.

S Q N-

✖✖✖✖✖✖✖✖✖✖✖✖✖✖✖✖✖✖✖✖✖✖✖✖

SONNETS.

SONNET I.

To R. Owen Cambridge, *Esq;*

CAMBRIDGE, with whom, my pilot and
      my guide,
Pleas'd I have travers'd thy Sabrina's flood;
Both where she foams impetuous, foil'd with
    mud,
And where she peaceful rolls her golden tide;

Never, O never let ambition's pride,
    (Too oft pretexed with our Country's good)
    And tinsell'd pomp, despis'd when understood,
Or thirst of wealth thee from her banks divide;

Reflect how calmly, like her infant wave,
    Flows the clear current of a private life;
    See the wide public stream, by tempests toss'd,
Of every changing wind the sport, or slave,
    Soil'd with corruption, vex'd with party strife,
    Cover'd with wrecks of peace and honor lost.

SONNET II.

To JOHN CLERKE, Esq;

WISELY, O Clerke, enjoy the present
   hour,
" The present hour is all the time we have,"
High God the rest has plac'd beyond our power,
 Consign'd perhaps to grief—or to the grave.

Wretched the man, who toils ambition's slave ;
 Who pines for wealth, or sighs for empty fame ;
Who rolls in pleasures, which the mind deprave,
 Bought with severe remorse, and guilty shame.

Virtue and Knowledge be our better aim ;
 These help us Ill to bear, or teach to shun ;
Let Friendship chear us with her generous flame,
 Friendship, the sum of all our joys in one :
So shall we live each moment fate has given,
How long or short, let us resign to Heaven.

S O N-

XXXXXXXXXXXXXXXXXXXXXXXXXXXXXXXXXXXXX

SONNET III.

To FRANCIS KNOLLYS, Efq;

O Sprung from Worthies, who with counfils
     wife
Adorn'd and ftrengthen'd great *Elifa*'s throne,
Who yet with virtuous pride mayft well defpife
    To borrow praife from merits not thy own;

Oft as I view the monumental ftone,
    Where our lov'd *Harrifon*'s cold afhes reft;
Mufing on joys with him long paft and gone,
    A pleafing fad remembrance fills my breaft.

Did the fharp pang, we feel for friends deceas'd,
    Unbated laft, we muft with anguifh die;
But Nature bids it's rigor fhould be eas'd
    By lenient Time, and ftrong Neceffity;
Thefe calm the paffions, and fubdue the mind,
To bear th'appointed lot of human kind.

S O N N E T IV.

To Mr. CRUSIUS.

CRUSIUS, I hop'd the little Heaven ſhall
  ſpare
 Of my ſhort day, which flits away ſo faſt,
 And ſickneſs threats with clouds to over-caſt,
In ſocial converſe oft with thee to ſhare ;

Ill luck for me, that wayward fate ſhould tear
 Thee from the haven, thou hadſt gain'd at laſt,
 Again to try the toils and dangers paſt,
In forein climates, and an hoſtile air ;

Yet duteous to thy Country's call attend,
 Which clames her portion of thy uſeful years ;
And back with ſpeed thy courſe to *Britain* bend :

If, e'er again we meet, perchance ſhould end
 My dark'ning Eve, Thou'lt pay ſome friendly
  tears,
Grateful to him, who liv'd and died thy friend.

❋❋❋❋❋❋❋❋❋❋❋❋❋❋❋❋❋❋❋❋❋❋❋❋❋❋❋❋

SONNET V.

On a FAMILY-PICTURE.

WHEN pensive on that Portraiture I gaze,
  Where my four Brothers round about me
    stand,
And four fair Sisters smile with graces bland,
The goodly monument of happier days;

And think how soon insatiate Death, who preys
  On all, has cropp'd the rest with ruthless hand;
   While only I survive of all that band,
Which one chaste bed did to my Father raise;

It seems that like a Column left alone,
  The tottering remnant of some splendid Fane,
   Scape'd from the fury of the barbarous Gaul,
And wasting Time, which has the rest o'erthrown;
  Amidst our House's ruins I remain
   Single, unpropp'd, and nodding to my fall.

U   SON-

SONNET VI.

To JOHN REVETT, Esq;

REVETT, who well haft judg'd the tafk too
    hard,
Of this fhort life throughout the total day,
To follow glory's falfe bewitching ray,
Through certain toils, uncertain of reward;

A Prince's fervice how fhould we regard?
    As fervice ftill—though deck'd in livery gay,
    Difguis'd with titles, gilded o'er with pay,
Specious, yet ill to liberty preferr'd.

Bounding thy wifhes by the golden mean,
    Nor weakly bartering happinefs for fhew;
Wifely thou'ft left the bufy buftling fcene,
Where merit feldom has fuccefsful been;
    In Checquer's fhades to tafte the joys, that flow
From calm retirement, and a mind ferene.

S O N-

S O N N E T VII.

To the Honorable PHILIP YORKE.

O YORKE, whom Virtue makes the worthy heir
　　Of *Hardwicke*'s titles, and of *Kent*'s eftate;
Bleft in a Wife, whofe beauty, though fo rare,
　　Is the left Grace of all that round her wait;

While other Youths, fprung from the Good and
　　Great;
　　In devious paths of pleafure feek their bane,
Recklefs of wifdom's lore, of birth or ftate,
　　Meanly debauch'd, or infolently vain;

Through Virtue's facred gate, to Honor's fane
　　You and your fair Affociate ceafelefs climb,
With glorious emulation; fure to gain
　　A meed, fhall laft beyond the reign of Time:
From your example long may *Britain* fee,
Degenerate *Britain*, what the Great fhould be!

U 2　　　　　　　　　　　　　S O N.

SONNET VIII.

On the Cantos of SPENSER's FAIRY QUEEN,
loft in the Paffage from Ireland.

WO worth the man, who in ill hour affay'd
  To tempt that Weftern Frith with ven-
 trous keel;
 And feek what Heav'n, regardful of our weal,
Had hid in fogs, and night's eternal fhade;

Ill-ftarr'd *Hibernia !* well art thou appaid
 For all the woes, which *Britain* made thee feel
 By *Henry's* wrath, and *Pembroke's* conqu'ring
 fteel;
Who fack'd thy Towns, and Caftles difarray'd:

No longer now with idle forrow mourn
 Thy plunder'd wealth, or liberties reftrain'd,
 Nor deem their victories thy lofs or fhame;
Severe revenge on *Britain* in thy turn,
 And ample fpoils thy treacherous waves ob-
 tain'd,
  Which funk one half of *Spenfer's* deathlefs
  fame.

S O N-

S O N N E T IX.

To the Memory of Mrs. M. PAICE.

PEACE to thy afhes, to thy memory Fame,
 Fair paragon of merit feminine ;
 In forming whom kind Nature did inſhrine
A mind angelic in a faultlefs frame ;

Through every ftage of changing life the fame,
 How did thy bright example ceafelefs ſhine ;
 And every grace with every virtue join,
To raife the Virgin's and the Matron's name !

In thee Religion, chearful, and ferene,
 Unfour'd by fuperftition, fpleen, or pride,
  Through all the focial offices of life,
To ſhed its genuine influence was feen ;
 This thy chief ornament, thy fureft guide,
 This form'd the Daughter, Parent, Friend, and
  Wife.

SON-

SONNET X.

To N. PAICE, Esq;

BROTHER and Friend, whom Heav'n's all-
gracious hand,
  In lieu of Brethren and of Friends deceas'd,
  To me a solace and support has rais'd,
And bound by Virtue's ever-sacred band;

To future times fair shall thy memory stand,
  (If aught of mine to future times at left
  Can reach,) and, for fraternal kindness blest,
Wide as good *Proculeius'* fame expand.

The fond remembrance of *Maria's* love
  Her friends and kindred to thy heart endears;
    With equal warmth thou dost their friendship
      meet,
And generous acts thy true affection prove;
  Thy kind compassion dries the Widows tears,
    And guides the lonely Orphan's wand'ring
      Feet.

SON.

❦❦❦❦❦❦❦❦❦❦❦❦❦❦

SONNET XI.

To the Author of Obfervations on the Converfion
and Apoftlefhip of St. PAUL.

O LYTTELTON, great meed fhalt thou re-
ceive,
Great meed of fame, Thou and thy learn'd
Compeer,
Who, 'gainft the Sceptic's doubt and Scorner's
fneer,
Affert thofe Heav'n-born truths, which you believe;

In elder time thus Heroes wont t'atchieve
Renown; they held the Faith of *Jefus* dear,
And round their Ivy crown or Laurell'd fpear
Blufh'd not Religion's Olive branch to weave;

Thus *Ralegh*, thus immortal *Sidney* fhone,
(Illuftrious names!) in great *Elifa's* days.
Nor doubt his promife firm, that fuch who own
In evil times, undaunted, though alone,
His glorious truth, fuch He will crown with
praife,
And glad agnize before his Father's throne.

SONNET XII.

To D. Wray, Esq;

WRAY, whose dear friendship in the dawn-
    ing years
Of undesigning childhood first began,
  Through youth's gay morn with even tenor ran,
My noon conducted, and my evening chears;

Rightly dost Thou, in whom combin'd appears
  Whate'er for public life completes the Man,
  With active zeal strike out a larger plan;
No useless friend to Senators and Peers:

Me moderate talents and a small estate
  Fit for retirement's unambitious shade,
     Nor envy I who near approach the throne;
But joyful see thee mingle with the Great,
  See thy deserts with due distinction paid,
     And praise thy lot, contented with my own.

SON-

S O N N E T XIII.

To the same.
Written in a fit of SICKNESS.

TRUST me, Dear *Wray*, not all these three
    months' pain,
  Though tedious seems the time in pain to wear,
Nor all those restless nights, through which in vain
  I've sought for kindly sleep to lull my care ;

Not all those lonely meals, and meagre fare,
  Unchear'd with converse of a friendly guest ;
This close confinement, barr'd from wholesome air
  And exercise, of medicines the best ;

Have sunk my spirits, or my soul opprefs'd :
  Light are these woes, and easy to be born ;
If weigh'd with those, which rack'd my tortur'd
    breast
  When my fond heart from *Amoret* was torn ;
So true that word of *Solomon* I find——
" No pain so grievous as a wounded mind."

✖✖✖✖✖✖✖✖✖✖✖✖✖✖✖✖✖✖✖✖✖✖✖✖✖✖✖✖✖

S O N N E T XIV.

O Sacred Love of Country! pureſt flame,
 That wont in *Britons*' honeſt hearts to blaze,
And fire them to achieve high deeds of praiſe,
Which earn the guerdon of eternal fame;

If aught of thee remain, beſide the name
 And ſemblance vain, to theſe degenerate days ;
 With all the effulgence of thy heavenly rays
Shine forth, and daſh the ſpurious Patriot's clame;

That bold bad man, who bellowing in the cauſe
 Of truth and virtue, and with fraudful ſkill
  Winning the giddy changing multitude,
Warps on the wind of popular applauſe
 To private wealth and power; pretending ſtill
  With hard unbluſhing front the public good.

S O N N E T XV.

To the Honorable CHARLES YORKE.

CHARLES, whom thy Country's voice ap-
　　plauding calls
　To *Philip's* honorably vacant feat ;
　With modeft pride th' awakening fummons meet,
And rife to glory in St. *Stephen's* walls ;

Nor mean the honor, which thy Youth befalls,
　Thus early clam'd from thy lov'd learn'd retreat,
　To guard thofe facred Rights, which elevate .
Britain's free fons above their neighbor thralls :

Let *Britain,* let admiring *Europe* fee .
　In thofe bright Parts, which yet too clofe con-
　　fin'd
　Shine in the circle of thy friends alone,
How fharp the fpur of worthy Anceftry,
　When kindred Virtues fire the generous mind
　　Of *Somers'* Nephew, and of *Hardwicke's* Son.

S O N N E T XVI.

To ISAAC HAWKINS BROWNE, *Efq;*

HAWKINS, whofe lips the Mufes have imbued
With all the fweetnefs of th' Aonian fpring;
Whom emuling I deftly learn'd to fing,
And fmoother tune my numbers rough and rude:

Truce with the jangling Law's eternal feud,
It's fubtile quirks, and captious cavilling,
Unlike the Mufe's gentle whifpering,
Which leads the Heaven-taught Soul to Fit and
Good:

Thee more befeems in Eloquence' fair field,
The Senate, war with Faction's chiefs to wage,
Bare the Mock-Patriot's ill diffembled crime,
Nor let fair Truth to feigned feeming yield;
With thy fweet Lyre to catch the lift'ning Age,
And fing thy Trimnell's charms in deathlefs
rhyme.

S O N.

SONNET XVII.

To the same.

ONCE more, my *Hawkins*, I attempt to raise
   My feeble voice to urge the tuneful song
  Of that sweet Muse, which to her Country's
    wrong
Or sleeps, or only wakes to *Latian* lays ;

Great is the merit, well-deserv'd the praise
   Of that last Work, where Reasoning just and
    strong
 In charming verse thy name shall bear along
To learned foreiners, and future days :

Yet do not Thou thy native language scorn ;
   In which great *Shakespear*, *Spenser*, *Milton* sang
    Such strains as may with *Greek* or *Roman* vie :
This cultivate, raise, polish and adorn ;
   So each fair Maid shall on thy numbers hang,
    And every *Briton* bless thy melody.

✕✕✕✕✕✕✕✕✕✕✕✕✕✕✕;✕✕✕✕✕✕✕✕✕✕✕✕✕✕

SONNET XVIII.

To the Right Honorable the Lord HARDWICKE,
Lord CHANCELLOR.

O THOU, to sacred *Themis'* awful throne,
  And the chief seat among the crowned
    Peers,
The Nation's laſt reſort, in early years
Rais'd by thy high deſert; Not this alone,
  Nor all the Fame thy Eloquence has won,
  Though *Britain's* counſils with ſucceſs it ſteers,
  And the rough *Scot* it's diſtant thunder fears,
Rank Thee ſo high above compariſon,

As that prime bliſs, by which thy heart is warm'd,
  Thoſe numerous pledges of thy nuptial bed;
    Who back reflect a luſtre on their Sire,
Taught by thy lore, by thy example form'd,
  With ſteady ſteps the ways of glory tread,
    And to the palm of virtuous praiſe aſpire.

S O N-

✖✖✖✖✖✖✖✖✖✖✖✖✖✖✖✖✖✖✖✖✖✖✖✖✖✖✖✖✖✖✖

SONNET. XIX.

To his Grace THOMAS *Archbishop* of Canterbury.

PRELATE, whofe fteady hand, and watchful
    eye
  The facred veffel of Religion guide,
  Secure from Superftition's dangerous tide,
And fateful Rocks of Infidelity;

Think not, in this bad age of obloquy,
  When Chriftian virtues Chriftians dare deride,
  And worth by Party-zele alone is tried,
To 'fcape the poifon'd fhafts of calumny;

No—though the tenor of thy blamelefs life,
  Like His, whofe flock is to thy care confign'd,
    Be fpent in teaching Truth and doing Good;
Yet, 'mongft the Sons of Bigotry and Strife,
  Thou too, like Him, muft hear thy Good ma-
    lign'd,
    Thy Perfon flander'd, and thy Truths with-
    ftood.

SON-

SONNET XX.

To the Right Honorable the Lord WILLOUGHBY of Parham.

PARHAM, if worth concel'd in reason's doom
 From want of worth be only once remov'd;
Nor can those virtues be esteem'd and lov'd,
Which listless sleep as in the silent tomb;

No longer let thy youthful years consume
 In thy retirement; Thee long since behov'd,
 In public life, with courage unreprov'd,
To shew those worths, which bloom so fair at home:

When Virtue, wanting to herself, will shroud
 Behind the veil of shameface'd bashfulness
 Those charms, which Action should produce
  to view;
No wonder if the forward, bold, and loud,
 In this world's bustling scene, before her press,
  Usurp her name, and rob her of her due.

SON-

SONNET · XXI.

For the Root-House at WREST.

STRANGER, or gueft, whome'er this hal-
lowed grove
  Shall chance receive, where fweet contentment
    dwells,
  Bring here no heart, that with ambition fwells,
With avarice pines, or burns with lawlefs love :

Vice-tainted Souls will all in vain remove
  To fylvan fhades, and hermits' peaceful çells,
  In vain will feek retirement's lenient fpells,
Or hope that blifs, which only good men prove :

If heaven-born truth, and facred virtue's lore,
  Which chear, adorn, and dignify the mind,
    Are conftant inmates of thy honeft breaft,
If, unrepining at thy neighbor's ftore,
  Thou count'ft as thine the good of all mankind,
    Then welcome fhare the friendly groves of
      Wreft.

SON-

SONNET XXII.

To the Author of CLARISSA.

O MASTER of the heart, whose magic quill
   The close recesses of the Soul can find,
  Can rouse, becalm, and terrifie the mind,
Now melt with pity, now with anguish thrill,

Thy moral page while virtuous precepts fill,
   Warm from the heart, to mend the Age de-
     sign'd,
  Wit, strength, truth, decency are all conjoin'd
To lead our Youth to Good, and guard from Ill:

O long enjoy, what thou so well hast won,
   The grateful tribute of each honest heart
     Sincere, nor hackney'd in the ways of men;
At each distressful stroke their true tears run,
  And Nature, unsophisticate by Art,
     Owns and applauds the labors of thy pen.

S O N

S O N N E T, XXIII.

To the Author of Sir CHARLES GRANDISON.

SWEET Moralift, whofe generous labors tend
　　With ceafelefs diligence to guide the mind,
　In the wild maze of error wandering blind,
To Virtue Truth and Honor, glorious end

Of glorious toils! vainly would I commend,
　In numbers worthy of your fenfe refin'd,
　This laft great work, which leaves all praife
　　behind,
And juftly ftyles You Of Mankind the Friend :

Pleafure with profit artful while you blend,
　And now the fancy, now the judgment feed
　　With grateful change, which every paffion
　　　fways ;
Numbers, who ne'er to graver lore attend,
　Caught by the charm, grow virtuous as they
　　read,
　　And lives reform'd fhall give you genuine
　　　praife.

X 2　　　　　　S O N-

SONNET XXIV.

To Miss H. M.

SWEET Linnet, who from off the laurel spray,
　　That hangs o'er *Spenser*'s ever-facred tomb,
　Pour'ft out fuch notes, as ftrike the Woodlark
　　dumb,
And vie with Philomel's inchanting lay,

How fhall my verfe thy melody repay？
　　If my weak voice could reach the age to come,
　　Like *Colin Clout*'s, thy name fhould ever bloom
Through future times, unconfcious of decay；

But fuch frail aid thy merits not require,
　　Thee *Polyhymnia*, in the rofeate bowers
　　　Of high *Parnaſſus*, 'midft the vocal throng,
Shall glad receive, and to her tuneful fire
　　Prefent; where, crown'd with amaranthine flowers,
　　　The raptured choir fhall liften to thy fong.

SON-

━━

SONNET LXXV.

To the most Honorable the Lady Marchioness GREY.

The Hermitage *at* TURRICK *to the* Root-House *at* WREST.

THE Beechen Roots of wood-clad *Buckingham*
    To *Bedford* Elms, their courteous breth'ren,
    send
  I Iealth and kind greeting, as from friend to
    friend,
And gladly join to celebrate their fame ;

Beyond all roots above ground we proclame
    You happieſt, deſtin'd all your days to ſpend
    In *Wreſts* fair groves, and *Graia* to defend
From *Eurus*' blaſts, and *Phœbus* ſultry flame ;

High Privilege to you, though dead, accorded,
  Which every living tree with envy views !
    We envy not, but pray for your ſtability ;
Proud, that ourſelves by *Graia* are regarded,
  At her command we not the fire refuſe,
    But chearful blaze and burn with * *Affability*

                X 3   S O N-

* A cant word uſed by the Builders of the Root-houſe.

SONNET XXVI.

On the Edition of Mr. Pope's Works with a Commentary and Notes.

IN evil hour did *Pope's* declining age,
   Deceiv'd and dazzled by the tinsel shew
   Of wordy science and the nauseous flow
Of mean officious flatteries, engage

Thy venal quill to deck his labor'd page
   With ribbald nonsense, and permit to strew,
   Amidst his flowers, the baleful weeds, that grow
In th' unbless'd soil of rude and rancorous rage.

Yet this the avenging Muse ordained so,
   When, by his counsil or weak sufferance,
      To thee were trusted *Shakespear's* Fame and Fate:
She doom'd him down the stream of time to tow
   Thy foul, dirt-loaded hulk, or sink perchance,
      Dragg'd to oblivion by the foundering weight.

S O N.

SONNET XXVII.

To Mr. WILSON WILLIAMS.

FRIEND of my Youth, Companion of my Age,
  Who faw'ft my rifing, feeft my fetting fun,
  And know'ft how faft the trembling minutes run;
Which lead me to this life's extremeft ftage,

Great is the power of Med'cine to affwage
  Thofe pains, which Nature gives us not to fhun,
  And much divine Philofophy has done,
To teach us decently to bear their rage;

But there's a Balm, which Art nor Nature knows,
  A Topic, by Philofophy ne'er taught,
    Which fheaths th' acuteft pains, and bids us fmile
At Age, at Sicknefs, and all earthly woes;
  A Confcience free from ill; a mind well fraught
  With Faith in Him, who will reward our toil.

SON-

✳✳✳✳✳✳✳✳✳✳✳✳✳✳✳✳✳✳✳✳✳✳✳✳✳✳✳✳✳✳✳

S O N N E T. XXVIII.

To George Onslow, *Esq;*

GOOD Son of the beſt Father, whoſe wiſe love
    And great example join thy breaſt to warm
With generous emulation to perform
That arduous taſk, which He has ſet before,

Mine own *George Onſlow*, oft reflect that more
    From thee the world expects, than from the
        ſwarm
    Of gay, miſtutored youths, who ne'er the charm
Of Virtue hear, nor wait at Wiſdom's door :

View then the pattern with a ſteadfaſt eye,
    By thy great Anceſtors from Sire to Son
      With a religious care tranſmitted down;
Firm to the cauſe of Truth and Liberty,
    In their fair ſteps the race of Glory run,
      Equal their worth, and equal their renown.

S O N-

SONNET XXIX.

To W. Heberden, M. D.

O *Heberden*, whose salutary care
  Has kindly driven me forth the crouded
    Town
  To *Turrick*, and the lonely Country down,
To breathe from *Chiltern* Hills a purer air,

For thousands' sakes may Heaven indulgent spare
  Long, long thy useful life, and blessings crown
  Thy healing arts, while well deserv'd renown,
With wealth unenvied, waits thy toil and care :

And when this grateful heart shall beat no more,
  (Nor long, I ween, can last my tottering frame,
    But soon, with me, this mortal coil shall end)
Do thou, if Calumny again should roar,
  Cherish his memory, and protect his fame,
    Whom thy true worth has made thy faithful
      friend.

S O N-

SONNET XXX.

To the Reverend Mr. HARVY.

HARVY, dear Kinsman, who in prime of youth
    (When Paſſions rule, or proud Ambition's
    call
  Too oft miſleads our heedleſs ſteps to fall
From the fair paths of Virtue, Peace, and Truth,)

For erring Souls touch'd with a generous ruth,
    Did'ſt vow thy ſervice to the God of All;
    Anxious to reſcue free the captive thrall
From the old Serpent's deadly poiſonous tooth;

Great is the weight, important is the care,
    Of that high office which thou made'ſt thy choice;
    Be ſtrong, be faithful therefore to thy beſt,
Nor pains, nor pray'ers, nor fair example ſpare;
    So thou ſhalt hear at laſt that chearing voice,
    " Well done, good Servant, enter into reſt."

SONNET XXXI.

To the Reverend Mr. LAWRY.

LAWRY, whose blissful lot has plac'd thee near
   To Wisdom's house, where thou mayst right-
    ly spell
Of the best means in Virtue to excell;
Science, which never can be priz'd too dear:

Where thy Great Patron, though in life severe,
   Is candid and humane, in doing well
   Constant and zelous, studious to repell
Evil by good, in word and deed sincere:

In this fair mirror see thy duty clear,
   Practice enforcing what his precepts teach;
    This great example study night and day;
If faithful thus thy Christian course thou steer,
   Though such perfection thou should'st fail to
    reach,
    Thy generous effort sure rewards will pay.

SON-

SONNET XXXII.

To the Editor of Mr. POPE's *Works.*

O Born in luckless hour, with every Muse
    And every Grace to foe! what wayward fate
Drives thee with fell and unrelenting hate
Each choiceft work of Genius to abuse?

Suffic'd it not with sacrilegious views
    Great *Shakespear's* awful shade to violate;
    And *His* fair Paradise contaminate,
Whom impious *Lauder* blushes to accuse:

Must *Pope*, thy friend, mistaken haplefs bard!
    (To prove no sprig of laurel e'er can grow
    Unblasted by thy venom) must he groan,
Now daub'd with flattery, now by censure scarr'd,
    Difguis'd, deform'd, and made the public show
    In motley weeds, and colors not his own?

SONNET XXXIII.

To the Memory of JOHN HAMPDEN, *Esq*;

O Hampden, laſt of that illuſtrious line,
     Which greatly ſtood in Liberty's dear cauſe,
  Zelous to vindicate our trampled laws
And rights which *Britons* never can reſign,

From the wild clame of impious Right Divine,
  Then when fell Tyranny with harpy claws
  Had ſeiz'd it's prey, and the devouring jaws
Of that ſeven-headed Monſter, at whoſe ſhrine

The Nations bow, threaten'd our ſwift decay;
  Neighbor and Friend, farewell—but not with
    Thee
  Shall die the record of thy Houſe's fame;
Thy grateful Country ſhall it's praiſe convey
  From age to age, and, long as *Britain's* free,
   Britons ſhall boaſt in *Hampden's* glorious
    name.

S O N-

● ●

SONNET XXXIV.

To Mr. NATHANAEL MASON.

NEPHEW, who soon design'st to pass the
   Sea,
To fix the basis of a useful trade;
With prosperous fortune be thy voyage made,
And safe return to home — if not to me;

Let these few precepts thy instructers be,
 In distant climes thy friendless youth to aid;
 Though interest, fashion, secresy persuade,
Yet keep thy morals pure, and conscience free:

In change of Countries God's all-seeing eye
 Is every where the same, Virtue and Vice
 Change not their nature; therefore be thou
  ware,
Shun follies haunts, and vicious company,
 Least from true goodness they thy steps entice,
  And Pleasure coil thee in her dangerous snare.

SONNET XXXV.

To Mr. J. PAICE.

JOSEPH, the worthy Son of worthy Sire,
    Who well repay'ft thy pious parents care
To train thee in the ways of Virtue fair,
And early with the Love of Truth infpire,

What farther can my clofing eyes defire
    To fee, but that by wedlock thou repair
    The wafte of death; and raife a virtuous heir
To build our Houfe, e'er I in peace retire?

Youth is the time for Love: *Then* choofe a Wife,
    With prudence choofe; 'tis Nature's genuine
        voice;
    And what fhe truely dictates muft be good;
Neglected once that prime, our remnant life
    Is four'd, or fadden'd, by an ill-tim'd choice,
    Of lonely, dull, and friendlefs folitude.

✖✖✖✖✖✖✖✖✖✖✖✖✖✖✖✖✖✖✖✖✖✖✖✖✖✖✖✖✖✖✖✖✖✖✖✖✖

SONNET XXXVI.

To the same.

" WITH prudence choofe a Wife " — Be
      thy firft care
Her Virtue, not confin'd to time or place,
Or worn for fhew ; but on Religion's bafe
Well-founded, eafy, free, and debonair,

Next rofe-cheek'd Modefty, beyond compare
   The beft cofmetic of the Virgin's face ;
   Neatnefs, which doubles every female grace ;
And Temper mild, thy joys and griefs to fhare ;

Beauty in true proportion rather choofe
   Than color, fit to grace thy focial board,
      Chear thy chafte bed, and honeft offspring
         rear ;
With thefe feek Prudence well to guide thy houfe,
   Untainted Birth, and, if thy ftate afford,
      Do not, when fuch the prize, for Fortune
         fquare.

SONNET XXXVII.

On the Death of Miss J. M.

YOUNG, fair, and good! ah why should
    young and fair
And good be huddled in untimely grave?
Muft fo fweet flower fo brief a period have;
Juft bloom and charm, then fade and difappear?

Yet our's the lofs, who ill alas can fpare
  The bright example which thy virtues gave;
    The guerdon thine, whom gracious Heav'n did
    fave
From longer trial in this vale of care.

Reft then, fweet Saint, in peace and honor reft,
  While our true tears bedew thy maiden herfe;
Light lie the earth upon thy lovely breaft;
And let a grateful heart with grief opprefs'd
  To thy dear memory confecrate this verfe;
Though all too mean for who deferves the beft.

SONNET XXXVIII.

To——

"SWEET is the Love, that comes with wil-
        lingnefs:"
  So fings the fweetoft Bard,* that ever fung;
  Ten thoufand bleffings on his tuneful tongue,
Who felt and plain'd true lovers' fore diftrefs!

Sweet were the joys, which once you did poffefs,
    When on the yielding Fair one's lips you hung;
  The forer now your tender heart is wrung
With fad remembrance of her ficklenefs:

Yet let not grief and heart-confuming care
    Prey on your foul; but let your conftant mind
      Bear up with ftrength and manly hardinefs;
Your worth may move a more deferving Fair;
    And fhe, that fcornful beauty, foon may find,
      Sharp are the pangs that follow faithleffnefs.

* Spenfer.

S O N N E T XXXIX.

To RICHARD RODERICK, *Esq;*

EQUALLY fkilful or the Lyric ftring
    To touch, and laugh in many a jocund lay,
  Or againft vice to rife with bold affay,
And Satire's burning brond with art to fling;

Roderick, why fleeps the Mufe, while jolly fpring
    In frolic dance leads-up the blooming May,
  And the fweet Nightingales on every fpray
Take the ear prifoner with their carolling?

Or, if thy verfe a higher theme demand,
    Mark the Mock-patriot, deck'd in proud array
    Of borrow'd virtues, which his foul ne'er
      knew,
Scattering fell poifon through the cheated land;
    And, while to private power he paves his way,
    Dazzling with public good the blinded crew.

SON.

SONNET XL.

To SHAKESPEAR.

SHAKESPEAR, whose heart-felt scenes shall
    ever give
  Instructive pleasure to the listening age ;
  And shine unrival'd on the *British* stage
By native worth and high prerogative ;

When full of fame Thou did'st retire to live
  In studious leisure, had thy judgment sage
  Clear'd-off the rubbish cast on thy fair page
By Players or ignorant or forgetive *———

O what a sea of idly squander'd ink,
  What heaps of notes by blundering critics penn'd
    [The dreams of ignorance in wisdom's guise]
Had then been spar'd! nor *Knapton* then, I think,
  And honest *Draper* had been forc'd to send
    Their dear-bought rheams to cover plums and
    spice.

* See 2 HENRY IV. Act 4. Vol. III. P. 511. *Theob.* 1st Edit.

SON-

SONNET XLI.

To the Rev. Mr. SHAW, *Rector of* Beirton.

O FRIEND, in fad affliction's ufeful fchool
  Long train'd and tutor'd, hard to humane
    fenfe,
And dark appear th' awards of Providence,
Though Truth and Goodnefs be their conftant rule;

The word of Truth has faid, and reafon cool
  Subfcribes, that wife and kind Omnipotence
  Does oft the bitter cup in love difpenfe;
While draughts of pleafure lull the profperous fool:

Omnifcience knows, and Goodnefs will beftow,
  What's righteft, fitteft, beft; let humble man
    With faith and patience bow fubmiffive down,
Secure, that GOD delights not in our woe;
  And, when we have meafure'd out this life's
    fhort fpan,
  If fore the trial, bright will be the crown.

SON-

SONNET XLII.

To Miss ————

SWEET are the charms of shamefac'd Mo-
desty,
 When, coyly shy of well deserv'd applause,
 She veils her blushing cheek, and meek with-
  draws
From general notice and the public eye;

But therefore shall exalted worth still lie
 Lost in oblivion? This the sacred laws
 Of Justice, the regard to Virtue's cause,
And honor of the lovely Sex deny;

Wherefore are giv'n the Muse-inspired lays,
 The Poet's lofty song, but to rehearse
The fair deserts of past or present days,
And bashful merit's doubting eye to raise?
 Ill he deserves the powers of tuneful verse,
Who can see Virtue, and forbear to praise.

SONNET XLIII.

MY gracious God, whose kind conducting
    hand
  Has steer'd me through this Life's tumultuous
    sea,
 From many a rock, and many a tempest free,
Which prudence could not shun, nor strength with-
    stand,

And brought at length almost in sight of land,
  That quiet haven where I long to be,
  Only the streights of Death betwixt, which we
Are doom'd to pass, e'er reach the heav'nly strand;

Be this short passage boisterous, rough, and rude,
  Or smooth, and calm—Father, thy Will be
    done——
  Support me only in the troublous stour;
My sins all pardon'd through my Saviour's blood,
  Let Faith, and Hope, and Patience still hold on
  Unshaken, and Joy crown my latest hour!

SON-

SONNET XLIV.

To MATTHEW BARNARD*.

MATTHEW, whose skilful hand and well-
worn spade
Shall soon be call'd to make the humble bed,
Where I at last shall rest my weary head,
And form'd of dust again in dust be laid;

Near, but not in the Church of God, be made
My clay-cold cell, and near the common tread
Of passing friends; when number'd with the
dead,
We're equal all, and vain distinctions fade:

The cowslip, violet, or the pale primrose
  Perhaps may chance to deck the verdant sweard;
    Which twisted briar or hasle-bands entwine;
Symbols of life's soon fading glories those——
  Do thou the monumental hillock guard
    From trampling cattle, and the routing swine.

* The Sexton of the Parish.

SONNET XLV.

To the Right Honorable Mr. ONSLOW, with the
Collection of SONNETS.

THOU, who fucceffive in that honor'd Seat
Prefid'ft, the feuds of jarring Chiefs to
'fwage,
To check the boifterous force of Party rage,
Raife modeft worth, and guide the high debate ;

Sometimes retiring from the toils of State,
Thou turn'ft th' inftructive *Greek* or *Roman*
page,
Or what our *Britifh* Bards of later age
In fcarce inferior numbers can relate :

Amid this feaft of mind, when " Fancie's Child,"
Sweet *Shakefpear*, raps the Soul to virtuous deed,
When *Spenfer* warbling tunes his Doric lays,
Or the firft Man from Paradife exil'd
Great *Milton* fings ; can aught my ruftic reed
Prefume to found, that may deferve thy praife?

INDEX

INDEX

OF THE

Passages in Mr. WARBURTON's Edition of SHAKESPEAR, remarked upon in this Volume.

I N D E X.

INDEX.

I N D E X.

INDEX

I N D E X.

I N D E X.

Z

I N D E X.

INDEX.

Z 2

INDEX.

INDEX.

INDEX.

F I N I S.

BOOKS printed for CHARLES BATHURST,

At the Crofs-Keys, *oppofite St.* Dunftan's *Church,* Fleet-ftrett.

1. THE Works of JONATHAN SWIFT, D. D. Dean of St. Patrick's, Dublin, accurately revifed: with fome Account of the Author's Life, and Notes Hiftorical and Explanatory, by JOHN HAWKESWORTH, LL. D. In Six Volumes Quarto, adorned with Copper-plates. Price 3 l. 12 s.

2. The Works of ALEXANDER POPE, Efq; with his laft Corrections, Additions, and Improvements, as they were delivered to the Editor juft before his Death; together with the Commentary and Notes of Dr. Warburton. In Nine Volumes large Octavo, of the fame Size as Dr. Swift's Works, Price 2 l. 14 s.

3. An Effay upon the Life, Writings, and Character of Dr. Swift, by DEANE SWIFT, Efq; To which is added, that Sketch of Dr. Swift's Life written by himfelf, and prefented by the Author of this Effay to the Univerfity of Dublin. Octavo, Price 5 s.

4. The Works of BEN JOHNSON, with Notes Critical and Explanatory, by PETER WHALLEY, late Fellow of St. John's College in Oxford. In Seven Volumes Octavo, Price 1 l. 15 s.

5. The Works of Sir WILLIAM TEMPLE, Bart. To which is prefixed, the Life and Character of the Author, written by a particular Friend. In Two Volumes Folio, Price 1 l. 10 s.

6. An Enquiry into the Foundation of the Englifh Conftitution: Or, An Hiftorical Effay on the Anglo-Saxon Government both in Germany and England. A new Edition with Additions. By SAMUEL SQUIRE, D. D. Archdeacon of Bath. Octavo, Price 6 s.

7. DEMOSTHENIS Orationes de Republica duodecim, cum Interpretatione Wolfiana denuo caftigata, et Notis Hiftoricis J. V. Lucchefinii. Acceffit Philippi Epiftola. Edidit. GUL. ALLEN. Two Volumes Octavo, Price 12 s.

8. Sermons preached upon feveral Occafions. By ROBERT SOUTH, D. D. late Prebendary of Weftminfter and Canon of Chrift-Church, Oxon —The chief Heads of the Sermons are prefixed to each Volume, and a general Index of the principal Matters is added to this Edition. In Eleven Volumes Octavo, Price 2 l. 10 s.

9. The great Hiftorical and Critical Dictionary of Mr. PETER BAYLE. The Second Edition, revifed, and greatly augmented, particularly with a Tranflation of all the Paffages quoted from eminent Writers in various Languages. Likewife the Life of the Author, by Mr. DES MAIZEAUX, F. R. S. In Five Volumes Folio, Price 5 l. 5 s.

10. BIOGRAPHIA BRITANNICA (a Supplement to BAYLE) or the Lives of the moft eminent Perfons who have flourifhed in Great Britain and Ireland from the earlieft Ages down to the prefent Time. In Four Volumes Folio, Price 6 l.

C :

Check Out More Titles From HardPress Classics Series In this collection we are offering thousands of classic and hard to find books. This series spans a vast array of subjects – so you are bound to find something of interest to enjoy reading and learning about.

Subjects:
Architecture
Art
Biography & Autobiography
Body, Mind &Spirit
Children & Young Adult
Dramas
Education
Fiction
History
Language Arts & Disciplines
Law
Literary Collections
Music
Poetry
Psychology
Science
…and many more.

Visit us at www.hardpress.net

Im TheStory

personalised classic books

UNIQUE
GIFT

FOR KIDS, PARTNERS
AND FRIENDS

Timeless books such as:

Kids

Alice in Wonderland • The Jungle Book • The Wonderful Wizard of Oz
Peter and Wendy • Robin Hood • The Prince and The Pauper
The Railway Children • Treasure Island • A Christmas Carol

Adults

Romeo and Juliet • Dracula

 Highly Customizable   **Change** Books Title   **Replace** Characters Names with yours   **Upload** photo the inside page!   **Add** Inscriptions

Visit

Im TheStory .com

and order yours today!

CPSIA information can be obtained
at www.ICGtesting.com
Printed in the USA
BVHW081819220819
556561BV00020B/4455/P